JAPANESE AMERICANS AT HEART MOUNTAIN

Japanese Americans at Heart Mountain

Networks, Power, and Everyday Life

Saara Kekki

UNIVERSITY OF OKLAHOMA PRESS : NORMAN

Library of Congress Cataloging-in-Publication Data

Names: Kekki, Saara, 1982– author.

Title: Japanese Americans at Heart Mountain : networks, power, and everyday life / Saara Kekki.

Description: [Norman] : University of Oklahoma Press, [2022] | Includes bibliographical references and index. | Summary: "Explores the networks of Japanese American inmates at the Heart Mountain, Wyoming, incarceration camp from 1942 to 1945"—Provided by publisher.

Identifiers: LCCN 2022022525 | ISBN 978-0-8061-9080-8 (hardcover) | ISBN 978-0-8061-9390-8 (paper) | ISBN 978-0-8061-9211-6 (ePub)

Subjects: LCSH: Heart Mountain Relocation Center (Wyo.) | Japanese Americans—Forced removal and internment, 1942–1945. | World War, 1939–1945—Concentration camps—Wyoming. | Japanese Americans—Wyoming—Social conditions—20th century. | Japanese Americans—Social conditions—20th century. | United States—Race relations—History. | BISAC: HISTORY / Modern / 20th Century / General | HISTORY / United States / State & Local / West (AK, CA, CO, HI, ID, MT, NV, UT, WY)

Classification: LCC D769.8.A6 K44 2022 | DDC 940.53/1773089956—dc23/eng/20220516

LC record available at https://lccn.loc.gov/2022022525

The paper in this book meets the guidelines for permanence and durability of the Committee on Production Guidelines for Book Longevity of the Council on Library Resources, Inc. ∞

Copyright © 2022 by the University of Oklahoma Press, Norman, Publishing Division of the University. Paperback published 2024. Manufactured in the U.S.A.

All rights reserved. No part of this publication may be reproduced, stored in a retrieval system, or transmitted, in any form or by any means, electronic, mechanical, photocopying, recording, or otherwise—except as permitted under Section 107 or 108 of the United States Copyright Act—without the prior written permission of the University of Oklahoma Press. To request permission to reproduce selections from this book, write to Permissions, University of Oklahoma Press, 2800 Venture Drive, Norman OK 73069, or email rights.oupress@ou.edu.

S|H|M|P   **The Sustainable History Monograph Pilot**
Opening Up the Past, Publishing for the Future

This book is published as part of the Sustainable History Monograph Pilot. With the generous support of the Andrew W. Mellon Foundation, the Pilot uses cutting-edge publishing technology to produce open access digital editions of high-quality, peer-reviewed monographs from leading university presses. Free digital editions can be downloaded from: Books at JSTOR, EBSCO, Internet Archive, OAPEN, Project MUSE, ScienceOpen, and many other open repositories.

While the digital edition is free to download, read, and share, the book is under copyright and covered by the following Creative Commons License: CC BY-NC-ND 4.0. Please consult www.creativecommons.org if you have questions about your rights to reuse the material in this book.

When you cite the book, please include the following URL for its Digital Object Identifier (DOI): https://doi.org/10125/75827

> We are eager to learn more about how you discovered this title and how you are using it. We hope you will spend a few minutes answering a couple of questions at this URL:
> **https://www.longleafservices.org/shmp-survey/**

More information about the Sustainable History Monograph Pilot can be found at https://www.longleafservices.org.

CONTENTS

Maps and Figures ix
Preface xi
Acknowledgments xiii
Abbreviations xvii

CHAPTER 1
Introduction: Network Analysis and the Study of Japanese American History 1

CHAPTER 2
From Immigration to Incarceration: The Japanese in the United States, 1890–1942 14

CHAPTER 3
Heart Mountain Community and Modeling the Networks 31

CHAPTER 4
Those Who Govern: Political Power 46

CHAPTER 5
Sense of Belonging 65

CHAPTER 6
Individuals of Power and Power Families 86

CHAPTER 7
Women of Heart Mountain 103

CHAPTER 8
Disobedience behind Barbed Wire: Passive and Active Resistance 122

CHAPTER 9
Onward: Routes to Freedom 152

Epilogue: Networks of Power and the Power of Networks 166

Methodological Appendix 171

Notes 179

Bibliography 203

Index 215

MAPS AND FIGURES

MAPS

Map 1 Locations of camps 27
Map 2 Postincarceration destinations of Heart Mountain segregates 149
Map 3 Postincarceration destinations of Heart Mountain inmates 160
Map 4 Destination states from Heart Mountain 162

FIGURES

FIGURE 1 Map of Heart Mountain blocks and streets 32
FIGURE 2 Connections between various institutions of Heart Mountain 38
FIGURE 3 Heart Mountain political network 50
FIGURE 4 Three young men shopping at the Heart Mountain canteen, 1944 62
FIGURE 5 Adult English class at Heart Mountain 72
FIGURE 6 Second community council, July 1944 88
FIGURE 7 Reach of the Fujioka family 97
FIGURE 8 Division of the full network by gender 105
FIGURE 9 The hospital at Heart Mountain 112
FIGURE 10 Breakdown of indefinite leave types 121

PREFACE

Whose stories do we remember? Do we note those who were vocal and prominent in their time, such as Kiyoshi Okamoto of the Heart Mountain Fair Play Committee? Or those who later tried to rectify a wrong, like Frank S. Emi, who spoke for redress and remembrance for the draft resisters? How do we recognize those who leave no paper trail or choose not to speak about their experience in public, like Toshiye Nagata? Dynamic historical network analysis can help us (re)discover people who have hitherto been lost to history. It allows us to discover actual networks of people and reconstruct past societies in an unprecedented way, taking us beyond what official history or even private diaries can offer.

This book explores the networks of Japanese American inmates at the Heart Mountain, Wyoming incarceration camp throughout its existence from 1942 to 1945. I created a dynamic network model of all the camp's 14,011 inmates, including familial connections among the inmates, as well as the compositions of political, employment, social, and geospatial networks. The network model forms the starting point for a unique analysis of the impact the incarceration and resettlement had on the Japanese American community of Heart Mountain.

The cover image of this book illustrates one practical aspect of creating those networks. The original caption of the image by WRA photographer Tom Parker read: "Salvaging lumber from the scrap pile, these evacuee residents are preparing lumber for use in making small items of resident furniture."[1] This practice of using scrap lumber, sometimes against the rules of the camps, was an integral part of the incarceration experience for many. In addition to providing necessities for the barren living quarters, salvaging scrap lumber and making small crafts created new bonds and a sense of community among inmates.

Few camps have been documented in as much detail as Heart Mountain has. Douglas Nelson's *Heart Mountain: The History of an American Concentration Camp* (1976) is credited as the first book-length study of a single camp. Mike Mackey has written several books on Heart Mountain, and newfound interest in the Heart Mountain Fair Play Committee has resulted in several works that necessarily shed light on the entire camp as well. All of these important books, however, relied on the *Heart Mountain Sentinel* and other newspapers and oral histories as their primary source material. While immensely valuable, they have one major shortcoming: they do not present an impartial point of view.

Despite its status as the most professionally run camp newspaper, the *Sentinel* was staffed by firm assimilationists and controlled by the government. Oral histories, especially by the twenty-first century, are limited by the willingness of a scant number of living survivors to share their ideas. My work has benefited enormously from the eagerness of people to record their memories, but these sources were always secondary to what the networks reveal. Whenever possible, I have looked for first-hand accounts by the people who were central in the networks. Eiichi Sakauye, for example, was an important person in the networks and has been active in sharing his stories. At other times, people that emerged in my model have not left a paper trail. One such example is Toshiye Nagata. When such firsthand accounts of key individuals have not been available, I have used other published narratives to supplement the story.

Through dynamic network modeling and the use of historical "big" data, I will discuss life at Heart Mountain in unprecedented depth. In creating the network model, I relied heavily on various theoretical and methodological frameworks, but in this book, I will only very briefly touch upon the theory when it is necessary for understanding my conclusions. Thus, this book will focus on the *results* of the network analysis. At times, this means that I use simplified terms from a theoretical standpoint. For example, I might say "connections" or "number of memberships" instead of "edges" or "outdegree." I trust this will make reading more enjoyable. A more detailed description of the method can be found in the appendix.

This book is about everyday life for members of a community under extraordinary circumstances. My starting point is not to say that the Japanese American incarceration communities were comparable to normal communities because, from their foundations, they were not. They were abruptly and artificially put together, the people had no choice in selecting their neighborhoods, nor could they opt to move elsewhere. Even the community government structure was fundamentally dictated from above. Many inmates became institutionalized and were afraid and unwilling to leave the camps when the time came. But life went on: marriages were formed, babies were born, people worked and engaged in politics. These everyday activities transformed the communities into something more ordinary. Despite the injustice, most individuals took charge of their own destinies.

ACKNOWLEDGMENTS

This book is the culmination of over a decade of studying Japanese American history. My interest in North America goes well beyond my years as a doctoral student, and even beyond my years as a university student. Twenty years ago, I was a sixteen-year-old high school exchange student in Sierra Vista, Arizona, and that year generated an interest in learning more. Academically, I became a North Americanist on the first week of my bachelor's studies in English philology at the University of Helsinki. I was given a study guide and told to choose a minor (and to start thinking about the topic for my master's thesis!), and there it was, North American studies. I felt welcome at the small Renvall Institute, and was especially welcomed by the (grand)father of Finnish American studies, professor emeritus Markku Henriksson.

What really pushed me toward the topic of this book (and the preceding dissertation), however, was an undergraduate exchange semester at the University of Idaho in Moscow, Idaho. Among the many exciting courses I took was "Idaho and the Pacific Northwest." I thought that the course's instructor, Professor Adam Sowards, challenged us more than the other professors did. In his class, I got my first in-depth insights into the incarceration of Japanese Americans. One essay turned into more research papers, a minor thesis on Japanese American incarceration literature, a master's thesis on the portrayal of Japanese Americans in the public sphere, a doctoral dissertation—and now this book.

I was fortunate to receive funding for the archival work, fieldwork, and writing parts of this project. Thank you to the Buffalo Bill Center of the West; the Ella and Georg Ehrnrooth Foundation; the Finnish Cultural Foundation (twice); the Finnish Konkordia Fund; the Kone Foundation; the University of Helsinki's Research Foundation, Jubilee Fund, Doctoral School for the Humanities and Social Sciences, Faculty of Arts, and chancellor; the Oskar Öflund Foundation (twice); and the Western History Association for their financial support.

I have been privileged to do research in various archives and libraries, where archivists and other staff have been very helpful and supportive of my efforts. Thank you to William Creech (National Archives), Oregon Nikkei Endowment, Cristine Paschild (Portland State University Library), Mary Robertson

(McCracken Research Library, Buffalo Bill Center of the West), Danielle McAdams and Dakota Russell (Heart Mountain Interpretive Center and Archives), James Stack (University of Washington Libraries), and Jordan Wong (Wing Luke Museum of Asian and Pacific American Experience).

Working in a small field in Finland means that few people share my exact research interest. As a consequence, several supervisors and, later, colleagues have had the possibly questionable pleasure of advising and reviewing work that was very far from their own fields—yet they did a remarkable job! Special thanks to Outi J. Hakola and Mikko Saikku for diligently reading countless versions of the manuscript, and for always pushing me to develop my argument. Similarly, thank you to everyone at the Department of Cultures, University of Helsinki, for the moral and practical support. And thank you to my friend Francis Flavin, without whom I would not have thought of applying network analysis to a historical event. In addition to challenging my brain to think "programmatically," he responded to countless pleas for help—for example, when I accidentally created a million new rows in my main data table.

Former and current fellow doctoral students and office mates Anna Koivusalo, Anna-Leena Korpijärvi, Jonathan Lagerquist, Tuire Liimatainen, Saara Rautanen, and Marina Vulovic offered support and, at times, badly needed "ventilation valves" in the tumults of (grad student) life. Laura Hooton and Philip Deslippe made me feel welcome at the University of California, Santa Barbara, and it was that feeling of collegiality that instilled in me the idea that there might be a career for me in academia. Boyd Cothran, the late Raymond J. DeMallie, Jeremy Johnston, and Joshua Reid have made me feel like a part of an international research community. My long-time friend and fellow North Americanist Heli Rekiranta made the beautiful maps for this book.

Toward the end of this project, I became virtually acquainted with several other people studying Japanese American history. Interactions with Stacey L. Camp, April Kamp-Whittaker, Chrissy Lau, Koji Lau-Ozawa, and Duncan R. Williams gave me an enormous boost to finish this book.

Professors Eric L. Muller, Greg Robinson, and Paul Spickard took the time to read different parts and versions of the manuscript and made insightful comments. I'm grateful to all three for their enthusiasm for this project. Exactly ten years ago, Paul signed his book for me with "I can't wait to read your book." That thought seemed quite laughable, but I'm proud to be able to deliver.

Finally, I want to thank the editors at the University of Oklahoma Press for their interest in this project from early on, when it was only a dissertation in progress. Alessandra Jacobi Tamulevich and Sherondra Thedford (Longleaf) deserve special credit for seeing this book through to the finish line.

My brother Tuomas and my pre-academia friends Tuuli, Katja, Matleena, and Riina have permitted the occasional "intellectual sloppiness" and have helped me see how mundane some of my worries are. Kalseat Poltot (Elina, Kati, Kaisa, Laura, Sinikka), my "singing buddies," have provided many laughs at times when they were critically needed.

Finally, the people that have dealt with me the most:

My parents, Marjaana and Simo—I think the only education-related advice I ever received was my father saying I should try to aim for a university education in general. I may have sometimes hoped for someone to make the choices for me, but I'm grateful you let me find my own path.

Rani, I don't think that a junior scholar often gets to honestly call her spouse one of her greatest advisors, but for me it's truly the case. It's not that I couldn't have done it without you—I wouldn't have. Your support has been crucial from the beginning, even before you and I became us. Thank you for always looking at my writings through your "orange"-colored glasses. Our children, Kaisla and Aarni, deserve thanks for forcing me to stop working at decent hours (though they still think I'm always working). Dragging them to conferences and archives has sometimes been like a second or third job, but I think it's been worth the effort, and I hope they'll look back on this time with memories as fond as mine.

ABBREVIATIONS

ACLU: American Civil Liberties Union
CWRIC: Commission on Wartime Relocation and Internment of Civilians
DNA: Dynamic network analysis
DYC: David Yamakawa Collection
FBI: Federal Bureau of Investigation
FPC: Heart Mountain Fair Play Committee
FSEP: Frank S. Emi Papers
HMWF: Heart Mountain Wyoming Foundation
HSTPL: Harry S. Truman Presidential Library
JACL: Japanese American Citizens League
JAERR: Japanese American Evacuation and Resettlement Records
NARA: National Archives and Records Administration
OAC: Online Archive of California
RHP: Ruth Hashimoto Papers
SNA: Social network analysis
USO: United Service Organizations
YBA: Young Buddhists' Association
YMCA: Young Men's Christian Association
YWCA: Young Women's Christian Association
WRA: War Relocation Authority

CHAPTER 1

Introduction

Network Analysis and the Study of Japanese American History

O N AUGUST 8, 1942, 302 people arrived at the railroad depot in Vocation, Wyoming, to become the first Japanese American residents of the Heart Mountain incarceration camp. In the next weeks and months, it became a town of over ten thousand residents with workplaces, social groups, and political alliances—in short, networks.

Networks and connections between people are the foundation of human societies. Human beings desire contact with others wherever they are, including and especially in times of crisis. This book explores the creation of networks at Heart Mountain and the mobility of inmates to and from the camp during its existence between 1942 and 1945. I focus particularly on manifestations of power, agency, and resistance in the incarceration community.

To investigate these forces at the individual and community levels, I developed a network model that recreated the structure, various types of networks, and their changes in the community during the war. The model applies historical "big" data and network analysis, but it also draws from traditional historical sources and methods. I use letters, diaries, government reports, and oral histories to complement the narrative and to support my findings.

This book explores how the Japanese American community at Heart Mountain organized itself, what kinds of structures and networks it established, and how power, agency, and resistance manifests in those structures and networks. I argue that, while one's ability to conform to the camp operator (War Relocation Authority) policy dictated many choices and opportunities, the spectrum of incarceration experience was even more varied than previously acknowledged. Network analysis allows me to draw conclusions beyond individual experience, taking into account groups and their interactions. Not only was the incarceration experience heterogeneous depending on one's ability to integrate into the incarceration community but the interpretation of it varies depending on the network under scrutiny. An individual could appear well integrated into one network and be completely absent from another. For example, being well integrated into the political network often meant being excluded from other networks, and, by extension, such exclusion meant a lower level of integration from the WRA point of view that certain types of behavior were signs of non-assimilation, "Japaneseness," and even disloyalty. Although community councils were typically considered the WRA's puppets, the councilmembers' actions often communicated the opposite: on average, they were more reluctant to leave the camp and they participated less in activities perceived as American that the WRA promoted.

I chose to study the networks at Heart Mountain because the camp was in many ways an average center: in population, in individuals' responses to the loyalty questionnaire, and in resettlement rate.[1] Contemporary authorities and early academic research dubbed Heart Mountain the "happy camp" because there were no major incidents like mass strikes, protests, or shootings by the military police. For the same reason, they considered the Heart Mountain community to have been less political than those at many other camps. As the historian Roger Daniels has noted, however, such a view is much simplified. Heart Mountain was perhaps peaceful considering its size and lack of physical acts of violence by or against the government, but politics were abundant. Heart Mountain was also the site of the only organized draft resistance movement, the Heart Mountain Fair Play Committee.[2]

The authorities justified incarceration as a wartime necessity and safety measure for both Japanese and "mainstream Americans."[3] The *Civil Liberties Act of 1987* acknowledged all those excuses as racially motivated lies. Once the camps were established, the authorities used them to learn about group formation to avoid ethnic clustering in the future. Ethnic neighborhoods—especially Chinatowns, Japantowns, and Indian reservations—were considered to hinder assimilation and thus to threaten the cultural uniformity many White Americans desired. Strengthening Americanism among the inmates of the Japanese American camps was a key priority.[4]

A resettlement or relocation program was created to discourage inmates from returning to their prewar communities. Many young inmates received practical and financial assistance to leave the camps to study in American universities outside the West Coast exclusion area. When the WRA closed the camps in late 1945 (and early 1946 in the case of Tule Lake, California), about 50 percent of inmates from all ten camps had resettled to other parts of the United States, while the other half had returned to the West Coast states—though, as I will demonstrate, not always to the places they had left behind in 1942.

Dynamic Network Analysis and the Study of a Historical Population

To explore the Heart Mountain community in a novel way, I employed dynamic network analysis to create a network model of all its adult inmates. Dynamic network analysis (usually abbreviated as DNA) stems from the more traditional social network analysis (SNA), which originates in the mathematics and computer sciences, specifically in graph theory. It is the study of relationships in any kind of a system: genes in the human body, an airline's connections, or websites on the internet. Graph theory was first introduced as a branch of mathematics in 1735 but the first textbook covering the topic dates only to 1936.[5]

Social network analysis is the investigation of human social ties and relationships. Its practitioners study the structures of a community, looking for patterns of relations to understand how communities work. It has roots in the work of early sociologists like Georg Simmel and Émile Durkheim, who emphasized investigating *patterns* that emerge in the relationships of social actors. The sociologist Harrison C. White is credited as the scholar who made social network analysis a universally accepted paradigm within sociology and anthropology in the 1970s. With eighteenth-, nineteenth-, and even late twentieth-century methods, researchers have only been able to focus on very limited numbers of relations and modest networks. The internet has enabled data sharing and cheap digital storage to allow for mapping extremely large networks. With the availability of bigger data, increasingly powerful computers, and versatile software, researchers of the twenty-first century can significantly expand their scope, not only in terms of network size but also time span. Following rapid developments in the power of computers, the key advocates of network analysis today are physicists. They have been involved in social network analysis since the 1950s, but only the works of Duncan Watts, Steven H. Strogatz, Albert-László Barabási, and Réka Albert in the late 1990s gained wider attention.[6]

The basic components of a network are nodes (the actors that form the network: individuals, organizations, etc., usually represented by circles) and edges (the links that connect two nodes, represented by lines). These edges can be *directed* (individual A belongs to organization X, where the visual link has an arrow pointing from A to X) or *undirected* (A and B are married to each other, where the link has no arrow). A multimode network consists of all individual-to-organization connections, including family groups, political organizations, workplaces, social groups, and geospatial areas. An individual-to-individual network contains direct contacts between two individuals. The number of nodes in a multimode network is thus higher, as it includes different types of nodes, while the individual-to-individual network omits all institutional nodes.

Social network analysis has typically focused on small networks with limited types of connections. This is also true of historical social network analysis. The seminal work in the field is John F. Padgett and Christopher K. Ansell's 1993 article on the Medici family in Renaissance Italy, which focuses on 215 families and nine kinds of direct ties that connect them. Padgett and Ansell do not, for example, include several types of actors (such as individuals and organizations), nor do they attempt to depict all the different kinds of relations between their chosen actors. Furthermore, they include only eight types of attributes, or background data fields, compared to the dozens in the present study. Similarly, in a much more recent article, Robert Michael Morrissey studied the marriage and godparent linkages of one community in eighteenth-century Illinois, resulting in a network of 823 individuals and five thousand connections among them. Finally, April Kamp-Whittaker has recently published on Japanese American networks at the Amache, Colorado incarceration camp. Her study focuses on sports networks and includes a sampling of events over the course of incarceration. In that sense, it is the least complete network example of the three.[7] In all three cases, one is left to wonder what other types of connections the researchers might have added. In comparison, my research consisted of a multimode network containing about twenty thousand nodes and ninety thousand edges and an individual-to-individual network with more than eleven thousand nodes and over three million edges.

In addition to the relative narrowness of the projects described above, traditional SNA has been criticized for its lack of focus on *change*—for not taking into account that actors in a network can learn and adapt and thus change the network.[8] DNA is a response to this criticism and the method I used to organize my data and findings.

Dynamic network analysis is multimode, multi-edge, and multilevel. Multimode means that the network consists of several types of actors—not only individuals or organizations but both, and in the case of this study also political groups, workplaces, and geospatial places. Multi-edge entails different types of links among places (family ties, membership in an organization, and movement between places, for example). Finally, multilevel means that one node can be a member of another node (or several), like an individual is a member of an organization.[9] In contrast, traditional SNA usually looks at the direct relationships among individuals or organizations. The benefit of multilevel (or multilayer) networks is that their multifaceted nature becomes evident.

The word "dynamic" can also imply the evolution of the network model itself—not just the network under consideration. In an open-source network model, for example, a user can add data as it becomes available and correct errors when they emerge. The creation of the Heart Mountain network model has been a dynamic process as well: data have been collected from multiple sources and formats and compiled into the most comprehensive model possible.

The network model itself is a significant research result. It should be kept in mind that my analysis in the printed output is not based on still screenshots or images but on a more complex model that has been queried in thousands of ways through partitions, filters, and statistical calculations.[10]

These queries measure individual and group-level influence and power in several different ways. The most frequently used concepts include:

Degree: The number of connections (edges) related to an actor (node). *Outdegree* measures the number of edges leaving a node (for example, an individual's number of memberships to different organizations). *Indegree* measures the incoming edges of a node (the number of members belonging to an organization).

Betweenness (centrality): The ability of a node to *bridge* parts of a network that would otherwise be unconnected. For example, if A and B know each other, D and E know each other, and C knows all four, C is a bridge between the two pairs. Another term used is *broker*.

Modularity: The grouping of the nodes in a network into communities based on their linkages. (Nodes that have many links between each other but fewer to other parts of the network are grouped together.)

Historical Data and Heart Mountain Networks

A historian engaging with quantitative data may sometimes wonder whether a dataset is big or small. To be clear, for physicists and economists, big data usually means millions if not billions of rows of data. Especially from the point of view of historical data, any dataset that is too large for an individual researcher to process manually constitutes big data. While data in the social sciences and humanities are often smaller in scale than in the natural sciences, each data point is more complex, allowing for more nuanced interpretations. And, as I noted above, my method of mapping all known relations of a community as large as Heart Mountain is novel in historical research, thus qualifying as historical big data.[11]

Almost anything web-based can be turned into a table readable by analysis and visualization tools. Social networking companies like Facebook and LinkedIn are dedicated to making big data available for researchers and advertisers. This may, in part, be due to their philosophy of openness, but sites like these are very interested in knowing the most profitable way of marketing either their own or their partners' products.

Using archival material and doing historical research is a different matter. In general, the older the data, the more likely it is to be written by hand and in completely narrative form. Optical character recognition (OCR) tools as well as data mining are developing so quickly that data that is nearly unusable this year may be available as a spreadsheet the next. In the meantime, a lot of manual labor is still needed. The researcher must first create a table of her findings—including the relationships between the actors and the type, strength, and duration of the ties—before being able to do data analysis. From a historian's perspective, this may not be a problem, as historians are used to collating large numbers of documents. Moreover, network analysis with numeric data cannot alone create a reliable reconstruction of a real historical community. Traditional documents and narratives are still essential, and manually processing one's data can significantly enhance the researcher's knowledge of the material she is using.

My model depicting the Heart Mountain networks is based on three large datasets: the "entry data," or the responses to form 26, which the War Relocation Authority collected from everyone taken to an incarceration camp; the "final roster," which accounts for the inmates' movement from the camps; and the *Heart Mountain Sentinel* dataset, which I collected from the *Heart Mountain Sentinel* newspaper. The convention of spelling Japanese names varied greatly across the documents. Sometimes Japanese names have received an English spelling (Kei/Kay). There was also a lot of variation in the use of diphthongs, as exemplified by the spelling of one name as both Yukie and Yukiye. Similarly, whether a name ends in an "o" or an "e" (Yukio or Yukie) did not seem to indicate two different names. Finally, authorities sometimes omitted the "ko" from female names without any apparent reason (Yuri/Yuriko). The order of first and middle names was not consistent in the datasets, with English names and Japanese names recorded in varying sequence. Unless clearly indicated in oral histories or other primary documents, I have used the names provided in the final roster. As an example, the entry data gives one of the female protagonists as Chiyoko N. Sashihara and the final roster lists her as Nina Chiyoko, whereas she referred to herself as Chiyo Sashihara. Based on the available information, I refer to her by the name Chiyo Sashihara. I use original spellings in the datasets instead of more detailed romanizations, which are occasionally used. And I use the Western order of first name–last name for *Issei* and *Nisei* alike, instead of the Japanese convention of last name–first name.[12]

The US National Archives and Records Administration provides on its website an online database of all incarcerated Japanese Americans as they entered the incarceration camps (later the entry database). In its entirety, it includes background data (such as education level, occupation, and length of stay in Japan) for over 109,000 individuals.[13] This "entry data" formed the first dataset for the networks.

My second large dataset was the final roster of the Heart Mountain Relocation Center, consisting of departure-day data for each inmate held in the camp. These included camp address (if resident on December 31, 1944), reason for departure (for example, indefinite leave for employment), and destination. In its final form, the dataset had 14,011 names. While the Heart Mountain peak population in January 1943 was 10,767, all arrivals, leaves, births, and deaths accounted for the larger number.

My third dataset was a collection from various sources, mostly the *Heart Mountain Sentinel* newspaper, published by the inmates (but supervised by White authorities). The newspaper launched in late October 1942 and appeared once a week until July 1945.[14] It typically had eight broadsheet English pages followed by four pages in Japanese. The English section contained images as well as advertisements, while the Japanese section was usually only text. The paper contained reporting on a variety of topics, including camp news, sports, and social life, as well as articles on incarceration and the war. Standard sections also included short news items from the nine other camps.

Like all camp newspapers, the *Sentinel* was accused of censorship and a pro-WRA and pro–Japanese American Citizens League bias. For example, this bias manifests in the wide publicizing of Nisei volunteers and draftees and the relative lack of reporting on the Fair Play Committee. To the paper's credit, however, it published a letter by FPC leader Frank S. Emi defending draft resisters.[15] Its editor, Bill Hosokawa, a former JACL leader, was a controversial figure, and his stance had an enormous impact on the content of the newspaper even after he resettled in Denver in 1943. As a result, he also influenced some of the networks explored in this book: although some of them were the result of WRA policy (such as the composition of workplaces or the creation of "American" social organizations), the newspaper had a say in what network elements were promoted.

Regardless of censorship or biases, the paper provides excellent material for data collection purposes. Its editors and reporters diligently reported on community government and activities, and listed the names of representatives and officers in various social groups (sports clubs, church activities). It offers a rich source of information on the construction and composition of the community. This material was central to identifying key individuals, or "hubs," who served in multiple roles in the camp.

The material would have allowed meticulous mapping of social activities (down to the participants of private tea parties). For my interest in power, agency, and resettlement decisions, it was most relevant to focus on the wider community, including involvement in political organizations, participation in camp activities, and membership in the camp labor force. Similarly, the newspaper would enable the construction of children's networks through Scout groups, boys' and girls' clubs, sports teams, and high school organizations.[16] While children's networks are important in their own right, I assume that in most cases they played little role in the adults' networks or resettlement decisions. They were therefore left outside the scope of this study.

Despite its wide scope and multiple contexts, this is an investigation of specific kinds of ties: those that were formalized in one way or another in official records or the newspaper. Not everyone participated in the formal operations of the camp, but they still had kinship and friendship networks. Some people engaged actively in the social network but did not assume official roles, and so they are absent from this model. Thus, even at its current depth and breadth, this network is extendable. This is the strength and challenge of historical network analysis: it is never complete and always evolving.

In addition to the evolution of the network, the key to historical network analysis is to investigate multiple viewpoints. The network model renders itself to analysis through several layers that form the basis for the chapters of this book. These subnetworks are political, employment, social, and geospatial. I begin by offering an overview of the full, "integrated" network, then peel back each layer to look at smaller segments of the networks before finally returning to the bird's eye view. The subnetworks also gave rise to themes, such as resettlement and power, that I analyze throughout.

The selection of subnetworks arose from the data and reflect the real-life networks that existed at Heart Mountain. The fact that the data allowed for the reconstruction of these particular networks demonstrates that the authorities and/or inmates considered them important. While the narratives promoted by the *Heart Mountain Sentinel* provide most of the network data, often the same communities appeared in administrative reports and other documents, thus validating my claim that these were the most important networks for the camp at large.

War Relocation Authority and Its Influence on Inmate Networks

In March 1942, President Franklin Delano Roosevelt established the War Relocation Authority and tasked it with creating and running "permanent" incarceration camps. Very quickly, the agency adopted the philosophy and policy of assimilationism as its guiding principle. The inmates were to be dispersed across the country to welcoming communities where they could more easily blend in. The WRA mandated that, while in camp, all effort should be expended on their education as idealized American citizens. By necessity, this had an enormous impact on the formal networks of the camps.[17]

While the WRA instructed inmates to create community governments and allowed for the establishment of various social groups, the ultimate power was always in the hands of the White administrators at each camp. Thus, the camp networks are easy to read from an assimilationist perspective: Which organizations and individuals appeared to conform to the WRA's wishes? It is, however, more interesting to consider these networks more deeply: How can we read both individuals and institutions as driving their own agendas, regardless of what the WRA promoted?[18]

Of course, these viewpoints are not separate or exclusive. I will uncover a variety and depth of relationships that sometimes show support for—and indicate—integration. At other times, networks enforced separation. My exploration of the Heart Mountain networks reveals that there was no unified "camp experience." I will show that there was a spectrum of reactions to incarceration with varying degrees and multiple strategies of outward resistance and accommodation. Although themes like agency, resistance, and power would traditionally be studied through narrative documents, I will show that historical big data and dynamic network analysis can, through the study of network structures, segmentation, and the spread of ideas and opinions, help us see trends and changes in a community that has received little scholarly attention.

Although an overall assimilationist spirit characterized the early twentieth century in the United States and many local programs were created to absorb immigrants into the "American mainstream," only Japanese Americans and Native Americans were the targets of federal assimilation programs. I rely on Mae Ngai's depiction of the WRA's programs as a form of benevolent assimilationism.[19] For example, my reading of WRA director Dillon S. Myer's speeches suggests that he wholeheartedly believed in a linear process of assimilation and, most importantly, that this process was not only inevitable but also desirable to members of the minority communities in question. While assimilation has without a doubt led to loss of identity and culture, on a community level, structural assimilation had the potential to benefit Japanese Americans. For example, it brought about access to a non-ethnic market and workplaces.[20]

Anglo-conformity as the desirable outcome of assimilation should not be automatically equated with racism. According to Gordon, one can exist without the other, although historically they have often occurred in parallel. Anglo-conformists were convinced of the cultural superiority of US institutions or simply believed that, since English culture had been dominant during much of the development of American institutions, it should be maintained. Similarly, American culture was seen as so strong that adapting to the new society would inevitably result in the loss of one's original group identity. The historian Lon Kurashige has pointed out that, compared to the extreme racism of the early 20th century, WRA assimilationism and Myer's role in creating the policies could be seen almost as "an antiracist response to the long history of Yellow Peril rhetoric."[21]

While some researchers argue that society should move and has moved on from emphasizing assimilation to embracing multiculturalism and multiethnicity, the expectation of "proper" assimilation has not disappeared. During the COVID-19 pandemic, some people again looked upon Asian Americans with suspicion, and open racism reignited. Former Democratic presidential candidate Andrew Yang went as far as to call all Asian Americans "to embrace and show our American-ness in ways we never have before. . . . We should show without a shadow of a doubt that we are Americans who will do our part for our country in this time of need."[22] Similar calls to demonstrate loyalty were also at the heart of the World War II incarceration debate, coming from both White and Japanese Americans. They prove that, while on the surface the United States may celebrate diversity, the underlying thinking has not disappeared. Minority ethnicities must conform to White cultural norms to avoid discrimination.

The ways to respond to a crisis called for in Yang's article are similar to the expectations that Japanese Americans faced during World War II. The authorities defined an assimilated person by citing certain characteristics. These were not necessarily words publicly proclaimed or printed in an administrative manual but adjectives and verbs that were used in reports to describe successful or unsuccessful adjustment and resettlement. For the authorities, an assimilated person spoke

English, identified as a Christian, received an education in the United States, and, in the incarceration camp context, participated in "American" activities organized by the authorities. In addition, they were ready to resettle in any part of the country, regardless of where their prewar homes, jobs, and families had been.[23]

My treatment of assimilation in this book arises from the perceptions of the White authorities. Because they had such a profound impact on the everyday lives of inmates, their assimilationist aspirations must be acknowledged. It is, however, not my intention to study the networks through assimilation theories or how we understand assimilation in a twenty-first-century context. Rather, I seek to show instances where inmates either conformed to or challenged authorities' requirements.

Key Concepts and Ethical Considerations

Researchers have long discussed and even argued over proper terminology to use when referring to the treatment of Japanese Americans during World War II. Writers agree on one issue: that the United States government frequently employed euphemisms to draw attention away from the prison-like conditions of the camps. "Evacuation" and "relocation" were the most common choices during the war, although "internment camps" and even "concentration camps" were also in use. After the war, internment became the most widely used term. More recently, scholars have commonly chosen words like "imprisonment," "detention," "incarceration," and "confinement." The historian Greg Robinson, for example, wrote of "internment," "internment camp," and "internees" in 2001, whereas by 2009 he had switched to "confinement" and "inmates."[24] Scholars have not found a term to suit all, but they increasingly agree that internment is an inappropriate concept, except when discussing the interned Japanese citizens.

Internment is a legal term that describes the possibly preventative imprisonment of non-citizens during wartime, and it is a procedure approved by the Geneva Convention.[25] It accurately describes the situation of the minority proportion of the Japanese Americans, the first generation Issei, and more specifically the Issei that were arrested after Pearl Harbor as leaders of the community. The majority—the US-born second-generation Nisei—were American citizens, whose incarceration was legalized by a presidential Executive Order.[26]

The museum curator Karen L. Ishizuka promotes the terms "concentration camp" and "inmate," referring to internment as a separate process. She has created a table of euphemisms the US government used, including the previously mentioned "evacuation" and "relocation" as well as "non-alien" for US citizens of Japanese ancestry and "native American aliens" for those who renounced US citizenship under pressure. The historian Brian Masaru Hayashi supports use of the term concentration camp, since that is what the camps essentially were. Nevertheless, he acknowledges the strong connotation with Nazi death camps, however false such an equivalence may be. Greg Robinson further argues that, despite the violation of civil rights, camp officials and outside workers sought "to ease the situation" of Japanese Americans.[27] The nonprofit Japanese American heritage organization Densho prefers the terms incarceration, concentration camp, and inmate. Hayashi, in turn, makes an argument against using inmate, pointing out that such a term would imply a violation of criminal law. For that same reason, I do not find "imprisonment" an appropriate term. Nevertheless, I consider inmate to be the closest appropriate term to describe the incarcerated Japanese Americans. I mostly use the terms incarceration and inmate. I also use the words "camps" and "centers" interchangeably, because both appeared in the official names of the places under discussion. In discussing events in the camp, I refer to "residents" and the "community." I agree that resident suggests a degree of voluntariness, but at the same time, the size (thousands of people), composition (people of all ages and sexes, families as well as single people), and government (while led by White administrators, in many ways modeled as a "regular" community) of the camps did generate communities, albeit from a non-voluntary starting point.

As I am using documents and texts that frequently use the terms "evacuation," "evacuee," and "relocation," I find it unavoidable to employ the same terms every now and then. It should be noted that the administration used the term relocation to denote two processes: the first phase of removing Japanese Americans from the West Coast and the second phase of forcing them to resettle from the camps across the United States. Similarly, resettlement referred not only to movement away from the West Coast but also to the return to old Japanese American neighborhoods. Many have considered resettlement the long process of reestablishing oneself, both physically and mentally, roughly from 1945 to 1955.[28] Since resettlement in the former sense of the word is a central theme in this book, I will use it in the exclusive meaning of moving to other parts of the country and will use "return" to describe those who went straight back to California, Oregon, or Washington when released from camp. Finally, it should become evident from context that sometimes the term "Japanese" denotes all Japanese Americans, both first-generation immigrants and Americans of Japanese descent.

Studying a group of real people—using census data and other data that identifies specific individuals—brings up certain ethical considerations. Some might argue that the National Archives should not make a database of all inhabitants of incarceration camps publicly available online. Since all primary sources used are more than seventy-two years old, I have deemed them appropriate for use.[29] When writing, I tried to avoid naming people unnecessarily.

To avoid issues relating to personal privacy, I only used publicly available census lists and official documents from the Census Bureau, the War Department, the War Relocation Authority, and other federal, state, and local governmental agencies. All non-governmental documents like journals, newspapers, and correspondences are from public sources. The use of details about court cases at Heart Mountain, although freely available from the *Heart Mountain Sentinel* and archival sources, was more difficult to reconcile. Should we afford additional privacy to people who committed crimes under such extraordinary circumstances? Most of the people involved in the trials were not otherwise central to my rendering of the networks. Therefore, I mention only few of them in passing.

The ensuing work is divided into ten chapters. Chapter 2 provides the context for the immigration, assimilation, and exclusion of the Japanese in the United States. It also provides an overview of the history of Japanese incarceration. Chapter 3 introduces the Heart Mountain networks as reconstructed through historical sources. Chapter 4 focuses on the Heart Mountain political networks, setting up the power relations in the camp community. Chapter 5 delves deeper into the social fabric of the camp through an examination of employment and social networks. Chapter 6 looks at "power families" and individuals of power, and chapter 7 brings the stories and experiences of women to the foreground. Chapter 8 emphasizes the active resistance of the Fair Play Committee and the more passive resistance of those who were segregated in Tule Lake. Chapter 9 explores the various paths to freedom from Heart Mountain, with a special focus on some of the more unusual routes. Chapter 10 is an epilogue, summing up the results, advantages, and future trajectories of network analysis on Heart Mountain and beyond.

CHAPTER 2

From Immigration to Incarceration

The Japanese in the United States, 1890–1942

To UNDERSTAND THE EXPERIENCES of Japanese Americans in the incarceration camps, we must first understand the histories of Japanese American communities in the US. Although it can be argued that the Japanese were already well integrated into American society at the start of the war in many ways, their collective history informed individuals' choices and opportunities.

Much of the pre-war Japanese American history has to do with interracial tensions and, more specifically, White discrimination against the Japanese. Racism (or, in milder terms, assimilationism) did not begin in the United States with the arrival of Japanese immigrants. Rather, it has as long a history as the country itself. All of these themes—the causes of migration, the culture of the migrants, and the culture of the new home country—must be brought into context in order to understand the relations between Japanese and WhiteAmerican communities.

This chapter will first discuss the history of Japanese immigration in the United States, then look at the racism, discrimination, and assimilationism that Japanese Americas faced. Following this prewar historical contextualization, I will present an overview of the incarceration policy.

Becoming Japanese American

For centuries, Japan was a closed society with little migration outside its borders. Even within Japan, peasants rarely traveled outside the boundaries of their prefectures. Historians consider the 1868 Meiji Restoration as the starting point of modern Japan, and in the latter half of the nineteenth century, the United States forcefully opened Japan to foreign trade and influence. The first Japanese immigrants to North America—mostly men—went to Hawaii (first an independent kingdom, then starting in 1898 a US territory) to work on its sugar plantations. Many of them came from the southwestern parts of Honshu Island, which had changed dramatically due to industrialization and left many families poor. Some emigrants escaped conscription into the Japanese army. Okinawans—members of a socially and politically marginalized group in Japan—also had reason to migrate. After initially large numbers of men arrived in the US, many sent for their wives to follow them, returned to Japan to get married, or found "picture brides"—women that intermediaries (*baishakunin*) arranged for the men to marry.[1]

In the beginning, the White elite welcomed the Japanese to the United States. They considered the newcomers hard workers who were eager to learn more yet accept modest wages. In many places, Japanese immigrants were considered cleaner and more intelligent than Chinese immigrants. Part of this favoritism had to do with protecting White interests: pitting the two racialized and discriminated groups against one another would stall them from organizing a labor union. At the same time, they were markedly different from the majority population in appearance, culture, religion, language, and tendency to form ethnic neighborhoods—a need arising from discrimination.[2] With the ban on Chinese immigration in 1882, the Japanese became targets of the fear of a "yellow peril." The fears were unfounded, and in fact the 1880 census found only 148 Japanese people living in the continental United States. The number began to grow rapidly, and by the early 1920s, one hundred and thirty thousand Japanese had come to the country, 70 percent of them living in California.[3]

Today, research literature continues to treat the Japanese as a "new" immigrant group, probably because the presence of this group in the US was virtually nonexistent before 1880. In terms of volume, however, it is important to bear in mind that the arrival of Japanese immigrants coincides with a mass immigration to the US. Their numbers are but a fraction in comparison with European immigrants during the same years.[4]

Many Japanese immigrants intended to stay in the US temporarily. Life's realities—either hardships that prevented return or relative prosperity that deferred such a decision—caused many to make a permanent home in the United States. Consequently, they made an effort to acclimate to life in the United States. A sizable number of Issei, although a minority, converted to Christianity. (Some of them did so when they were still living in Japan as a result of American Christian missionary work in the 1870s and 1880s.) Christianity had its appeals: Protestant denominations offered Sunday school and social welfare activities like English language classes, help in finding jobs, and childcare for working parents. Children found friends across ethnic lines in church activities. Those Japanese Americans who remained Buddhist allowed the religion to evolve, adopting Western elements like congregational services, Sunday schools, and ministers, all unknown in Japanese Buddhism. At the same time, Japanese Americans began creating ethnic institutions, including the Japanese Association, newspapers, and religious groups. They retained close ties with the homeland, sent money to relatives in Japan, and kept in close contact with the many consulates of the Japanese government.[5]

Japanese social structure entailed horizontal instead of vertical identification: identification with one's family or employer rather than with one's peer group or profession. Similarly, it was crucial to avoid causing shame to one's family (more important, for instance, than avoiding shame to oneself). These features reinforced the power of the group and encouraged individuals to handle conflict without outside help, which resulted in the low use of community resources. Loyalty to the *ken* (Japanese state or prefecture) sometimes led to occupational concentration: The first Japanese barber in prewar Seattle was from Yamaguchi-ken, and once his enterprise was established, he helped people from that ken to start up their own barbershops. Eventually, this led to a domination of barbers from that particular ken. Because people patronized companies owned by people from their ken and helped "their own" to advance their careers, the owner of a large and successful company was almost certain to be from one of the more populated kens. Loyalty to one's employer, grocery store, or medical care provider were fundamental even in a situation of conflict or dissatisfaction.[6]

Japanese society—and, by extension, prewar Japanese American society—was hierarchical. As described by the sociologist Forrest E. LaViolette, "Each member's position in the family, and the family's position in the community, [was] defined in express and minute detail." A person's rank and status in the society were dependent on age, sex, order of entrance, and period of service, instead of competence, efficiency, or training.[7]

Japanese Americans in the early twentieth century were statistically a relatively homogeneous group. Having immigrated in the United States over the course of just a few decades, between 1890 and 1924, the majority had arrived young and were close to each other in age. As a result, the number of their American-born children, the Nisei, grew rapidly. Adding to the homogeneity of the Nisei and Japanese Americans in general, most of them continued to practice Buddhism and many actively spoke Japanese. Japanese Americans were also racially homogeneous. Japanese social norms discouraged marrying someone who was not Japanese, and those who were willing to act against those norms faced an obstacle in the California and Oregon miscegenation laws that prohibited Asian (and Black) people from marrying Whites until 1948 and 1951, respectively.[8]

The Nisei, the historian David Yoo argues, comprised such a cohesive group that they can truly be treated as a generation. As a distinction from other minorities, the second-generation Japanese Americans not only shared the experience of having been born in a country not native to their parents but also shared the experience of growing up in the same years. On the other hand, as the historian Cherstin M. Lyon points out, within the Nisei there are two generations that grew up in very different societies. The "older Nisei," born between 1910 and 1917, constituted less than a quarter of the Japanese American (*Nikkei*) population. During their formative years, the political debate as well as public opinion focused more on the perils of immigration (i.e., the supposed threat posed by their parents) than on the status and degree of assimilation of the Nisei. The majority of the Nisei were born between 1917 and 1925, and their youth coincides with the assimilationist movement.[9]

It would be an oversimplification to claim that *all* Nisei unanimously supported the same values. They were split into cliques and factions, and as I will discuss in subsequent chapters, the presence of *Kibei* further complicated the matter. Kibei is the Japanese word for those American-born children of Japanese descent who received some or all of their education in Japan. Sometimes the stays were shorter and included the entire family traveling, but many children were sent to Japan on their own and spent most of their childhoods there.

The Japanese American Citizens League was the most vocal and well known of the Nisei groups. It was also the most assimilationist and barred aliens from membership. From the launch of the organization in 1929, its purpose was to establish and promote the identity of the Nisei as Americans. In the spirit of White American ideology, the JACL promoted assimilationism and opposed causing friction between Japanese and White Americans. Furthermore, the JACL wanted the Nisei to express patriotism and prove their loyalty to the United States. Such pro-American sentiment became even more important after the Japanese attack on Pearl Harbor, when the JACL began to support the incarceration of all Japanese Americans as a way of proving the Nisei's loyalty to the United States. However, the Japanese American community did not unanimously support this decision. The JACL's strong alliance with the WRA earned JACL activists a poor reputation, and other Japanese people at the camps often shunned them for their questionable loyalties. Some Nisei were also active in Young Democrat clubs, which were more radical in their calls for reform of not only the Japanese American community but American society in general.[10]

The top JACL leadership—most notably its national executive secretary, Mike Masaoka—lived outside the exclusion area and avoided incarceration. As a consequence, the JACL continued to directly influence inmates. For example, when the first sixty-three Heart Mountain draft resisters were awaiting their trial (they were tried together), JACL influencers Joe Grant Masaoka and Minoru Yasui visited them in the Cheyenne County Jail and tried to talk the resisters into reversing their conviction. According to the JACL, draft resistance drew negative attention onto all Japanese Americans at a time when they should be exhibiting loyalty to the United States.[11]

Many White Americans expressed suspicion over the continued identification and formal ties with Japan. In particular, the practice of sending American-born children to Japan to receive an education may be a significant reason why Japanese Americans were collectively labeled as disloyal. The estimates about the number of Nisei having studied in Japan for at least a year range from about 15 percent to up to 50 percent. At the time of the Pearl Harbor attack, this would have amounted to some eleven thousand Kibei.[12] The Heart Mountain data reflects the lowest percentage figure: the number of American citizens with any amount of schooling in Japan was 993. This corresponds to about 11 percent of all citizens in camp and about 14 percent of those who were of school age any time before the war broke out. I will discuss this issue in chapter 8.

It is unclear why parents chose to send their American children to Japan. Most likely, the Issei were uncertain about the length of their stay in the United States; they were, after all, unqualified to apply for citizenship. In a 1944 report, the War Relocation Authority stated that the Issei wanted their sons to have a combined American and Japanese education that would increase their chances of a good job. Girls, in turn, were to be taught to adhere to traditional behavioral norms to increase their marriage options. Most Kibei returned to the United States after a few years of schooling, usually to find themselves in a conflicting role. Many Nisei did not perceive the Kibei as properly American, as the Kibei often acquired Japanese cultural traits and forgot the English language. The assumed immersion into Japanese culture and values led the US authorities to view the Kibei as potentially disloyal. Nevertheless, some Kibei qualified for the armed services, and they formed the core of the group that served in the Pacific with the US Army's Military Intelligence Service as interpreters.[13] As I will later show, many Kibei were also in central positions in the Heart Mountain networks.

For the Nisei, becoming Japanese American was never, as the historian Gary Okihiro notes, a black-and-white question of choosing America over Japan.

External and internal forces directed the process, as the Nisei negotiated the demands of mainstream US culture on the one hand and the values of the Japanese community on the other. For many Nisei, being American meant rejecting their parents' culture. True Americanizers claimed that the Issei were old-fashioned, while the Nisei represented the future. Issei parents were accused of causing confused cultural identities, which the Nisei expected to overcome by distancing themselves from the parents. Okihiro argues that much of the confusion and generational conflict had to do with anti-Japanese hostility that simultaneously sought to exclude the Japanese from American life and demanded their complete assimilation. As a result, some Nisei became what Okihiro called "religiously Oriental" while others strove to become as "intensely American" as possible. In fact, hybridization, becoming *Japanese American*, was quite impossible in such a context.[14]

In this book, I discuss both Issei and Nisei experiences. In general, the Nisei have been studied in more detail; they came of age during incarceration and produced plenty of written material. The Issei often wrote in Japanese, limiting the number of researchers able to incorporate their views. Without Japanese language skills, I, too, am restricted to English and/or translated text when it comes to the Issei point of view. In the network analysis part of this book, the Issei become part of the story naturally. Although they were the seniors of the community, many of them were not advanced in age at the time of incarceration. The Japanese American community moved toward an era of Nisei leadership, but the Issei were in power coming to the camps.[15]

Discrimination and Racism Lead to Incarceration

The prewar stereotype of Japanese Americans mostly consisted of negative attributes. The stereotypical Japanese American, according to early incarceration historians Jacobus tenBroek, Edward N. Barnhart, and Floyd W. Matson, was "inscrutable, treacherous, and disloyal." After the attack on Pearl Harbor, these characteristics seemed reason enough to make the entire group suspect of sabotage. In a 1943 congressional debate about the fate of Japanese Americans, Democratic representative Alfred J. Elliott of California called them not only "treacherous" but also "tricky." One of Elliott's main arguments against the loyalty of the Japanese was that a truly loyal American would have warned the United States about the Pearl Harbor attack, which "not even one of these J—— rascals" did. As late as 1945, Democratic representative Harry R. Sheppard of California stated that "lessons sternly learned" proved that Japanese Americans prided themselves "on their refusal to assimilate, indeed, on their *innate* inability to assimilate." This, Sheppard argued, was because the Japanese belonged "to an utterly alien race, a race which teaches its members that it is superior, that it is destined to rule the world."[16]

The anti-Japanese movement had begun and was always at its strongest in California, a state where 95 percent of the residents were White. Already in 1905, the California legislature passed an anti-Japanese resolution calling the "mode of living" and "general characteristics" of Japanese immigrants undesirable and expressing the fear that, by accepting wages that were below subsistence level, the Japanese would drive away White labor. Many Californians also felt that "Japanese laborers do not evince any inclination to assimilate with our people, or to become Americans."[17]

Of course, the Issei were not allowed to "become Americans." Although a few hundred had managed naturalization (for example, through military service in World War I), the Takao Ozawa v. the United States case in the Supreme Court in 1922 cemented the status of the Issei as "aliens ineligible for citizenship."[18]

Where the late nineteenth-century public image had portrayed the Japanese as hard workers, attitudes across the country began to change after 1905. Japanese workers were beginning to establish their own enterprises and became a threat to White farmers and businesspeople. This also meant that available labor became scarcer. Japanese success challenged the presupposition of White supremacy. At the same time, Japan increased its military power and became the dominant naval power in the Pacific, and thus made all Japanese people less trustworthy to many White Americans.[19]

Perhaps most significantly, White Americans viewed the practice of dual citizenship as a threat. Many felt that American citizens who also held Japanese citizenship would be loyal to the Japanese Emperor, even though dual citizens were American-born and thus likely to be first and foremost loyal to the United States. This perceived threat led to anti-Japanese legislation, most notably the Alien Land Law of 1913, which prohibited people ineligible for citizenship from owning land. Previously, Californians had initiated a campaign to stop Japanese immigrants from moving to the United States, leading to the Gentlemen's Agreement of 1907. According to the agreement, Japan began to place restrictions on emigration to the United States, while the US government allowed the family members of existing Japanese immigrants to move to the country.[20]

While some expressions of American culture today valorize cultural and ethnic diversity, in fact the country's policies and programs have promoted cultural homogeneity throughout much of its history. George Washington, the first president of the nation, said in his farewell address that the people of the United States shared "the same religion, manners, habits, and political principles."[21] In Washington's time, and until the late nineteenth century, members of the White majority could by and large keep themselves isolated from ethnic minorities and foster the ideal of White, Anglo-Saxon America. By the turn of the century, however, industrial expansion and increasing immigration brought different groups much closer to each other. There emerged a new need to define the nation, which gave rise to requests for immigrants and non-White individuals to assimilate.[22]

Americanization entailed an appreciation for democracy, representative government, law and order, capitalism, general health, and the use of English. A Protestant ethic (in other words, being self-reliant, hardworking, and morally upright) was understood as the key to success. These values were taught in schools—indeed, their promotion was the primary reason for the establishment of public schools.[23]

Japanese immigrants embraced educational opportunities in the United States, whatever the underlying goal of the White-led government. In late nineteenth-century Japan, at least four years of education were compulsory, and often another four years followed. When the Issei came to America, most had several years of schooling and an understanding of (and respect for) the educational process. In Japanese culture, the teacher was the ultimate authority and always right, whereas the student should be unquestioning, conforming, and competitive.[24] With parental appreciation for schooling and a culture emphasizing diligence, the Nisei were particularly prone to Americanization.

Postwar scholarship has often claimed that the Japanese have an "inherent" ability to adapt. But according to psychologist Harry L. Kitano, such a claim is not compatible with Japanese actions in the South Pacific, Philippines, and Asia, where the Japanese government behaved in much the same way as European colonial powers. Thus, he argues, the Japanese were *willing* to adjust to life in the United States; many of the core values (such as hard work) were easy for them to adopt because they already held those values. Clearly, says Kitano, the relative success in acculturation can be attributed to the ability of the Japanese culture to "teach, shape, and reinforce certain behaviors over others."[25]

Indeed, to counter the racism they faced, the Issei were active in promoting Americanization. They organized patriotic (that is, pro-American) celebrations, emphasized the use of the English language for their children, and reorganized the Japanese language schools (though they didn't go so far as to close those schools).[26] The persistence of language schools was also a protective means.

Japanese American children would need to be familiar with Japanese language and culture, should families be forced out of the country.[27]

Locked-up Citizens

In the fall of 1941, before the Japanese attack on Pearl Harbor, President Franklin D. Roosevelt had already commissioned a report to review the loyalties of Japanese immigrants living on the United States West Coast and in Hawaii. The Munson report, named after the State Department special representative and head investigator Curtis B. Munson, concluded that the Japanese, both non-citizens and citizens, were "remarkably," even "extraordinarily," loyal to the United States. The contents of this report, however, remained unknown to various relevant authorities throughout the war. On the other hand, access to the report did not necessarily affect decision-making: among the chief executives of incarceration were people who knew about the report's contents.[28]

Immediately after the attack on Pearl Harbor, the FBI was authorized to arrest enemy aliens, Germans and Italians as well as Japanese, who had been deemed dangerous. About two thousand Issei were arrested, and the Navy ordered all Japanese-owned fishing boats beached to prevent the fishers from aiding Japanese ships. All assets of Japanese nationals were frozen, although First Lady Eleanor Roosevelt managed to persuade the Treasury Department to allow each family to withdraw one hundred dollars per month for living expenses. The Justice Department issued a list of "contraband" items that Japanese citizens were not allowed to possess. The list included such everyday items as cameras and radios. The search for contraband caused many Issei to destroy anything from Japan or representing Japanese culture in their households: clothes, books, and personal artifacts.[29]

Issei were arrested based on their leadership (or mere membership) in "suspect" organizations, not necessarily for suspicious individual actions. Removing such a large number of leaders "paralyzed Japanese American community structures" and prevented the community from organizing a group response to unfolding events.[30] The Nisei were too young, often still underage, and too inexperienced to create a unified front against accusations. They managed to hold their first meeting to consider a strategy only after President Roosevelt issued Executive Order 9066 on February 19, 1942. The order enabled the military to prescribe restricted areas from which "any or all persons may be excluded."[31] In theory, the order could have also applied to German and Italian immigrants, both more significant minorities with 97,080 and 113,847 non-naturalized residents, respectively, living on the Pacific Coast. In practice, the exclusion only extended to the 110,000 Japanese Americans, only 36,000 of whom were not US citizens.[32]

As a result of the executive order, the Western Defense Command (the office in charge of coordinating the defense of the Pacific Coast) designated western California, Oregon, Washington, and the southern part of Arizona as a military area, requesting all people of Japanese descent to be removed from it. For the first couple of weeks, people were allowed to relocate voluntarily. Most of the residents of the coastal areas were unable to close their businesses and sell or store their property in the short time given them, and few had a home or a job waiting elsewhere. Furthermore, inland communities were not any more tolerant of the Japanese, and migrants were constantly shunned. Thus, voluntary relocation proved ineffective. The process was halted and authorities began to plan new measures. During those few weeks, about eight thousand Japanese people relocated outside the military area, but some of them were forced to return to the excluded areas due to housing and employment problems and were thus incarcerated.[33] My data includes individuals entering Heart Mountain from places of residence outside the military area. I interpret this to mean that they voluntarily joined their families in incarceration.

Although the incarceration policies are normally attributed to a few high-level military and civilian officials, some of the key decisions were made by request of local authorities. The governors and attorneys general of the states neighboring the restricted coast—states where camps were to be located—opposed voluntary relocation and even more fiercely the idea of establishing "free" Japanese American communities in their states. These actors demanded the construction of fenced and guarded camps.[34]

Contrary to what the opposition to Japanese Americans in the inland states might suggest, Japanese Americans did live outside the West Coast. Wyoming, for example, had 643 residents of Japanese background in the 1940 census, down from a peak population of 1,596 in 1910.[35] After Pearl Harbor, Wyoming Governor Nels H. Smith ordered a list of all Japanese Americans and their addresses, which yielded the information of 398 people of Japanese ancestry. Sheriff W. R. Silver of Converse County reported that he had found three Japanese American families, the members of whom were "according to my findings, good citizens."[36] Little has been written about free Japanese Americans in the vicinity of the incarceration camps, but Gretel Ehrlich imagines that experience in her novel *Heart Mountain*, in which an elderly Issei working on a Wyoming ranch marvels at the appearance of his compatriots, who were suddenly isolated from the rest of the society.[37]

Following the final evacuation order, the evacuees had to close their businesses and sell their properties in less than two weeks. The government offered storage of property "at the sole risk" of the owners, an arrangement that few dared to trust. Many sought to take advantage of the difficult situation of the Japanese Americans, buying property at nominal prices or making threats to force sales. A postwar survey indicated that the caretakers destroyed, stole, or illegally sold 80 percent of privately stored goods during the absence of the owners.[38]

Some authorities urged the mass incarceration of the Japanese Americans of Hawaii. This move met vigorous opposition because the Hawaiian economy was so highly dependent on Japanese labor. The historian Ronald Takaki estimates that the Japanese accounted for 90 percent of Hawaiian carpenters and transportation workers and made a significant input to local agriculture. A few thousand were evicted from their homes near military areas and either forced to find housing elsewhere or sent to mainland camps. The evicted group contained some one thousand Japanese people, almost all of whom were US citizens. Although the authorities claimed that the internees were volunteers, in practice the authorities selected them. The inmates included some who were considered potentially dangerous and others who simply did not represent a big enough asset for the economy of the islands. About 150 Japanese were excluded from Alaska.[39]

Canada also incarcerated its relatively small West Coast Japanese population of twenty-three thousand, of which 75 percent were Canadian citizens. In many ways, Japanese Canadians were treated in an even harsher manner than Japanese Americans. Canadian and Japanese citizens alike were moved to labor camps and deserted mining towns and they were permitted to return to the Canadian coast only in 1949. On the other hand, Japanese Canadians were not under military guard during their evacuation and were free to move elsewhere in Canada without restrictions if they had the resources and networks to do so. Most often, they did not.[40]

In addition to jailing its own residents and citizens, the United States successfully lobbied some of its Latin American allies to round up their Japanese residents, many of whom were sent to US camps. Altogether, some 2,200 Japanese inmates came to the United States from thirteen Latin American countries, most of them from Peru. More than eight hundred Japanese Peruvians were exchanged with Japan as prisoners of war. After the war, Peru refused to readmit inmates who were not Peruvian citizens. Most of them received permission to remain in the United States but were considered to be there illegally.[41]

War Relocation Authority

To take care of the practicalities of incarceration and the day-to-day running of the camps, President Roosevelt established the War Relocation Authority in March 1942. Many of the WRA administrators—including both of its directors, Milton Eisenhower and Dillon S. Myer—hailed from the Department of Agriculture and the Bureau of Indian Affairs. They shared collegial networks and a New Deal philosophy toward the organization of their work. Eisenhower and Myer both followed the practices of the era in thinking that people must be governed with close supervision, but they also firmly believed in listening to their subjects and helping incarcerated people.[42]

From the beginning of incarceration, Eisenhower believed the Japanese American population should not be kept locked up in camps but encouraged to scatter across the country. Even Eisenhower was not progressive enough to suggest unrestricted relocation; his vision included the establishment of planned communities rather than relocation to existing communities. The plan was quickly abandoned as Eisenhower became familiar with the extent of hostility toward the Japanese in the United States, especially on the West Coast. Although the original purpose of Executive Order 9066 was to quiet anti-Japanese hysteria, it worked to the contrary, suggesting to the public that Japanese Americans were indeed suspect and disloyal. It appeared that only confined communities would be a satisfactory solution to the "Japanese problem" during the war.[43]

Eisenhower resigned his post as WRA director in early June 1942 to join the Office of War Information, which he had helped design. The historian Greg Robinson points out that Eisenhower was greatly "sickened and disheartened" by the treatment of the inmates and wanted to step down. Still, he did not give up his conviction that the initial evacuation of the West Coast had been justified as a wartime necessity. Eisenhower recommended Dillon S. Myer, his former colleague at the Department of Agriculture, as the new director of the WRA, and after some political disagreements across governmental departments, President Roosevelt asked Myer to take over the agency.[44]

Among the appointed personnel (a term used to distinguish WRA administrators from inmates) were anthropologists, or community analysts. Their task was to generate information about the functioning of the inmate communities, which in turn helped the government in policymaking. Importantly, as the anthropologist Orin Starn argues, they were also to promote a "positive image" of incarceration and the Japanese Americans to the general public.[45]

The impact of the anthropologists should not be underestimated. Although their role was not public, in that they typically did not represent the WRA outside the camps, my analysis of Dillon S. Myer's speeches shows that there were many parallels in the phrases of anthropologists' reports and Myer's public speeches.[46] Furthermore, it became evident as I reviewed archival records for this study that the Heart Mountain anthropologists were very detailed in their descriptions of community sentiments, and while they usually refrained from making direct recommendations, their thoughts on many matters, such as resettlement, come through in their reports.[47]

Although President Roosevelt authorized the actions of the WRA, he remained uninterested in the actual incarceration or relocation processes and met only once with Myer during the war. He let lower-level officials handle publicity issues and would not speak favorably of the inmates (to show his support for the WRA policy), even when other administrators asked him to do so. When Roosevelt finally stepped up to laud the loyalty of Japanese Americans, they had been incarcerated for a year and public opposition to Japanese Americans had increased tremendously.[48]

Life in Incarceration Camps

Following the initial evacuation, all evacuees were moved to fifteen assembly centers—hastily built barracks on former horse racetracks and fairgrounds—that were operated by the Wartime Civilian Control Agency. During the summer of 1942, the WRA assumed control of the inmates and moved them to more permanent "relocation centers," as they were named. These barrack communities were mostly located outside the military area, most of them in very harsh desert conditions: two each in Arizona, Arkansas, and California, and one each in Colorado, Idaho, Utah, and Wyoming. The camps accommodated between seven thousand (in Granada, Colorado) and nineteen thousand (in Tule Lake, California) people. In addition, there were several actual internment camps, operated by the Department of Justice, that held a small number of probably disloyal German and Italian citizens.[49]

Map 1 presents the locations of the assembly centers, incarceration camps, internment camps, and isolation centers. The two incarceration camps in Arkansas, Rohwer and Jerome, were on lands that the Farm Security Administration had originally bought to aid poor southern farmers. Tule Lake (California), Minidoka (Idaho), and Heart Mountain (Wyoming) were on federal reclamation lands.[50] The camps of Manzanar (California), Topaz (Utah), and Granada

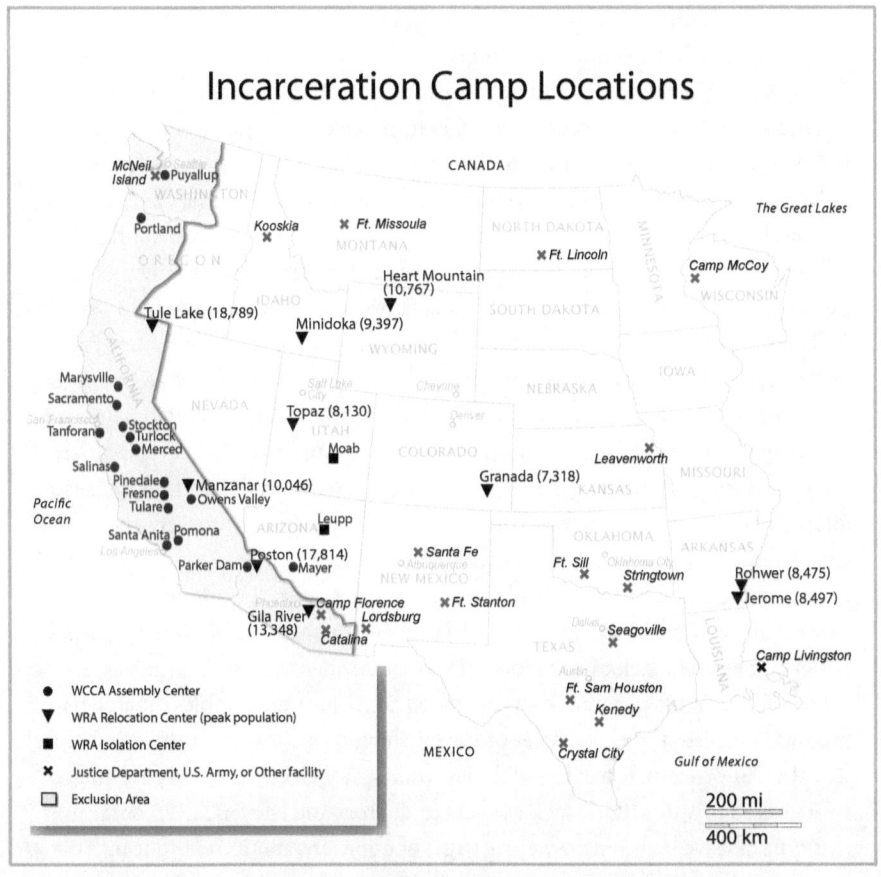

MAP 1. Locations of assembly centers, incarceration camps, and internment camps. Map by Heli Rekiranta.

(Colorado) were on lands obtained from various different sources—federal, municipal, and private. Finally, both Arizona camps, Gila River and Poston, were located on Indian reservations, the former on the lands of the Pima and the Maricopa, and the latter within the Colorado River Indian Reservation of the Mohave, Chemehuevi, Hopi, and Navajo.[51]

Barbed wire fences surrounded the camps and the military police stood guard. Each family got a one-room apartment with communal toilets, showers, and mess halls.[52] Inmates were encouraged to work in the camps, and eventually they provided many camp services, including food, education, and medical care—at least partly. Wages were small, ranging from twelve to nineteen dollars a month. In addition, the government paid a clothing allowance. Still, the War Relocation Authority employed altogether three thousand people, all so-called "Caucasians," in the camps and in administrative offices across the country.[53]

Incarceration brought sudden changes to the lives of all Japanese Americans, but women especially. Most of the Issei women had remained in the sphere of their homes, which sometimes extended to farms and small businesses that their husbands owned. Second-generation women, the Nisei, had been encouraged to study, but mostly for lower degrees; because of their sex and race, their parents saw them as future housewives.[54] In the camps, meals were provided in mess halls and there were few other household chores to do in the tiny one-room apartments. This left older women with much more free time and freed younger women from the expectations of learning domestic skills. Many women were able to get various kinds of jobs in the camps, for example as teachers and nurses.

In the spring of 1942, sugar beet growers began to demand that the authorities allow them to hire inmates for work in the fields. Upon the approval of the Western Defense Command, some nine thousand inmates were employed outside the camps by the end of the year. Students were quickly given the opportunity to resume their studies outside the restricted coastal area, and the National Japanese American Student Relocation Council was established to facilitate the process.[55]

The WRA leave program soon extended to include all eligible inmates. The program consisted of three types of leave: "short-term," "work group," and "indefinite." Short-term leaves lasted for less than a month and allowed the inmates to attend to private affairs, such as visits to doctors and lawyers. Even obtaining this type of leave required answering pages of questions about the applicant's history and affiliations. Work group leaves were issued for temporary agricultural labor. To be permitted to leave camps "indefinitely," inmates had to go through a complicated process wherein their "eligibility" was tested. They also had to agree to keep the WRA informed about their subsequent jobs and hometowns. To obtain leave clearance, inmates had to answer a questionnaire under oath that asked them to promise to stay away from "large groups of Japanese" and to inform authorities of "any subversive activity" they might encounter. Inmates were also "to try to develop such American habits which will cause you to be accepted readily into American social groups."[56]

It soon became clear that the designed leave program was not encouraging a sufficient number of inmates to leave camps. The process of acquiring a leave permit was bureaucratic, but the inmates were also reluctant to move again. Finding a suitable job was not easy and inmates feared the reactions of White

Americans to their arrival in communities that traditionally had no Japanese population. To encourage and facilitate mass resettlement, the WRA decided in the first months of 1943 to conduct a loyalty questionnaire for all inmates. Among the questions were two that created great turmoil among the inmates: number twenty-seven asked inmates about their willingness to serve in the United States Army and number twenty-eight asked them to "swear unqualified allegiance" to the United States and to "forswear any form of allegiance or obedience" to Japan. This questionnaire turned out to be one of the most controversial WRA policies, driving generations further apart from each other, but also causing splits within age and family groups. In general, the Issei were afraid of admitting loyalty to Japan because of the risk that they would be deported. At the same time, they were hesitant to pledge allegiance to the United States, as they were unqualified for citizenship. The Nisei could not understand why their loyalty as US citizens was being questioned in the first place. Despite these apparent controversies, the WRA's administrators were surprised to see that 25 percent of draft-age Nisei males responded "no" to the questions.[57]

The eligibility of the Nisei to serve the United States military was, from the beginning of the war, a highly controversial issue. Following Pearl Harbor, the Nisei draft status was lowered, and the Nisei were excluded from military service based on the government's suspicions about their loyalty. At the end of January 1943, President Roosevelt authorized the recruitment of Japanese Americans—believing in the propaganda value of Nisei service, argues Robinson.[58] The campaign to recruit Nisei volunteers was not as popular as the army had anticipated. Only some 1,200 volunteers—about a third of the number expected—enrolled. The number for Heart Mountain was only thirty-eight. In 1944, the government reinstituted the draft, after which more than twenty-five thousand Japanese Americans from Hawaii and the mainland United States served in the military, their two Nisei-only units being among the most decorated units of war.[59]

Those who refused to respond to the questionnaire or swear allegiance to the United States were moved to the Tule Lake relocation camp, which had the highest number of "no-noes" to begin with.[60] In this segregated camp, the WRA made a few changes to policy: the inmates could establish Japanese schools and they had more freedom to participate in Japanese cultural activities. This accommodation of Japanese culture was due to the presumption that the Tule Lake inmates had chosen Japaneseness and eventual repatriation to Japan. The authorities saw little value in trying to continue their Americanization efforts. In comparison to other camps, and clearly to emphasize the administrators' distrust of the inmates, they did not allow self-government, although Tule Lake had an advisory board of inmates and a few smaller councils that cooperated with the camp administration.[61]

In addition to the large-scale segregation of the Tule Lake residents there were other incidents related to power struggles within the camp communities and linked to wider dissatisfaction among the inmates. In 1942, newspapers reported on the strike at Poston and the Manzanar riot. The next year, inmates at Tule Lake staged a demonstration that lasted several days. At Heart Mountain, potential for larger conflicts was brewing in the motor pool and hospital strikes of 1943. Considering the scale and nature of incarceration, most of these incidents can be characterized as minor troubles. Nevertheless, the military police shot four people to death in the camps during incarceration. Most of these deaths occurred in somewhat unclear circumstances, demonstrating hot-headedness and poor judgment on the parts of the military police rather than actual danger.[62]

CHAPTER 3

Heart Mountain Community and Modeling the Networks

WHEN THE FIRST RESIDENTS of Heart Mountain arrived in early August 1942, they found an unfinished barrack community built in the middle of the arid Wyoming landscape. The Heart Mountain Relocation Center, named after the Heart Mountain (8,123 feet, 2,476 meters) that looms on the background of the site, was located halfway between the towns of Cody and Powell in northwest Wyoming. The area was a Bureau of Reclamation irrigation project, part of which was unfinished at the outbreak of the war. When it became evident that incarceration camps would be established, Wyoming politicians and businesspeople saw a local camp as an economic opportunity and a way to get laborers to the Cody-Yellowstone highway and sugar beet fields. Indeed, inmates completed the Heart Mountain canal, which provided drinking water and irrigated the fields at the incarceration camp, and later enabled farming and ranching in the area.[1] Today, the site houses the Heart Mountain Interpretive Center and Archive with a few original buildings and a walking tour of the premises.

Once the incarceration process began in earnest in May 1942, Japanese Americans typically had only a week or two to pack their belongings. First, they were taken to assembly centers (usually close to their hometowns) and then divided into camps based on city of residence. The inmates did not know where they were headed or how long the voyage would take. Heart Mountain residents mostly came from Los Angeles County, California (6,448 people); Santa Clara County, California (2,572); San Francisco County, California (678); and Yakima and Washington counties, Washington (843). Consequently, the biggest assembly centers through which they came were Pomona, California; Santa Anita California; Portland, Oregon; and Pinedale, California. The center's peak population was 10,767 in 1943, but with births, deaths, and transfers, 14,011 people lived there.

The camp consisted of thirty blocks of 467 barracks, including administrative buildings. While some Caucasian employees lived in the nearby towns of Powell and Cody, many stayed in the camp. A few children of the Caucasian

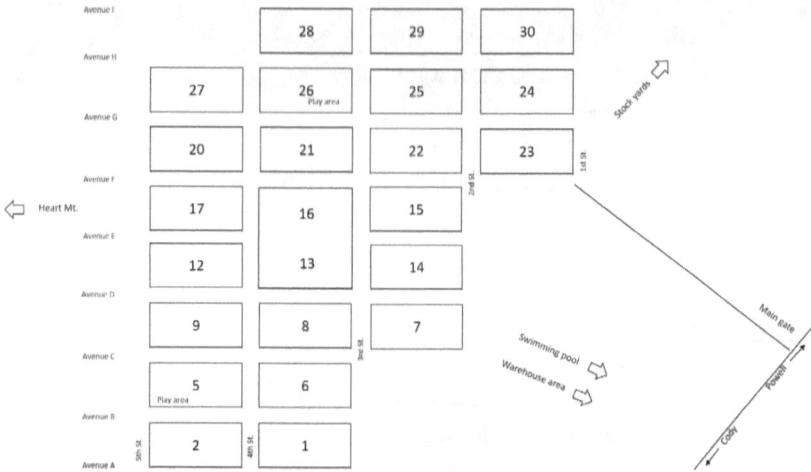

FIGURE 1. Map of Heart Mountain blocks and streets. Based on a schema from Heart Mountain Interpretive Center. Created by author.

employees also lived in the camp and went to school there. The living quarters of the staff were separate from those of the inmates, but the buildings were constructed in the same way. Living quarters for staff, however, did have indoor plumbing. Importantly and in comparison to the inmates, the Caucasians also had more privacy.

Each barrack was about 120 feet (thirty-seven meters) long and twenty feet (six meters) wide. The rooms varied slightly in size depending on the number of family members, and sometimes large families occupied two apartments. A couple or a small family, on the other hand, might have to share a room with strangers. The average room size was twenty by twenty feet (six by six meters) with only a coal stove and cots installed when the inmates arrived.

Once all the permanent camps were populated, the people living at each adopted slightly different practices and community dynamics. Solutions depended on the WRA administrators in each camp, as well as the origins, personae, and power relations of the inmates themselves. The highest administrative official at Heart Mountain was the Caucasian Project Director, first C. E. Rachford and after his retirement, Guy Robertson. They had their own office and staff. The rest of the camp administration was divided into five divisions or offices: Community Management, Operations, and Administrative Management divisions, and the offices of the Reports Officer and the Camp Attorney. The divisions and offices were further broken into sections and departments.[2] The structure was very hierarchical and required many levels of leadership from "foremen" to "managers" and "directors."[3]

To prove to the inmates and possible outside critics that the incarceration camps were democratic, the WRA wanted the camps to resemble normal communities. This practice was outlined before the permanent camps were established, in the early weeks of assembly centers. The purpose was to create "an equitable substitute for the life, work, and homes given up." Furthermore, "the standards of living and the quality of community life [would] depend on their [the inmates'] initiative, resourcefulness, and skill."[4] The WRA, in other words, sought to have the inmates run all the camps' basic services, from administration to service production. For the most part, the mess halls, for example, were in the hands of the inmates.

To cater to the needs of the residents, the WRA allowed the establishment of various enterprises through what it envisioned as a cooperative system. The co-ops had an extensive network of services, ranging from barbershops and office supply stores to food and clothing. Such a system was also in place at Heart Mountain, but the residents objected to an actual cooperative, voting instead for a trust-based model. The operation of the community enterprises was the cause of some of the most heated disputes at Heart Mountain, causing divisions within groups of inmate administrators.[5]

On an everyday level, though, the enterprises did what they were meant to do: they provided daily necessities as well as variation to the lives of the inmates. The little shops sold supplies like soap, fabric for clothing, and toys and sweets. Inmates with the financial means could also buy products through mail order catalogs like the Sears-Roebuck. It soon became evident, however, that the centers would not become completely self-sustaining. The WRA blamed this development on the "labor-hungry employers from agricultural areas" who wanted to recruit inmates for seasonal work. At the same time, the resettlement program drew work-age people from the centers, thus decreasing the available workforce within the camps.[6]

In addition to envisioning a self-sustaining community, the WRA imposed its ideal of democracy through community government. The establishment of community councils created frictions especially between the Issei and the Nisei. The War Relocation Authority originally intended for only the Nisei to be eligible to hold office in the community government. Many Issei and Nisei alike opposed this policy. The administration justified it as an effort to restore some of the citizens' privileges to alleviate the bitterness incarceration caused. It is evident that members of the administration were afraid of letting power slip to the Issei, partly because of the dominance of the Japanese language and thus the difficulty of controlling the Issei. Even without a language barrier, administrators simply trusted the Nisei more. At the same time, the Nisei only constituted about one third of the adult population in the camps and the older generation of Japanese considered them too young and inexperienced for leadership. It is therefore understandable that the Issei resented the Nisei being in charge.[7]

Councils tried to overcome the Issei representation issue by establishing advisory boards and other organs where the Issei could hold power, and at Heart Mountain, the very first (temporary) council included a Nisei and an Issei member from each block. The rules eventually changed in the spring of 1943, allowing the Issei to hold office.[8] After that, the older generation—and perhaps the Nisei themselves—elected the more experienced Issei to leadership positions. Consequently, the camp administration appointed Nisei block managers "to work in liaison capacity between the appointed personnel and the evacuees."[9] Block managers, all male at Heart Mountain except for Ruth Hashimoto in 1943 and Betty Aoyama in 1944, represented the oldest age group of the Nisei, in their thirties at the time.

Some historians, most notably Brian Hayashi and Douglas Nelson (especially in the Heart Mountain context), have criticized the community governments, the latter labeling them as puppet governments and calling the WRA form of democracy as a hoax. Mike Mackey has been more lenient, saying the councils were valuable in that they were "able to present grievances."[10] I would be careful about dismissing these bodies as nothing but WRA puppets and would give them more credit than Hayashi, Nelson, or Mackey. Although it is true that they had little formal power and the WRA could veto all their decisions, the community councils emerge in my data and network analysis as significant ways of bringing the community together and of making the inmates' voices heard. Despite the occasional lack of candidates, elections were held on schedule and votes were cast even when there was no contest. Councilmembers had visibility and the ability to act as bridges between groups of people, even if they did not have formal power. Voting behavior shows that these people were respected.

Origins

Two thirds of inmates were American born and, overall, birthplaces were concentrated in California. In Japan, the region labeled Southern Division was by far the most common birthplace, followed by Kyushu.[11] Several hundred people were born in Hawaii, but most of them had migrated to the continental United States before incarceration. Only thirty-five Heart Mountain people came directly from Hawaii to camps—primarily to Jerome—before transferring to Heart Mountain. These were usually families in which the father had been interned in Hawaii, and in order to be reunited as families, they succumbed to incarceration on the mainland. While most of the Nisei had been born in coastal states (and some in mountain states as well), there was a sizable number of additional birthplaces—altogether twenty-seven states. One birth is listed each for Canada and Mexico.[12] This data shows that, despite the prevailing narrative that the Japanese concentrated on the West Coast (which is true in purely statistical terms), many people did venture to other parts of the country and even the continent before their exclusion.

While the Japanese moved across the country in search of work and welcoming communities in the early decades of the twentieth century, many eventually returned to the West Coast. When incarceration started, only about fifteen thousand Japanese people lived in states other than California, Oregon, and Washington. The list of pre-evacuation addresses for Heart Mountaineers named 255 places. The largest city of origin for Heart Mountain was Los Angeles with 4,736 people, followed by San Jose with 1,133. After these two large origin cities, the Heart Mountaineers hailed from diverse locations, although mostly from California (from altogether 167 places). In general, inmates spread across the ten incarceration camps based on previous residence, but family ties also played a role. The list includes dozens of towns from which only a few people came to Heart Mountain. In comparison, practically all of the Japanese American population of Palo Alto and Pomona, both in California, was sent to Heart Mountain. The 544 inmates hailing from Wapato, Washington, constituted a third of the town's entire population before the war. Interestingly, the 1940 census listed San Jose as having 423 residents of Japanese origin, whereas in Heart Mountain alone, there were 1,133 inmates from San Jose. This is likely a reflection of movement within California due to the war and especially following Pearl Harbor.[13]

Once at Heart Mountain, people were divided into blocks at least partly based on prewar residence. Residents of Los Angeles and San Jose were present in almost every block. In fact, block 20 was the only one with no Los Angelenos. Pacific Northwesterners, particularly those from Toppenish, Yakima, and Wapato in Washington, were concentrated in blocks 15, 21, and 22.

The concentration of people from specific cities into the same camps and blocks suggests that there were sizable groups of people who knew each other before incarceration. In the first-hand accounts, inmates usually speak about the difficulty of constantly associating with new people. Their experiences emphasize new encounters rather than familiar people, although hardly anybody came to camp without knowing at least some people beforehand. Younger Nisei, especially, later recalled associating with their old friends.[14] Factions, nevertheless, arose between residents of different cities. In terms of leisure, many sports and Scouts' groups were organized by former hometown, and the high school yearbook always listed students' previous high schools. On a more political level, the Heart Mountain Social Service Department stated in its report on the camp housing situation that inmates had said that "Los Angeles people can't live near San Francisco people."[15]

Inmates recognized this geographical division and its effect on attitudes in postwar interviews. Those who spent their childhoods in camp reminisced about city children being boisterous, loud, and even "scary," as the Hawaiian Marjorie Matsushita outlined. There was also a division between mainland inmates and Hawaiians: "They [Hawaiians] talked funny. . . . They would be walking barefoot. . . . Just these different customs." Young adults, too, made a distinction between Los Angelenos and the country people. Mits Koshiyama, for example, attributed much of the camp politics—probably referring especially to the Fair Play Committee—to the Los Angelenos, "who had an understanding of what politics were really about." In contrast, Koshiyama, himself a San Josean, thought Northern Californians were naive. Frank Sumida, a Tule Lake segregate, further classified the city youth as individualistic. By contrast, he said of those from the countryside, "You could get 'em as a group"—referring in this case to the Japanese nationalistic groups forming at Tule Lake, but more broadly explaining the reasons why some young men joined while others did not.[16]

Similarly, a strong leader from one's previous place of residence could have an impact for a significant segment of inmates. In his trend report in May 1945, community analyst Asael T. Hansen reported that a Yakima councilmember had so much influence in his block that the block had a lower than average departure rate in the first half of the terminal departure period. Hansen is probably referencing Shinji Fujimoto, who was a councilmember for block fifteen throughout his incarceration, apart from the second council in 1943, when he was out on seasonal leave.[17]

On the other hand, camp life could also unite people from different parts of the West Coast and even influence their future paths in life. George Yoshinaga, from Mountain View, California, later maintained that camp dances and other social activities brought together people from different backgrounds: "That's one of the things that I feel was an important part of our life is that I got to know so many people that if it wasn't for evacuation I would have never had the opportunity to do so. And today I wouldn't be here [a retired professional], I'd be driving a tractor on our farm."[18]

Finding Each Other: The Creation of Networks

The first residents of Heart Mountain were about three hundred volunteers who agreed to help finish building the infrastructure for the rest of the inmates. Not only did they help create the physical environment; we can also speculate about their contribution to the development of the camp network. As an example, the first arrivals famously included Bill Hosokawa, who became the editor of the *Heart Mountain Sentinel*, one of the most long-lasting elements in the network. Four other *Sentinel* employees were also among the first residents, all of them later working as managers or directors.

Many of the first arrivals were young men, who were needed for physical labor like finishing the construction of the barracks. The background of the early residents is evident also in the network model, with many first arrivals populating the segments containing men's sports clubs and some of the workplaces demanding physical labor. The Fair Play Committee (FPC) had a staggering number of members from this group: nineteen, including one of the leaders, Paul (Takeo) Nakadate. The number of early arrivals constitutes almost 10 percent of the organization's membership. Four of the first arrivals were among those FPC members with the highest number of other connections, indicating they may have served as some of the organization's underlying influencers. Arriving voluntarily to prepare the camp probably gave them a head start in learning the politics and dynamics of Heart Mountain, putting them in a good position to exert influence on topics important to them. Early arrival could also correlate with heightened disillusion: if conditions were basic at their best, they must have been primitive in the beginning. Only two of the first arrivals, however, went to Tule Lake and five were among the imprisoned FPC members, which is a lower share than for the organization overall. Twelve first arrivals left for the army. There was, therefore, a high concentration of both those who wanted to emphasize their civil rights through the FPC and those who wanted to show their loyalty and compliance through military service.

Eventually, almost a third of the Heart Mountain adult population, 2,881 people, participated in the formal networks of the camp. In my model, this

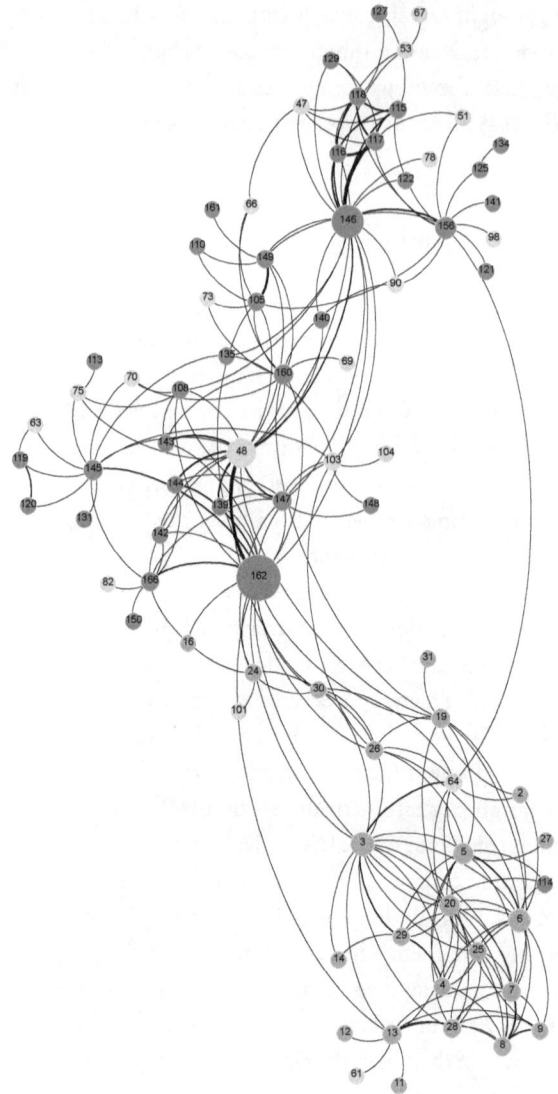

FIGURE 2. Connections between various institutions at Heart Mountain. A connection appears when two institutions share a member. (Included in the figure are organizations with more than one shared member.) The thicker the edge, the larger the number of shared members. The medium-dark nodes at the bottom of the figure represent the political network, the darkest are the social organizations, and the lightest color are the workplaces. The node size reflects the betweenness centrality of the organization. For example, the USO appears often on the path from one organization to another. Created by author. Additional visualizations can be accessed on the University of Oklahoma Press author website.

Key to Figure Labels

1: Agricultural Committee
2: Community Activities Board
3: Community Council 1942 October
4: Community Council 1943 March
5: Community Council 1943 August
6: Community Council 1944 February
7: Community Council 1944 October
8: Community Council 1945 February
9: Community Council 1945 August
10: Community Enterprises Advisory Council
11: Community Enterprises Board of Trustees
12: Community Enterprises Liquidation Committee
13: Community Enterprises Trust Committee
14: Consumer Co-Op Committee
15: Cooperative Education Committee
16: Coordinating Council for the Prevention and Disposition of Juvenile Delinquency
17: Fair Labor Practice Committee
18: Farm Advisory Board
19: Heart Mountain Scholarship Fund Committee
20: Judicial Committee
21: Manpower Commission
22: Mess Hall Advisory Board
23: Physical Education Board
24: Relocation Committee
25: Relocation Coordination Committee
26: Relocation Planning Commission
27: Space and Coordinating Committee
28: Study Committee for Opening the West Coast
29: Temporary block chairmen
30: War Savings Committee
31: Wounded Soldier Fund
32: City Planning Board
32B: Administrative Management Division
33: Finance Section
34: Mess Hall Section
35: Office Service Section
36: Poster shop
37: Timekeeper's office
38: Placement Section
39: Procurement Section
40: Statistics Section
41: Supply Section
42: Post office
43: Attorney's Office
44: Community Management Division
45: Community Activities Section
46: Community Activities Adult Department
47: Community Activities Athletic Department
48: Community Activities Clubs & Organizations Department
49: Community Activities office
50: Community Activities Group Activities Department
51: Community Activities Maintenance & Supply Department
52: Orchestra
53: Community Activities Recreation Department
54: Community Activities Technical Department
55: Community Activities Youth Activities Department
56: Community Services Section
57: Community Enterprises Section
58: Barbershop
59: Beauty salons
60: Community Enterprises office
61: Stores
62: Community Government Section
63: Block clerks
64: Block managers
65: Education Section
66: Adult Education Department
67: Camp public library
68: Education office
69: Elementary school
70: High school
71: High school office
72: Kindergarten
73: Night school
75: Hospital
77: Maintenance Section
78: Garbage crew
79: Police
81: Shoe repair shop
82: Social Welfare Section
83: Operations Division
84: Agricultural Section
85: Farms
86: Fields
87: Engineering Section
88: Plumbing crew
89: Pump crew
90: Fire department
91: Manufacturing Section
92: Canning project
93: Ceramic project
94: Sewing project
95: Tofu plant
96: Transport and Maintenance Section
97: Milk stations
98: Motor pool
99: Project director's office
100: Relocation Division
101: Relocation office
102: Reports Division
103: Heart Mountain Sentinel
104: Mimeograph Department
105: Buddhists
106: Bukkyo-kai
107: Catholics
108: Christians
109: Episcopalians
110: Nishi Hongwanji
111: Salvation Army
112: Seventh Day Adventists
113: Heart Mountain Golf Club
114: Heart Mountain Judo Club
115: Men's baseball
116: Men's basketball
117: Men's football
118: Men's softball
119: Women's basketball
120: Women's softball
121: Block 1 Nisei club (Ace of Hearts)
122: Block 12 Nisei club
123: Block 14 Nisei club
124: Block 15 Nisei club
125: Block 17 Nisei club
126: Block 2 Nisei club
127: Block 20 Nisei club
128: Block 21 Nisei club
129: Block 22 Nisei club
130: Block 25 Nisei club
131: Block 27 Nisei club
132: Block 28 Nisei club
133: Block 29 Nisei club
134: Block 30 Nisei club
135: Block 6 Nisei club
136: Block 7 Nisei club
137: Block 8 Nisei club
138: Block 9 Nisei club
139: Boy Scouts
140: Boys' clubs
141: Block 23 Nisei club
142: Coordinating Council for Girls Clubs and Scouts
143: Girl Scouts
144: Girls' clubs
145: Rho clubs
146: Senior boys' clubs
147: Student Y Club
148: Tau clubs
149: Young Buddhists' Association
150: American Assoiation of University Women
151: Army volunteers' Americanism group
152: Block 25 elementary school PTA
153: Block 7 elementary school PTA
154: Gyotoku Kai
155: Heart Mountain Country Club
156: Heart Mountain Fair Play Committee (FPC)
157: Heart Mountain Fishing Club
158: Heart Mountain Music Club
159: Mess Hall Workers' Club
160: Red Cross
161: Seiro Kai
162: United Service Organizations (USO)
163: USO parents
164: YMCA
165: YWBA
166: YWCA
167: 5th war loan drive 1944
168: 6th war loan drive 1944
169: Buddhist convention dance 1943
170: Buddhist New Year's party committee 1942
171: Buddhist Thanksgiving dance committee 1942
172: Carnival organizing committee 1943
173: Carnival organizing committee 1944
174: Center-wide picnic committee 1945
175: Christian church toy drive 1942
176: Christmas celebration committee 1942
177: Christmas play 1943
178: Clean-up week committee 1943
179: Clean-up week committee 1944
180: Sewing school graduation 1, 1945
181: Sewing school graduation 2, 1945

translates into 3,055 nodes and 4,780 edges. The rest of the nodes can roughly be grouped as follows: seventy-seven relating to social activities (including fifteen one-time events), seventy to employment, and thirty-two to the political sphere.

The network graph divides into three segments: one including almost exclusively social groups, another including social groups and workplaces, and the third containing most of the political elements with limited other types of institutional nodes. This segmentation indicates a division in the network between the politicians and members of other types of institutions. While there were politicians with workplace and social connections, the majority of politicians had connections mostly within one category. The concentration was especially evident for the community council members: none of the councils appear at the center of the full network graph, which shows that councilmembers had extremely few other types of connections. Although council membership was a political (not paid) position, it was full-time work, which allowed little outside activity. The council met twice (and sometimes more) a week for two hours in the morning, and sometimes the meetings reconvened in the afternoon. Especially in the beginning, the councilmembers reported spending up to sixty hours a week taking care of community affairs. Sometimes they complained about the near impossibility of combining employment and council duty.[19]

If we look more closely at the emerging communities (groups of nodes that have more connections among themselves than to other network actors), we see that the strongest connections were between various social organizations, especially men's sports teams and most block clubs. Another community formed around girls' clubs and Scouts and included schools as workplaces. Finally, a third community formed around the community councils, several other political groups, and the community enterprises workplaces. The three large social institutions bridged different types of organizations: the United Service Organizations, the umbrella organization of the YMCA-affiliated senior boys' clubs, and the Fair Play Committee. The Community Activities Clubs and Organizations Department is the workplace that bridges the largest amount of other workplaces, while the Community Enterprises Trust Committee and the Heart Mountain Scholarship Fund Committee (hereafter Scholarship Fund) serve in a bridging position from among the political groups. Apart from the Fair Play Committee, all these institutions had a strong alliance with the WRA. One could speculate about the appearance of the FPC on the list of broker organizations, but its importance is partly computational: because it had such a large recorded membership base, its weight becomes larger than some of the other organizations that had a different membership tracking system.

Interestingly, the block manager department becomes the second most important bridge among workplaces. This is a surprising finding because, as I will explore later, block managers were not very active in the networks otherwise. It seems that the few block managers with a very high outdegree make the entire group central. This means that one would have had to know specific block managers—most notably Hidenobu George Nakaki, Eiichi Sakauye, and Ruth Hashimoto—to gain direct access to other organizations.

When we shift focus to gender, the network becomes almost split in half or into sectors with two thirds men and one third women. Women occupy the part of the network with the hospital, schools, girls' clubs, and women's sports teams, while men dominate the part with the political groups, men's sports teams, and many of the workplaces. Religious groups and block clubs are in the middle, although men occupy a slight majority in those organizations as well. Thus, although women's presence was strong, especially in the employment network, large divisions in the placement of the sexes are evident in the integrated network. Women and men concentrated in different types of institutions, both by selection (sports groups) and by outside direction (appointment of women as block clerks).

At its peak in the early part of 1944, the full network had about 1,600 individuals and 2,300 edges. The composition of this snapshot network did not change drastically from the network that depicted the entire existence of the camp from 1942 to 1945: 70 percent remain Nisei citizens, but two leadership-related matters emerge. First, the political part of the network is less clearly distinguishable than in the mapping of all organizations across the camp's existence. Second, the Issei all but disappear from the network's top players. Whereas in the full network, Issei account for five of the ten most active members, here only one Issei makes the cut. The lack of active Issei has to do in part with the structure of the most popular Issei organizations. The community council elections were held twice a year, and thus most of them disappear in a snapshot like this.

By the summer of 1945, the appearance of the network changed again. Many workplaces became more peripheral because so many former employees left the camp. Similarly, the political organizations were reinforced because "politicians" stayed in the camp relatively longer. As a result, the Issei regained some of their prestige when it came to their degree: there were three Issei among the ten most active members of the network. The share of Nisei in the network overall, however, dropped more dramatically: they only constituted 44 percent of actors. This was due to their faster departure from the camp throughout its existence and especially in its final months.

Impact of Prewar Residence on Heart Mountain Networks

Geospatial elements were added to the actor-centered networks to explore possible linkages between places of origin and the positions of individuals in the camp networks. A first glance suggests extreme dominance of Californians. This is true in terms of absolute numbers: 11,115 individuals (79 percent) hailed from California, 1,883 (13 percent) from Washington, and only 252 (2 percent) from Oregon, the third largest state of origin. What is more, in considering the power relations in the camp, all individuals with a high outdegree were Californians, as we will later see. The same is true of the individuals with the highest-ranking jobs.

The inclusion of the geospatial layer changes the appearance and composition of the network drastically. While in the other networks people's appearance in any given network was at least partly due to volunteerism and active participation in an institution, the geospatial data brings many new people into connection with the previously elite network. Block residence, for example, ties 80 percent of the camp population to their neighbors, even though they may have been absent in the other types of networks.

At the same time, the network becomes increasingly messy visually: there are so many places that the number of nodes expands, and more importantly, places like Los Angeles have so many residents, that they obscure the attention from in-camp institutions. Editing the data table to separate the top places allows for geospatial analysis without losing sight of the camp networks. When the threshold is set at twenty residents from within the integrated network members, the pre-evacuation place of residence list comes to twenty-one places and the destination list to seventeen places.

As in all levels of the network, Los Angeles was the largest place of origin. Strikingly, only 386 people in the formal networks were from the smaller places that fell below the above-mentioned threshold of twenty residents. A comparison of the largest places of origin for the formal network members with that of the entire camp shows that the top six are the same for both sets: Los Angeles, San Jose, San Francisco, Wapato, Mountain View, and Hollywood. The next four places of prewar residence are in slightly different order, but the comparison shows that people from any given place were not overrepresented in the camp network.

There were only two institutions in which non-Californians, in this case Washingtonians, had a majority. These were the block 15 and block 21 Nisei clubs. Block 21 had only two Californian officers from a total of twenty-three officers, while block 15 had three Californians out of fourteen officers. Although

Californians (and Los Angelenos specifically) were present in most residence blocks, blocks 15 and 21 had more Pacific Northwesternern residents. Similarly, large organizations like the rho clubs, the senior boys' clubs, and the FPC had a fair number of Washingtonians. The few Oregonians in the network were more scattered throughout the institutions, though there were many working at the hospital.

This overview of all the Heart Mountain formal networks forms the basis from which to start exploring different aspects of the community in more detail. It will become evident that the different layers of the network—specifically, the political, the employment-social, and the women's—had their particularities. Different people, families, and groups emerged as powerful, but two topics should be kept in mind when considering an individual's rise to a position of power: the importance of prewar education attainment and the versatility of in-camp contacts. Education level and camp contacts also played a big role in people's decisions to leave the camp. This theme will carry through all of the ensuing chapters.

Resettlement and Return

What would happen to the Japanese after incarceration became a pressing issue for the WRA even before all inmates had been placed in camps. The first WRA director, Milton Eisenhower, drafted the first resettlement plan before the permanent camps opened. Soon, resettlement became a top concern for the WRA, and at times, the personnel appeared outright anxious about the situation. It is no wonder, then, that journalists for the *Heart Mountain Sentinel* were recruited to write encouraging reports of successful resettlers. The reports started with a list of people who had been granted indefinite leave and then expanded into a weekly "relocation in review" section published between August 1943 and April 1944. This section included a few lines of information on people who had left Heart Mountain either to seek an education, to pursue previously acquired jobs, or to look for work. Longer articles recounted people's experiences, detailing job markets in various larger cities.[20] These articles became even more valuable in the terminal departure period in 1945, when the administration was growing desperate due to the large numbers of people remaining in all camps. At that point, administrators desired name lists just to prove to inmates that other people were leaving camp.[21]

Nisei could apply for indefinite leave as soon as they arrived at Heart Mountain, and little by little, Issei who fulfilled the WRA's loyalty criteria were allowed to apply as well. At first, most departees went on seasonal leave to participate in

TABLE 1. Departures from Heart Mountain by Leave Category in Final Roster

Leave Category	Number of individuals	Percentage
Indefinite Leave, excl. institutionalized or interned	3,444	24.6
Armed Forces	185	1.3
Imprisonment	89	0.6
Institutionalized (e.g., hospitalized)	61	0.4
Interned	34	0.2
Repatriated	27	0.1
Transferred, excl. Tule Lake	276	2.0
Transferred to Tule Lake	991	7.1
Terminal Departure, excl. institutionalized or interned	8,710	62.2
Death	181	1.2
Unknown	12	NA
Total	14,011	100

There were essentially two broad leave categories: indefinite leave and terminal departure. Within each category, there were different types of leave, depending on the reason for the leave, and sometimes on whether the person leaving received government aid to leave. In addition to these two broad categories, I grouped the table above to separate all institutionalized, interned, and transferred people, regardless of the year of departure. The number in the "interned" category mostly contains family members of men interned after Pearl Harbor who sometimes requested to join their husbands or fathers if they were not granted parole. These were concentrated in the Crystal City Internment Camp in Texas.

nearby harvests and were not recorded as having resettled. Individual inmate records show that some young men went back and forth between Heart Mountain and places like Idaho and Montana at least three times.[22] The administrative classification of "indefinite leave" lasted until the end of December 1944. Indefinite meant that if conditions on the outside were unsatisfactory, the inmate could return to incarceration. As unappealing as it may have been, many did so. Katie Koga Uchiyama worked as a domestic attendant in Illinois but developed a skin condition in her hands and had to return to Heart Mountain: "At least in camp, I don't have to cook, because they have the mess hall. I had to get my hands well."[23] Likewise, students tended to come back to Heart Mountain for summer.

By contrast, "terminal departure" started when the exclusion orders were revoked starting in January, 1945. Soon, authorities became worried about people leaving and returning to camps and began restricting such movement. At this point, the WRA intended to make the leaves permanent.

During the fall of 1942, only fifty-six people left Heart Mountain on an indefinite leave permit. Thirty-four of them left for employment, fifteen were students, five joined their families on the outside, two were invited by either an acquaintance or one of the organizations helping resettlers, and two were listed as going into the armed forces. In 1942, all Nisei had been reclassified to draft status IV-C, aliens not acceptable to armed forces. Since both men listed as armed forces recruits in 1942 went to Fort Snelling, Minnesota, where one Japanese language school was located, my interpretation is that they had enlisted before Pearl Harbor and were recruited as language teachers for training soldiers, not as actual soldiers.

Because the West Coast remained an exclusion zone until the end of 1944, anyone leaving before that had to resettle to a new part of the country. I mostly refer to these people as resettlers or indefinite leave resettlers. People in the terminal departure category also had destinations outside the West Coast, and if a distinction needs to be made, I call them terminal departure resettlers. While I fully acknowledge that resettlement decisions were multifaceted (and the fact that an individual did not resettle might not always indicate reluctance to do so), I refer to resettlers to emphasize their apparent willingness to make lives elsewhere in the United States. For the purposes of mapping migration, I believe the term is appropriate. In contrast, I speak about returnees when referring to those who returned to their former homes.

CHAPTER 4

Those Who Govern

Political Power

ALTHOUGH THE WAR RELOCATION Authority had the formal power in all incarceration camps, inmates had both direct and more subtle opportunities to exert power. The most obvious source of this power was the community council, but the council was also a source of disputes and distrust: the Nisei were suspicious of the body due to Issei dominance, while many Issei considered all councilmembers, regardless of nationality, too American to be trusted. Block managers, whom the War Relocation Authority selected, faced a similar dilemma. Both Issei and Nisei sometimes accused the block managers of being government accomplices, even spies. Nevertheless, to dismiss either political body as redundant would be a severe underestimation of camp power relations.

Terminology relating to the community government positions is confusing, reflecting the evolving situation and complex power relations. The concept of block manager was fairly straightforward in all sources. But the position to which I refer as councilmember was variously also called block chairman and coordinator. To complicate matters further, many older Issei did not accept the Nisei councilmembers as de facto block leaders; instead, they unofficially selected one or more older men as *kucho* (district heads), who were considered the true leaders of their respective blocks.[1] These men were leaders by virtue of an unofficial, even tacit, agreement among block residents; their names did not appear in any documents or rosters.

Not all Heart Mountain groups in this network were political in nature. Some, like the Farm Advisory Board or the Scholarship Fund, focused on community administration and improvement. Nevertheless, inmate participants often referred to themselves as "politicians," and to further separate the inmate politicians from the WRA appointees, I refrain from using the word "administration." In any case, the functions of the different groups were so closely intertwined that treating them separately as "administrative" or "political" would misrepresent the distribution of power.[2]

Political analysis shows that relatively few people held power. There were several types of bodies, ranging from inmate-initiated groups with little decision-making power to WRA-sponsored community councils that had some formal authority over community affairs and plenty of influence on inmate attitudes. In addition to community councils that the inmate community directly elected, there were committees and councils that the WRA unilaterally appointed. The general population did not necessarily agree with the WRA administration in the selection of representatives: less than a third (28 percent) of block managers also served in the community councils. Block managers' membership concentrated in less powerful groups, in which representation was often based on (camp) occupational merit or membership in social groups.

Political Network

I identified twenty-four boards and committees and seven community councils. Their purpose and size varied from the four-person Fair Labor Practice Committee to the Community Enterprises Trust Committee, which had sixty-nine members through its existence. Some of the committees had inmate-only membership, while others had a mixed membership of WRA administrators and inmates. I included in my analysis those boards where inmates held the power, at least in theory.

The community councils appeared as the most powerful and active political group based on the number of members, the frequency of occurrence of both elections and mentions in the *Sentinel*, and the fact that it was the largest body with camp-wide elections. There were, however, numerous other political bodies. Some of them were short-lived, providing solutions to pressing issues, like the Community Enterprises Liquidation Committee that only functioned for a few months. Others were permanent, like the Judicial Committee.

The most active committees beyond the council, including nominations to the boards and reports on the committees' activities, were the Relocation Committee, the Relocation Planning Commission, the Judicial Committee, the Community Activities Board, and the Community Enterprises Trust Committee.[3] The prominence and relevance of the various political bodies depends greatly on viewpoint. The WRA administration put together some of them, like the relocation committees, and although members were selected from various organizations in the camp, they were some of the most pro-WRA inmates. The community councils, the Judicial Committee, and the Community Enterprises Trust Committee, meanwhile, were products of camp democracy—bodies that the inmates designed and elected, although under supervision and veto power of the WRA. Several committees arose purely from inmate needs, including the Study Committee for Opening the West Coast (or the West Coast Study Committee) and the Wounded Soldier Fund; the WRA probably had minimal control over them. Finally, some committees, such as the Community Enterprises Board of Trustees, combined different selection processes and included elected and appointed members.

Besides the community councils, the Community Enterprises Trust Committee and the Judicial Committee were by nature the most influential groups at Heart Mountain. Both were elected by inmates, but their prominence manifested in different ways. The Community Enterprises Trust Committee was important for the community because it was involved in operating the camp shops. It also became a political body over which councilmembers and other leaders tested their powers. The Judicial Committee, meanwhile, had practical power over criminal cases that were not severe enough to be handled by state court.

Without taking the councils into account, the remaining groups were strongly connected; the twenty-three groups have many shared members. An interesting exception is the Physical Education Board, whose members were not connected to any other group. It was a small committee with only five listed members in January 1943, but it is remarkable that none of the members were on, for example, the Community Activities Board. Community activities was the branch of WRA administration that ran a wide range of programs in the camp, from sports groups to movie theaters, among others. The Physical Education Board was basically a working group from within the Community Activities Section, but apparently the two committees were unrelated. Other boards that were weakly connected to the rest of the group (through only one member) were the Mess Hall Advisory Board and the Fair Labor Practice Committee (although the one connecting member in the latter committee was particularly active, participating on three other committees). The rest of the boards formed a tight cluster, where the Judicial Committee, the West Coast Study Committee, and the Relocation Planning Commission had the most members with connections to other boards.[4] Certain groups were also understandably close to each other: the Agricultural Committee and the Farm Advisory Board; the Community Enterprises Trust Committee and the Community Enterprises Liquidation Committee (with only one member of the former who did not belong to the latter);

and the Relocation Planning Commission and the Relocation Committee. The Relocation Committee was formed in April 1943 to collect and distribute information about resettlement. This work included distributing job listings and statements from those who had already relocated.[5] Surprisingly, the Community Enterprises Advisory Council members were more connected to other boards than to the two other community enterprises boards. It seems this council was a controlling organ that consisted of outsiders whose task was to oversee the budget of the community enterprises.

Councils gravitate to the center of the graph, demonstrating the significance of the council as a governing body in the political sphere. The Manpower Commission, which was not remarkably connected in the depiction of the other political bodies, became one of the hubs outside the councils, with all but two members belonging to at least one other committee or council. The Manpower Commission consisted of an equal number of inmates and WRA administrators and is therefore an exception among the committees. It was established in the summer of 1943 by the initiative of the community council to assess camp workforce, which was expected to deteriorate due to resettlement. Nurse's assistants (nurse's aides) and coal crew workers, especially, were often in high demand.[6]

The political network was at its largest in the fall of 1944—later than the full integrated network. This difference in the peak time has two implications: that politicizing increased as time went on and that, whereas the employment and social networks began to diminish due to resettlement, the political network seems to have grown.

People in Charge

The total number of people in the political network was 359. The average camp politician was an Issei man in his fifties: 60 percent of politicians were Issei with the mean birth year being 1888 and all but one of the five most common birth years being in the 1880s. Only seventeen politicians were women. None of them stood out for her number of connections, but to make sure their service does not go unnoticed, I discuss them in chapter 7.

The political group's educational background was diverse. A third of its members had at least some high school education in Japan, while 15 percent had an equivalent education from US schools. When it comes to higher degrees, the shares turn around: 16 percent had some college in the US, while only 8 percent had the same level from Japan. Finally, as many as twenty-four individuals (7 percent) had pursued postgraduate studies in the United States. Apart from

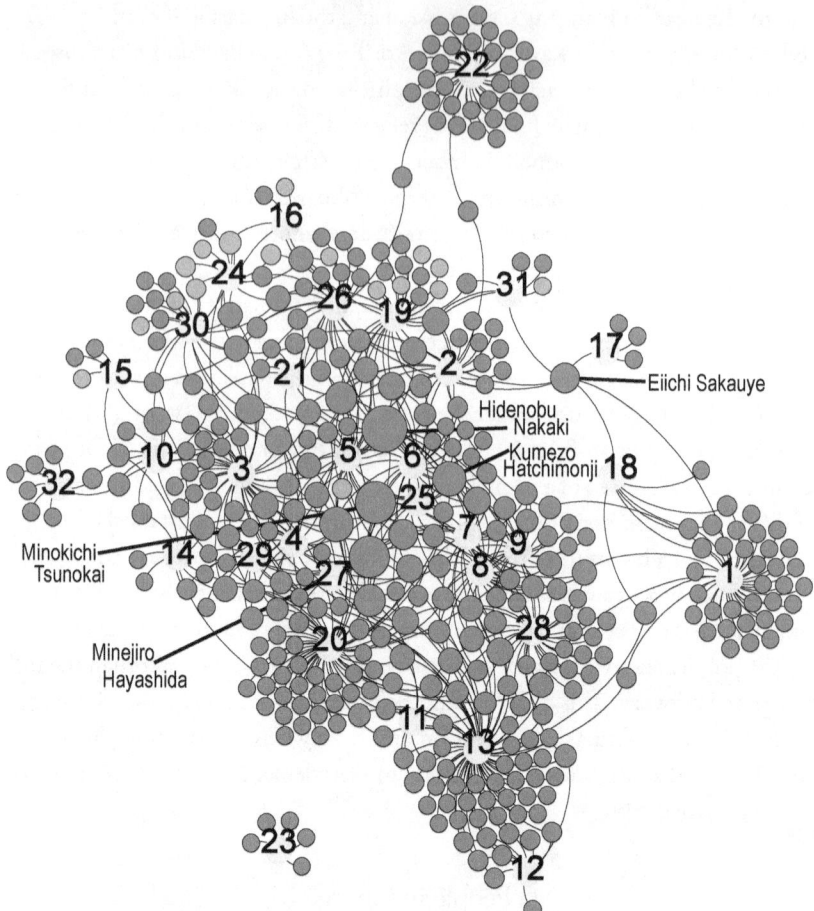

FIGURE 3. Heart Mountain political network. Political organizations are numbered. Darker nodes represent men and lighter nodes represent women. Nodes are sized based on outdegree, the number of memberships an individual has. Some of the significant individuals are labeled. See number key in figure 2 (chapter 3). Created by author.

the community enterprises committees (which had a heavier concentration of Japanese-educated people), people with different educational backgrounds were fairly evenly spread across the network. There was, however, a concentration of the more highly educated individuals in the most central—or connected—groups.

Importantly, there is a significant number of Kibei in the political network, a fifth of the network's American citizens. A third of them had more than ten years of schooling in Japan. Their number was the highest in the Judicial

Committee and the Community Enterprises Trust Committee, groups whose members the inmates elected. Their participation in elected bodies proves that although Nisei, in general, had less power, a Japanese education helped individuals rise to positions of power in the incarceration community. At the same time, none of the Nisei with the largest number of connections had any education in Japan at all. Furthermore, the lack of Kibei in the community councils demonstrates that those were considered the camp's most powerful governing bodies, where the younger generation was not easily admitted.

Occupationally, the group was perhaps less diverse, with a third reporting as managers upon registering for incarceration.[7] The second-largest occupational group was entrepreneurs, mostly truck or fruit farmers and some hotel owners. Although the managerial category is ambiguous, it is likely that a significant majority of politicians were small-scale entrepreneurs or workers in a family enterprise. This was also true of college-educated politicians, of whom only about 29 percent worked in white-collar jobs. In this light, the prewar occupations provide stark proof of Japanese Americans' difficulty finding employment matching their credentials. The sociologist Dorothy Thomas claimed that the adult Nisei were economically worse off than their parents. The Issei had been able to establish their own enterprises and rise in status in comparison to their homeland and especially their starting point in the United States. For many Nisei, employment in the family business was not so much a matter of choice as a result of the discrimination they faced in the larger employment market.[8] Even if we consider managerial positions broadly, especially for the Nisei, occupational status does not reflect education level.

In addition to valuing education, the Japanese appreciated family status. In Heart Mountain politics, though, individual attainment appeared to be more important than family background. Taking "father's occupation" both abroad and in the United States as an indicator of status did not have an effect overall. That said, as was the case with the education level, the most central individuals had a high socioeconomic status. About half of the politicians had fathers with a high socioeconomic position (managerial, professional, and skilled positions), while the other half had unskilled fathers. This category, however, included fathers whose occupation was "farm operator," which is an ambiguous term, as it can refer to work on anything from a small self-sustaining plot of land to a large-scale farm. Based on literature, I assume it means, at most, the ownership of a medium-sized family farm, and have thus included them in the "lower" socioeconomic category. Men from both types of family backgrounds could become politicians and men with the highest degrees were found equally in both categories, with one case standing out: the person with the highest degree, Hidenobu George Nakaki, had a father who was listed in a professional position both in Japan and in the United States.

Among the ten most connected politicians, Nakaki is the only Nisei, demonstrating that although individual Nisei could become powerful, the Issei dominated the political sphere. This group was also exceptionally well educated: seven of the ten had pursued college or postgraduate studies. Beyond the most connected ten, education level and connections were more equally distributed. In the next most connected group of ten people, five had elementary or high school education, while the other five had university-level education. In this group, two were Nisei, one with college and one with postgraduate education. Despite this slight drop in education level, it seems that a high education level was a more important prerequisite for a Nisei than an Issei to become powerful. The high education level of the Nisei indicates that members of the community (mostly the Issei) valued education and were willing to allow younger people to access positions of power, especially if they were well educated.

The overwhelming majority of political group members came to Heart Mountain via the Pomona and Santa Anita Assembly Centers in California. This is logical, since they were the top two centers of origin for all Heart Mountain inmates. Sixteen of the network members (slightly over 4 percent) came from actual internment camps, where they had been placed immediately after Pearl Harbor because they were prominent in the Japanese American community. These internees resumed their leadership positions and were not considered suspicious or undesirable within the incarceration community. Unfortunately, little background data is available for these men, because most of them came to Heart Mountain after the collection of the entry data. The WRA administration seemed to consider the internees (or parolees, as they were often referred to) as harmless. A report by the Heart Mountain Welfare Section, which was in charge of the camp housing arrangements and several social services, described the arriving internees as grateful for "the care which was given to them by the government ... as well as ... for the privilege of again being reunited with their families." This sentiment is naive and patronizing, but communicates the WRA's willingness to consider them loyal once approved by the Department of Justice.[9]

The largest group of people not "originating" at Heart Mountain (that is, arriving via another facility) were the transfers from Tule Lake, California (just over 5 percent). They were on many of the committees and community councils, most notably the Community Enterprises Trust Committee and the Relocation Planning Commission. Most of the Tule Lake transfers arrived in September

1943, meaning that they had to integrate into a new community that already had a year-long history. In all camps, there were reports of animosities between the "original" residents and the "newcomers," arising especially due to feelings of inequality: newcomers felt that the best apartments and jobs had been given out to existing residents, while older residents were reluctant to give up their potentially more spacious living arrangements to accommodate the new inmates.[10] At the same time, many institutions, such as the community council, had only recently taken their final shape, so the transferees appear to have found ways to integrate. Each block elected a community enterprises trustee, which further speaks to the integration of the former Tuleans.

The new arrivals were keen on improving their new community through the community enterprises, but they also clearly had an interest in facilitating resettlement. Their participation in the Relocation Planning Commission makes sense, since presumably transferees from Tule Lake already had at least a slightly more open attitude toward resettlement, whereas those staying at or transferring to Tule Lake were generally fearful of leaving the camps. Those who moved away from Tule Lake had sworn unqualified allegiance to the United States despite the rumors that they would be forcefully resettled across the country. This would perhaps make them more willing to take such steps and relocate voluntarily. In practice, out of all the politicians arriving from Tule Lake, only four left during the indefinite leave period, and out of those, three were on the Relocation Planning Commission.

Conversely, eight politicians (2.2 percent, compared to 7 percent of the entire camp) moved to Tule Lake, which suggests that participation in the early stages of community politics encouraged a "yes-yes" response to the questions on unqualified allegiance in the loyalty questionnaire. Only two of the Tule Lake transfers were members of community councils, while the other six were members of either the Mess Hall Advisory Board or the Agricultural Committee, two of the less connected groups.

Resettling the Politicians

For the rest of the political network, camp closure (various types of "terminal departure" during 1945) was the most common leave type (59 percent), compared to 62 percent in the entire Heart Mountain population. This suggests that political positions within the camp had little effect on a person's decision to leave the camp. Early departure due to more connectedness and presumed willingness to comply with the administration's wishes would be equally plausible. At the same time, the political group was predominantly composed of the older segment of men, who in general found it more difficult to resettle due to the lack of available funds for resettlement, difficulty in finding employment, and denied leave permits.

These camp politicians may also have been among those who delayed departure in hopes of being allowed to return because they owned real estate on the West Coast. In most cases, these would have been rural Issei (although their Nisei children officially owned those lands due to the laws preventing Issei landownership) or urban Issei with small businesses like hostels. The WRA also reported about a small but tenacious group that considered it the government's duty to figure out what to do with them. Many believed that the camps would not be able to close during 1945 if a substantial proportion of inmates refused to leave. Some of the most vocal members of this group were councilmembers and block managers. Minejiro Hayashida—long-time chairman of the community council—seems to have been in this group. According to community analyst Asael T. Hansen, making noise about the impossibility of closing the camps was a "deliberate policy," although never officially recorded in community council minutes. Hansen wrote that the councilmembers attempted "to apply to the administration exactly the same strategy that the WRA uses on them," in that the WRA maintained that the camps were being closed (when they were struggling to keep the schedule), while the council insisted it would not be possible (when in fact they secretly believed it would happen). The purpose was to "scare" the WRA into making provisions like offering larger resettlement grants.[11]

While Hansen's view of the inmates trying to scare the WRA may be somewhat exaggerated, it is true that the council vehemently opposed sending inmates away without proper financial and practical support. In a 1944 meeting of Issei with the relocation team, Shinji Fujimoto and Kumezo Hatchimonji pointed out that running the camps cost four hundred dollars per year per inmate. They suggested that government funds would be better used by paying each incarcerated individual eight hundred dollars to resettle. This way, they would have a true incentive to leave the camps and would have funds to help them start their lives over.[12] Instead, resettlers received transportation and twenty-five dollars, often not enough to get started.

Hansen's reference to the community council and its alleged policy of non-resettlement speaks to the underlying power of the community council. Inmates that actively participated in the political network, especially, were less likely to leave the camp before 1945. The five most active individuals in the camp all left during the terminal departure period, and three of them only in the last three months before the camp closed.

Clarence I. Nishizu, a college-educated Nisei and a block manager, claimed in his resettlement report that the "squatters," the most persistently anti-resettlement individuals, were among the wealthiest inmates and so experienced little financial pressure to leave. An unnamed man of such status, an owner of a dry-cleaning service, was cited as saying, "I don't want to go. I sort of like it here. My work is interesting. I have time for golf and fishing. I have a lot of friends. I have no worries."[13]

The above quote is a revealing and multifaceted description of camp life by someone who was well integrated and connected in the camp community. This individual may have felt discriminated against on the West Coast, despite having a successful business. As a small business owner, the profits of the enterprise probably were not high enough to make his life comfortable, whereas at Heart Mountain he felt his status had risen and his quality of life had improved. With his background, it seems likely that he worked for the Community Enterprises Section, found friends, and felt more in control of his own life. People like him were at an extreme end on a spectrum of camp experience. What differentiated him from the average inmate was his connectedness to camp institutions on several levels. He was well integrated into the camp community and also appeared connected to the WRA administration.

Nevertheless, he otherwise paints a portrait of the typical inmate in the "terminal departure" category: an older Issei who struggled to make a living before the war, got a physical respite from hard labor through incarceration, and did not have the financial or educational means to resettle anywhere but his prewar home.

Another example of a well-connected person—someone with a large number *and* wide range of connections to different kinds of institutions—was Eiichi Sakauye. Sakauye was prominent in the camp network and his entire family were what I call a "power family": a family that had many members in various camp networks and had a strong volume of connections to many different types of organizations (political, employment, and social). In an oral history interview, he explained why he decided against early resettlement even though he was young and well educated. His father operated several farms in California and had loyal and competent friends take care of them during incarceration. The father had, according to Sakauye, "no desire to go out and start over again," which led Sakauye to stay in camp until early 1945 as well. To Sakauye, it was not only about resignation and pleasing his father, however. He had actively run the farms alongside his father and, even decades later, one can detect his enthusiasm about getting back to work: "If I get back home, I want to do this and I want to do that. Because rapidly things—modern technology, in other words—[were]

creeping in. . . . So back of my mind, when I get back to California, I got to acquire a forklift to do something. I got to improve my method of farming." Because of his positive attitude—and because of the competent and trustworthy operators of the family property—Sakauye's readjustment to normal life was "very good and very easy."[14]

Since members of the political network deviated from those of the employment and social networks in that they left the camp later, I wanted to investigate the ratio in which members of the political network either resettled or returned to their homes. It was especially meaningful to see whether Issei politicians reflected the overall camp population. It turned out that, of all the politicians, regardless of nationality or time of departure, 39 percent returned to West Coast states and 61 percent resettled to a new state. Thus, the resettlement rate of the politicians is significantly higher than for the general population, as I will discuss in chapter 9. The Issei politicians, meanwhile, resettled at a rate that corresponded to the average resettlement rate. More importantly, although the Issei politicians were as reluctant to leave the camp as the Issei in general, their resettlement rate during terminal departure was significantly higher than that of other inmates during that period of time. In other words, while the Issei politicians may have been anxious to leave the camp or wanted to secure help for their peers as discussed above, their camp experiences and networks seem to have helped them once they made the decision to leave.

As noted in the beginning of this chapter, the camp political structure was often confusing even for those involved. Block managers complicate the situation even further, forming a specific niche in the camp networks. My data includes sixty-nine block managers, but only forty-five appeared elsewhere in the political network. In part, the lack of block managers was due to the fact that in the WRA administrative structure, block managers were employees in charge of the administration of their block. Contrary to secondary literature, block managers were not the highest political officers in all camps; at Heart Mountain, the community councils were more powerful and the roles of block managers and councils often conflicted.[15] In the next section, I consider the block managers as a network of their own.

Block Managers

Block managers' main duty was to act as a liaison between the Caucasian administrators and the inmates. This included practical work, such as distributing goods, but it also meant passing on information about WRA policy. The papers of block manager Ruth Hashimoto revealed that, in the early months of incarceration, block managers kept records of various topics from vaccination needs to voluntary block fire fighters and Santa Claus's schedule and route.[16]

Block managers were a complicated set of actors in the networks. Appointed by the WRA, they received a salary and worked as camp employees. Although they served in a similar position as the councilmembers, they had more practical power than the councilors over everyday matters like the operation of laundry facilities. Finally, their role was highly politicized by the inmates, who alternately considered block managers their allies and administrative spies, depending on an individual manager's position and reputation in the community.

As the camp government was taking shape, the WRA appointed a group of nineteen men as the temporary block chairmen to serve as Issei representatives alongside the Nisei block managers. Men in this group became more influential in the political network than the block managers because they were more often elected into the permanent councils and other political bodies. Of the nineteen, only two were absent from other committees, while the rest subsequently became members in eighteen of the thirty-two other committees. Ten of them became members of the first community council but none was named block manager.

There were sixty-nine known block managers throughout the existence of Heart Mountain, on average three for each of the residence blocks. Only two of them were women: Ruth Hashimoto and Betty Aoyama. Little is known about Aoyama. Her block managership was her only official task at Heart Mountain. Hashimoto, meanwhile, will be discussed in detail later on. Thirty-five of the block managers were additionally connected to at least one other political group—twenty-three to social organizations and twelve to other workplaces—but twenty-two were not connected to any institution in the political, employment, or social networks. Thus, as a group, they were at the fringes of the formal networks.

A submodel of the block managers is much smaller than the full political model, but it also shows connections across various groups more clearly. As noted above, a third of the block managers did not seem to have any connections besides their block managership. This may be a proof of residents' distrust toward WRA-appointed officials. Although it would seem that the block managers were not formally very connected, their informal networks were, by default, extensive: they knew all the affairs of their blocks and had tight relations with the White administrators.

Other inmates considered the block managers "trustees" of the Caucasian administrators. Although some accounts report that the community councils were pro-WRA, this was more openly the case for the block managers, who were not elected by the residents (although they could make suggestions as to the selection) but by the WRA administration. Some of the block managers were targets of rumors questioning their loyalty and some were even attacked. Judy (Nomura) Murakami, whose father, Howard Nomura, had been the Portland JACL president just before the war and then became a block manager at Heart Mountain, described her father receiving anonymous messages and even said that a burning newspaper was thrown into their barrack room.[17]

In that sense, it is not surprising that a large proportion of the block managers were not members of the councils or other committees that the residents elected. However, I expected them to have been more active in other organizations and to have a high degree of social links in the community. This was not the case: including social organizations in the block manager network only compounded their apparent isolation.

On the other hand, simply stating that inmates did not trust the block managers would be a simplification. Rather, as often happens, personality traits played a role. Shigeo Masunaga, just like Howard Nomura, was a former JACL leader, yet he was both a block manager and elected to three councils. In comparison with Nomura, Masunaga had the benefit of being incarcerated with many acquaintances from his native San Jose, whereas Nomura was separated from many of his associates, who were sent to Minidoka. Masunaga's friend and coworker John Hayakawa credited Masunaga for avoiding some conflicts in camp with his attitude. He did not want the block managers to protest the construction of a barbed wire fence around the Heart Mountain camp perimeter, nor did he want them to meddle in the affairs of the Fair Play Committee, and, in Hayakawa's view, "it came out alright."[18]

Contrary to the WRA's original regulations restricting block managership to US citizens, eleven block managers were Japanese citizens. Eight of them were listed as having arrived in the United States after the 1907 Gentlemen's Agreement banning new immigration from Japan, one as late as in 1937. They may have been children—born to Issei parents while visiting Japan—who were never registered or eligible for US citizenship. Even so, their selection as block managers is extremely surprising. Not only were they "disloyal aliens," they were very recent immigrants, which should have made them more, not less, mistrusted. What is more, two of the men had been interned before coming to Heart Mountain.

Educationally, the block managers were less diverse than the larger political group. Reflecting the fact that they were Nisei, 43 percent had high school education from the United States and another 12 percent from Japan. A fraction of a percent had only elementary education but close to 25 percent had at least some college studies (20 percent undergraduate and over 4 percent graduate studies). Although the share of college-educated people was lower than it was in the larger political network (where 31 percent had attended college), it was still much higher than in the camp on average (about 8 percent of adults). The largest occupational category for block managers was farmers (18 percent), but 23 percent of block managers reported some type of managerial occupation before camp. If we categorize managerial positions as requiring high school education, it seems that in this small subgroup, educational background and occupation corresponded better than in the political network. Block managers' departure details were close to those of employees—48 percent in the terminal departure category and 43 percent indefinite. One block manager was sent to Tule Lake.

The single largest political unit with block manager membership was the first community council, in October 1942. Its eleven block manager members had started in their managerial positions in September, at most a few weeks after arriving at Heart Mountain. Their inclusion in the first community council probably says more about the need to organize the government than a change in trust from endorsing the block managers to not voting for them. As for candidacy, five block managers ran for the community council once but were never elected. Others won their elections at least once. It does not look like block managers were actively shunned in camp politics, although their number dropped in the later councils, indicating that they did not have the inmates' unqualified support. There were of course exceptions, like one of the powerful individuals from the political network, Hidenobu George Nakaki, who served in almost all community councils as well as several committees and social groups.

Other notable political organizations among the block managers were the August 1943 and the February 1944 councils, the Community Activities Board, the Judicial Committee, and the Relocation Planning Commission. On the individual level, Hidenobu George Nakaki had by far the most memberships at twelve. Through his memberships, he was connected to about half of the other committees with block managers. Two men, Eiichi Sakauye and Toyosake Kimoto, each had five memberships, but Sakauye's reach was fairly limited; he was connected to many of the less central groups (such as the agricultural sector committees), while Kimoto connected to both a larger number of individuals and more prominent groups like the Judicial Committee. In this example, the block managers all knew each other and could at least theoretically have accessed all the political groups through fellow block manager members. Accessibility becomes relevant when we consider that a person wants to exert their influence on a group of people, for example, in persuading acquaintances against or in favor of resettlement. In such situations, the reach of an individual block manager or other inmate politician could make a difference.

More generally, the block managers, while each heading their own blocks, also acted as a body of inmate administrators. They met at least every other day as a unit and also divided into smaller task-specific subcommittees. Despite the persistent inmate claims that block managers were pro-WRA, they had disputes with the White administration. As an example, in February 1943, the managers complained to their boss, Assistant Project Director Douglas M. Todd, that "unauthorized" tasks were being "shoved" on them by other departments. In addition to their regular tasks, departments heads had ordered the block managers to arrange the maintenance of sewing rooms in each block and to assist fellow inmates in filing income tax returns. The inmates also entrusted the block managers with many "personal problems" such as marital troubles, seeking for their opinion and assistance. On a more general level, disagreements arose in the practices of not allowing Issei to work in the defense industry and of prohibiting reentry to the camp from indefinite leave in 1944, and more generally in the resettlement policies.[19]

Internal Politics

One of the biggest internal disputes at Heart Mountain, however, arose from the organization of the community enterprises. It was not only a conflict between the WRA administration and the inmates but one that also divided camp politicians. One group advocated for a cooperative—the model proposed by the WRA—while another favored a trust. The WRA model included the provision that the cooperative would be the employer of its workers. In other words, the inmates would become responsible for some of their own salaries. This was the biggest point of disagreement between the WRA and the inmates, and the WRA abandoned the plan to avoid negatively impacting the camp's morale.[20] Among the inmates, members of the two sides sometimes went quite far in taking a political stand, such as refusing to attend meetings in order to prevent the Community Enterprises Trust Committee from reaching a quorum. The disputes got personal. According to Camp Attorney Byron Ver Ploeg, "The majority group is motivated above all considerations by a desire to discredit and humiliate Hayashida, while the Hayashida group has exactly the same desire with regard to the present Trustees."[21]

The factions among inmates roughly followed the presumed assimilationist-nonassimilationist line. Some Nisei, like Yoneo Bepp and Teresa Honda, were active in promoting the cooperative. Honda, who otherwise was not a politician, served on the Cooperative Education Committee, while Bepp was a fairly well-connected politician. One of the most powerful supporters of the cooperative model was council chairperson Minejiro Hayashida, whom the WRA considered a progressive Issei. Meanwhile, the opponents of a co-op were often older Issei businessmen, who opposed WRA meddling in general and were particularly offended by the idea that they should take classes in running a cooperative.[22]

Certain delegates who were considered peacemakers said they were not in favor of either system, but wanted a democratic referendum on the matter. This dispute went on for over a year and included disagreements over the councilmembers' qualifications to be trustees. The organization of the enterprises—the fight between the co-op faction and the pro-trust faction—captured the interest of the camp residents, but toward the spring of 1945, interest in the selection of trustees dwindled.[23]

In addition to the specific dispute over community enterprises, the block manager–community council relations were sometimes strained. As noted, block managers had a more conflicting role within the inmate community than councilmembers. In addition to the doubts about loyalty that arose from their employment status, conflict seemed to have roots in generational disputes. More Nisei were mature and experienced enough to become community leaders, but in the camps, the White administration rather than community members chose new leaders. Members of the community council frequently sought to partner with the block managers—perhaps in an attempt to attach themselves to actual power—but the block managers more often expressed their preference for the younger generation of leaders.

This is evinced, for example, in a 1943 memorandum by a group of block managers to newly elected councilmembers Shig Masunaga, Tom Oki, Hidenobu George Nakaki, and Min Yonemura. The block managers write: "We hope the Nisei Quartet will sing in harmony and outdo the Elders in giving them 'music' that's in the groove. Please give the Community 'something to sing about'— and let's have no more discordancy. God bless America, the WRA, and the new Heart Mountain Community Council (especially, the last)."[24] With the addition of Kiyoshi Okamoto, these five were the only Nisei in the twenty-three-member

FIGURE 4. Three young men shopping at the Heart Mountain canteen, 1944. Although the organization of community enterprises was the source of some of the most heated debates at Heart Mountain, various shops also played a vital role in the daily lives of inmates. Photograph by Frank Hirahara. Reproduced by permission from the George and Frank Hirahara Photograph Collection, SC 14, Washington State University Libraries' Manuscripts, Archives, and Special Collections.

council, but Okamoto is not addressed as a hope in "outdoing the elders" along with Masunaga, Oki, Nakaki, and Yonemura. There are two main reasons for his exclusion. First, born in 1888, he was not one of the young men, though he was an American citizen by virtue of his birth in Hawaii. Second, he seemed to have already severed ties with the apparently more assimilationist politicians at this point. Okamoto was one of the most vocal opponents of incarcerated Nisei volunteering for the army, and later in 1943 he went on to establish the Heart Mountain Fair Play Committee. Since Okamoto had already earned a reputation as a potential troublemaker, the block managers trusted more that these four other men would side with them. After all, they had all also been or would become block managers and were thus likely to share some values with the unit.

Nakaki himself later estimated that the lack of Nisei councilmembers was due to their own unwillingness to run for the position, not so much to the Issei voting them out. Looking at voting results, this seems to be the case: the first council needed both Issei and Nisei representation, so they appear on that list. In the second council election in February 1943, the number of Nisei candidates dropped from forty-four (out of ninety-six) to twelve (out of fifty-two), only one of whom was elected. In the August election that prompted the letter from the block managers, the number of Nisei candidates had further sunk to seven, but the number of successful candidates was five. The Nisei clearly did not want to participate. It seems the Nisei had grown tired of negotiating with the Issei, as evidenced in the block managers' letter.

Another likeminded pair that supported increasing Nisei power was Kiyoichi Doi and Rikio Tomo. Both were older Nisei born in Hawaii in 1898 and 1899, respectively. Doi was an attorney and had a lot of formal power at Heart Mountain, while Tomo was officially a member only in the City Planning Board and the first community council. Despite this scarcity of formal connections, however, Tomo was a key inmate from the WRA perspective as a potential hindrance to the WRA agenda. I will return to both in chapter 6.

According to Hidenobu George Nakaki, the leaders that emerged at Heart Mountain were new to these roles regardless of nationality because the old leaders had to step back due to their internment record.[25] The most important community leaders probably remained interned for the duration of the war or at least long enough not to be able to regain their status in the camps. Nevertheless, many former internees participated in the political network, especially on the community enterprises committees.

The fact that the inmates elected the councilmembers did not prevent them from accusing the councilors of being pro-WRA. In fact, although the block managers may not have been thoroughly integrated into the full camp networks, councilmembers bore the most direct attacks. Four-time member Charles Tozaburo Oka was threatened several times and assaulted at least twice in 1944. Although the motive was not revealed on either occasion, his political activity seems to have angered his fellow block mates. Byron Ver Ploeg speculated about the attackers' connection to the Fair Play Committee, although neither of the named aggressors nor their family members appeared on the membership roster.[26]

This was not the only time law intertwined with politics. The Judicial Committee tried three men in the political network for misdemeanors. Two of them were only members of the Mess Hall Advisory Board, but the third was a community leader: Kiyoichi Doi, an attorney, the chairman of the Judicial Committee, and a member in multiple camp institutions. Doi was a part of a large gambling ring, where nine men were fined seventy-five dollars each for operating a gambling establishment and another fourteen men were suspected of frequenting it in the spring of 1945.[27]

By leaning on Issei leadership during incarceration, residents showed a desire for continuity despite disrupted lives. Allowing Issei to take power also speaks of the Nisei's respect for their elders: the Nisei could have complied with the WRA's orders to keep Issei from elective office but instead advocated for the Issei's inclusion. The Issei became prominent on the councils as soon as their full membership was allowed in the spring of 1943, but interest in community council participation seems to have dwindled as time passed, as exemplified by the decreasing number of candidates in the elections. Although the Issei were more reluctant and less able to resettle, they did not step up as candidates in the elections. One can, of course, speculate that this was sign of satisfaction with the administration, and indeed, Asael T. Hansen said that the community council "reflects as well as represents the community."[28]

Similarly, one can speculate that the community suffered election fatigue, as community council elections were held twice a year and other committee elections even more often. Hansen reported that some blocks had little interest in nominating candidates for the Community Enterprises Trust Committee. According to Hansen, people felt that "it's no use thinking of changing now the center is going to close."[29] Although the question was only about the elections for one committee, the community enterprises were very important to many Heart Mountaineers—both in practice and as a matter of policy debate—and the lack of interest in its composition expresses the general mood.

CHAPTER 5

Sense of Belonging

> My services at the hospital gave me a very agreeable chance of working with all my might without ever thinking of money matters. Those were really the happiest days of my life.
>
> —Peter-Maria Suski

THIS CHAPTER'S EPIGRAPH FEATURES a quote by Peter-Maria Suski, an Issei surgeon who worked at the Heart Mountain hospital until the very last train left in November 1945. In addition to surgeries, Suski attended over half of all childbirths at the hospital. His experiences provide a powerful example of how employment can instill a sense of self-worth.[1]

The political network, while important to its members, was cocooned, allowing for limited interaction with other networks. While camp politicians invested both time and mental effort in their activities, it also meant that they remained, for the most part, outside the core of the camp's social community. In contrast, the employment and social networks were entangled both due to network structure and the behavior of individuals. Many of the biggest workplaces were also the most important sites of social interaction. The Community Activities Section organized social activities, such as girls' and boys' clubs and Scouting, especially to children and young adults. The Adult Education Department and the night school, both under the Community Management Division, especially employed Issei (but also Nisei) and brought the adult population together in learning activities ranging from artificial flower arrangement to American history and from weightlifting to vocational sewing skills. These activities undoubtedly also contributed to the many marriages in camp: between October 1942 and August 1945, at least 245 marriages took place. The majority of them were formed between individuals from different prewar hometowns. Although there were many ways to find a spouse, and while many still used matchmakers in the 1940s, social and employment activities were an opportunity for the modern Nisei to make new contacts.

Social activities and employment therefore necessarily became intertwined, and so it is sometimes difficult to perceive whether a mentioned person was a volunteer or a paid employee. Sometimes the roles also changed. Whenever possible, I have included the paid employees as part of the Community Activities Section (where these clubs were placed administratively) and voluntary officials in the more loosely constructed social groups category. At the same time, I wanted to recreate the relationships of the paid employees and the volunteers and have thus recorded both types of attachment. This may place unwarranted weight on some individuals, who will have a link both to community activities as a workplace and to a social group, even though they would have only served in one capacity.

Important Employment

Fully realizing the irony of using the terms "employer" and "employee," I have not found better words to describe this aspect of the incarceration community. Despite the general incarceration conditions, the people discussed here received a salary, however meagre it may have been, and had all the responsibilities of employees in a similar workplace outside.[2]

I have recreated the employment network in a way that captures the dynamics of each workplace.[3] The unraveled employment network in this chapter shows a highly educated and professional workforce segment, but also people with less formal training. The network evinced little turnover for reasons other than resettlement: few people appear to have switched jobs except to take up seasonal work outside the camp or to resettle more permanently. In this network, the interconnections are brought about by the organizational structure—even the hierarchy of the administration—and the resulting collegial relationships, rather than by the sheer number of institutional connections, as was the case in the political network.

Employment information was available for 1,343 individuals for the life span of the camp. Many more people must have been employed, but they were not in positions to be named in sources. The second issue of the *Sentinel* gave the number of camp employees as 4,464, which corresponds to 44 percent of the entire camp population and 50 percent of the adult population. At the same time, the claims in research literature that "all" inmates were "assigned" jobs or that "most" inmates worked in camp do not seem warranted, at least beyond the initial months of incarceration. There were also unemployment benefits available in camp. Most sources describing life in camp emphasize that the Issei, and especially Issei women, had a lot of free time, sometimes for the first time in their lives. Community analyst Asael T. Hansen wrote in his June 1944 weekly report that, for many, the center provided better living conditions than life on the outside, and if not, then it did provide "compensating benefits [of] leisure and an abundance of Japanese associates." It thus seems more likely that "everyone" supposedly working refers to the younger men or heads of families. It is true, too, that all camps used "over-employment," or hiring more people than were needed, simply to keep inmates busy and prevent protest. According to the *Sentinel*, the largest employers were the mess halls, with over fifteen hundred employees, followed by the much smaller maintenance section with seven hundred employees.[4] Available employee name lists, meanwhile, show the biggest workplaces as the hospital and the Community Activities Section. The number of employees speaks to the value of these organizations in the camp community: while the mess halls and the maintenance section were crucial for the operations of the camp, the hospital and community activities were more important in imparting a sense of personal meaning to daily life.

Inmates ran many of the camp services, especially food production and the hospital operations. Wages were next to nominal, between twelve and nineteen dollars a month. In comparison, a Caucasian nurse working in the camp hospital would earn $150 per month.[5] Some inmates had small private businesses, offering services like carpentry, but most worked in the various sectors of the WRA administration.

The employment network differs from other types of networks in this study because linkages between departments occurred more often due to organizational hierarchy than movement of people. This is obvious for the short timespan studied, but the data nevertheless shows that people switched jobs across departments, creating a connected web of camp offices. Over a hundred people had a connection to more than one organization. For the most part, linkages were logical. Kindergarten, elementary school, high school, and night school shared employees, as did community services, community activities, and the athletic department. The strongest links were between the Mimeograph Department and the *Heart Mountain Sentinel*, which housed many similar jobs, such as typing and advertising. Both under the Reports Division, the *Sentinel* was strictly focused on transmitting the news, while the Mimeograph Department produced copies of camp communications, like newsletters, administrative orders, and advertisements. An equally strong connection existed between the Community Activities Recreation Department that organized events like movie screenings and the camp library. The actual numbers, however, are low—only four shared workers—which emphasizes an abstract connectivity through hierarchy. Certain departments were connected to each other through administrative practices.

All employees were young: the largest age group was those born between 1920 and 1925 (a third of the workforce) who were between eighteen and twenty-five years old during the war. Another quarter were born between 1915 and 1919, meaning that over half of the workforce was under thirty years old.

In fact, the youth of the workforce prompts consideration of the placement of Nisei born in 1924. They were to graduate high school in the spring of 1942 but most of them had to drop out due to discrimination or their "evacuation" date taking them away from their schools. Some were able to get their diplomas at Heart Mountain (and still others have received symbolic diplomas by their West Coast high schools and colleges in the twenty-first century to acknowledge the wrongs of 1942).[6] At Heart Mountain, there were 370 people born in 1942, of whom 144 showed up in the formal networks. Thus, their participation rate in the formal networks was much higher than it was for the population on average. Similarly, over half of these potential dropouts left the camp early and the most common leave category was indefinite leave for employment. They do not seem to have shied away from employment opportunities or the chance to leave the camp, at least to any greater degree than other young adults.

Reflecting the young age of the people in the employment network, most of the employees had at least some high school education. The number of college students and graduates is remarkably high, 329 (25 percent, compared to under 6 percent in the entire camp population). As could be expected, college-educated inmates were concentrated in the education department and the camp hospital, but they appeared in lower-level jobs as well. The fact that highly educated inmates accepted jobs below their education level is further proof of the importance of work itself to the inmates—of having a meaningful way to spend the day. The department with the highest education levels was the Attorney's Office, where two out of the nine employees had a high school background, four had attended at least some college, and three had pursued postgraduate studies. The jobs in the Attorney's Office were some of the most expert assignments available in the camp: many of the employees gave legal advice to inmates, such as assisting with divorce disputes related to property ownership.

Given the age distribution in the camp, no prewar occupational information was available for more than a third of the workforce. For those who did have pre-war work experience, the five most common job titles were salesclerk, retail manager, truck farmer, maid, and farm hand. These occupations were very spread out across the network, but there was an evident concentration of former maids in the hospital, working as nurse's assistants or in similar assisting positions. Many inmates that were unemployed or underemployed before the war found incarceration to be a turning point in their careers. Ironically, for these individuals, incarceration brought along new employment opportunities.

Career-Building in Incarceration

Inmates were eager to take up jobs in the camp, if only to alleviate the stress of incarceration. As Eiichi Sakauye said, "I kept busy. That's the only way that I could've survived all this. At [the] same time, it was educational to me. I learned [a] lot of things. I learned even how to speak Japanese a little more fluently than I did before."[7] At one point, the WRA administration wanted to start limiting the number of persons employed in camp from each family. This was partly to make jobs available to as many people in a given family as possible, but also to encourage unemployed family members to resettle.

Those who were employed in the camp were predominantly US citizens (76 percent), but Issei could also get jobs. Several Issei doctors, for example, worked at the camp hospital. In that organization, the ability to speak Japanese was essential, while a lack of English skills could be overlooked, and Caucasian doctors could treat patients who only spoke English.

Chieko Otsuki, a thirty-year-old female Issei, was both a doctor and a chemistry teacher at the night school. This unusual combination of workplaces, coupled with her membership in the American Association of University Women, also made her a broker in the employment network, something I will discuss later. Born in 1912, Otsuki had arrived in the United States at age eighteen in 1930 on a student visa. Her parents, Iwajiro and Hichi Otsuki, had made several trips between Japan and the US West Coast before and after the daughter's birth, finally staying more permanently in 1921. It seems likely they left their daughter in Japan in the care of her uncle when they traveled or returned to the United States.[8]

After Otsuki's arrival in the United States, she studied at Oregon State College as a graduate student, and in 1941, she completed a PhD in chemistry at the University of Michigan.[9] Otsuki's father was by now a hotel manager listed with the status of "employer" in the 1940 census. Given that members of the family were well-educated, successful, and seemingly assimilated, authorities may have seen the family as unlikely to repatriate. Nevertheless, both Chieko Otsuki and her father were among twenty-seven people who repatriated or expatriated to Japan on the MS *Gripsholm* in an exchange of prisoners of war.[10] There were no public records for Otsuki and her father after their departure date, August 24, 1943, on the final roster, so they probably stayed in Japan. Otsuki is interesting as a female doctor and a bridge in the network, but the fact that she repatriated in August of 1943 slightly decreased her value as a broker in the camp networks. Her time to act was relatively short.

In general, the Issei were quite evenly spread across the departments, although in the agricultural section of the Operations Division they comprised 43 percent of the workforce. Many of the jobs available there were practical, such as fieldwork that did not require English skills. Although these tasks did not require specific training, the education level of the employees in this section was not particularly low; it included high school and even college-educated inmates. In fact, some of the main advisors in the camp farm project—the experimental farm that was to provide most of the camp's food supplies—were Issei. One influential employee was Kumezo Hatchimonji, who had years of experience working with different types of soils and plants. His insights were needed: the purpose of the farm project was to produce as much of the camp's food as possible but little farming had taken place in the area before. By the end of its first season in late 1943, the farm had produced over 900,000 eggs, more than 500,000 pounds of potatoes, and other vegetables and fruit.[11]

At age fifty-four, in 1942, Hatchimonji was an established member of the West Coast Japanese American community. One of the first (and few) Issei to graduate from an American university, he had a degree in business administration from Columbia and he spoke fluent English. Before the war, he had been a commercial seed distributor in Arizona and California, hence his ability to participate in the Heart Mountain farm project as a researcher. Although instrumental in the success of camp agriculture, Hatchimonji also became prominent in the political network, participating in several committees and councils. It seems that despite his connectedness in the prewar Japanese American community, political activity was new to him: the only mention of his prewar political participation is his personal achievement of getting his sons admitted to an integrated school instead of a segregated one.[12]

The exception to the inclusion of the Issei in the employment network was the basic education sector (kindergarten through high school), where only one employee was Issei. Meanwhile, in the Adult Education Department, the Issei constituted about half of the employees. Their considerable activity in this department is understandable from several perspectives. First, basic education was to be conducted according to American standards and ideals. Therefore, head teachers were all White Americans, while inmates could act as assistant or apprentice teachers. The assistant teacher status was seen as more often suitable for young Nisei women than for Issei, who often had too much teaching experience for apprentice roles but who were not proficient in English. Second, the Adult Education Department and the night school, which employed many Issei, offered more informal courses, ranging from English to embroidery. Issei were logical teachers for courses aimed at their peers, and the ability to teach in Japanese was essential.

Women made up nearly half of the workforce, which is somewhat surprising considering that they were underrepresented in the political sphere. There does not seem to be an obvious explanation for women's strong participation. It is true that, especially in the beginning, all adult inmates were encouraged to work, but typically the male heads of the family received offers of work. Although many of the core jobs in the camp (such as education and hospital work) were associated with women, the structure of the employment network shows that there were plenty of other types of work available, both for men and for women. Men did not leave for the army until 1943 (as volunteers) and 1944 (as draftees), so that does not explain the large number of women, either. It simply seems that women, and young women in particular, were eager to take the opportunity to work. Perhaps they were motivated to seek employment in an environment where they did not experience discrimination for their race or gender.

Interestingly, adult education shared only a few employees with the rest of the educational sections but was connected via one person (Kiyoye Inouye) to the Mess Hall Section and the Community Enterprises Section. Starting in December 1943, adult education was part of the Education Department instead of the Community Activities Section, but its curriculum contained hobby-like classes, while more academic courses for adults were offered in the night school. The less formally educative content of the adult education classes did not equate to a lower education level for the department's workers. Of the ninety-five teachers, twenty-three (24 percent) had a college-level education. However, it appears that the placement of employees in the Adult Education Department was based more on extracurricular skills than preincarceration occupation or education. Indeed, their occupational backgrounds were diverse, including farmers, teachers, musicians, dancers, artists, and dressmakers.

As early as October 1942, the camp's general information bulletin announced a course on "American history and current topics" in both English and Japanese. From the beginning, two Japanese-language groups were organized due to high demand. In 1945, the *Heart Mountain Sentinel* produced English exercises as part of its supplement series.[13]

Part of the in-camp and on-the-job training, of course, had its roots in the larger WRA ideology of benevolent assimilationism: of "helping" inmates become "true" Americans. When the adult education program started in the fall of

FIGURE 5. Adult English class at Heart Mountain. Photograph by Tom Parker for the War Relocation Authority. (Original title: At the Heart Mountain Relocation Center, night school classes in advanced English are very popular. For the first time, many of the older people are now able to take advantage of the opportunity to read and write the language of their chosen country.) War Relocation Authority photographs: Japanese-American evacuation and resettlement, BANC PIC 1967.014 v.11 BE-591—PIC. Courtesy of the Bancroft Library, University of California, Berkeley.

1942, its program statement announced as one of its basic aims "to equip the person with the training and preparation which will enable him to become a more effective and functional worker and citizen." Behind this veil of good intentions lies the assumption that inmates possessed few useful skills. The program statement further outlined that particular emphasis was to be "placed upon preparation in democratic citizenship," again falsely implying that the inmates were undemocratic, or at least uninterested in democracy, when the Issei could not participate in the country's democratic system in the first place.[14]

The training went on until the very last months of the camp's existence. In March 1945, the *Sentinel* announced the graduation of seventy-five people from sewing school—one of the largest groups to receive a diploma through the vocational training program. In the same issue, the paper advertised new short-term courses in many other practical fields, as well as openings for on-the-job trainings.[15]

The data demonstrates the significance of employment in situations of transition: in the first and last months of incarceration, the WRA kept people busy in order to build a sense of community and individual purpose. Takashi Hoshizaki worked around the clock at the Pomona Assembly Center mess hall to feed all the inmates before new mess halls opened but felt his job so meaningful that, upon moving to Heart Mountain, he wanted to keep working at the mess hall with the same people. He described a sense of camaraderie, an ease of working together that arose from familiarity.[16] In addition to the important mess hall jobs, especially in the beginning, there were many jobs related to construction. These jobs were most often given to young men to keep them from becoming frustrated. Toward the end, there was an increase in club advisors and group activity leaders. These were often either older Issei or very young Nisei whom the WRA clearly wanted to keep occupied and motivated for their upcoming resettlement or return.

These transitional jobs served a dual purpose: in addition to offering avenues to resettlement and new careers to individual inmates, they produced social activities for the masses. Despite announcing the teachers or advisors in the newspaper or the information bulletin, though, the WRA kept these activities informal, and did not typically track the names of the participants. Next, we will explore the formal social networks at Heart Mountain.

Social Bonds Strengthened

Heart Mountain residents could choose from a wide range of free-time activities. All of the most popular American organizations were present at camp, including the YMCA and the YWCA, as well as the Boy and Girl Scouts. The relative importance of these institutions in the eyes of WRA administrators is evident, as they employed several people. In comparison, Japanese organizations like the Young Buddhists' Association were permitted but required volunteers. Although the presence of paid employees shows the prestige of certain clubs, these organizations were by no means unfamiliar to the Japanese American community. They had been an integral part of Japanese American life from the beginning of the twentieth century.[17]

The social network in this chapter portrays a web of the most active members of the various organizations. Typically, a link to an organization indicates that a person took up some level of additional responsibility in a group, such as becoming a member of a board or a committee. I divided social groups into four categories: religious, sports, young adult, and other. Organizations within the religious category consist of parishes in the center, although there were also several youth clubs connected to religious institutions. Many, such as the YWCA, gained large memberships at Heart Mountain, but I separated them into the "other" category, as their function was primarily social rather than religious. Membership in these organizations did not always follow religious affiliations; for example, people could be members of both the YWCA and the Buddhist clubs.

In the sports category, there were numerous teams and even several different levels and types of leagues in each of the available sports. To keep the network from getting too big and confusing, I grouped all teams of one sport together, such as "men's baseball." The assumption is that, since all the teams competed against each other, these people knew each other. Furthermore, there was considerable turnover on the teams, with people moving from team to team during the season or playing for several teams at the same time. Judo club belongs in the other category because, unlike the sports leagues, the *Sentinel* did not report its activities with equal precision. Apart from the occasional tournament results, their club officials most often represented all the participants, the judokas, whereas basketball, baseball, football, and softball were organized and reported through full leagues.

The number of organizations in the young adult category reveals the primary audience of most groups: the Nisei. Girls' clubs and boys' clubs consisted of adult volunteers (or sometimes employees, as seen in the employment section of this chapter) who led the clubs, while "rho clubs," "tau clubs," and the "senior boys' clubs" included officials and active members of individual clubs. Rho clubs were originally intended for young women between eighteen and twenty-one years of age, while the tau clubs were for women over twenty-one (but usually younger than YWCA members). The tau clubs of Heart Mountain seem to have only been active for a few months, after which they ceased to exist or possibly merged with the rho clubs. The senior boys' clubs had members from around age seventeen to twenty-five years old and they further divided into smaller groups based on prewar residence or extracurricular interests. Although there were numerous clubs under the umbrella organizations, I have grouped them together, because membership varied from season to season, which would have made the network appear denser than it probably was. The clubs had a large number of shared activities, making it highly probable that at least all officials knew each other.

The other category is the most diverse in composition, but the clubs' memberships consisted mostly of older inmates. This was the case, for example, for the Red Cross and the USO Parents, both of which especially attracted parents with children in the army. The USO included young members but was not specifically targeted at young adults, hence its characterization not as a young adults' organization but as one in the other social organizations category. Its popularity at Heart Mountain speaks to two trends: it was popular among those whose lives military service directly affected (soldiers and their family members), but it also seems linked to participation in the war effort on the home front and thus to expressing the kind of Americanness acceptable to the Japanese American Citizens League and the WRA.

The sheer number of organizations and their members shows that they served an important function in inmates' daily lives. Engaging in social organizations sometimes resulted from a sense of duty, as described by Art Okuno, who took part in setting up the Heart Mountain Boy Scouts: "[A] group of parents in [from] San Jose were worried about their kids running wild, maybe out of control ... but some message must've gone out saying I was an Eagle Scout in Troop 12, San Francisco. It was a prestigious troop ... I guess sort of a loyalty to what I got out of scouting myself, how it helped me."[18] Participation in the Scouts and other formal social activities also created opportunities to get permission to leave the camp for recreational trips. These included hikes to the Shoshone River and the Heart Mountain, and also camping excursions to Yellowstone National Park.

People had a need to find like-minded companions, but the abundance of block clubs also shows that there was a desire for community building on the neighborhood level. The number of attendees also demonstrates that social organizations were crucial in network building. These organizations brought people together from different backgrounds and introduced them to new ideas.

Originally, the WRA had been worried about "the danger of block consciousness" and consequently designed recreational activities on a center-wide level. Reports do not state why or at what point they began to promote the block clubs. We could infer that the center was becoming too unorganized and thus the WRA wanted young people to identify with smaller units. The block clubs' purpose, according to the community activities final report, was "to be of service to the community and to create interest in community affairs, welfare, and politics. The bringing about of a better understanding between boys and girls ... [was meant to] to help curtail juvenile delinquency, to help with center morale and to teach and lead the youth."[19]

Structure of the Social Network

As an isolated network, the Heart Mountain social network consisted of 1,860 individuals, sixty-two groups, and fifteen one-time events. The people in this network are those who were active enough in an organization to be named in the *Heart Mountain Sentinel*. Excluding the Fair Play Committee, the largest groups were the senior boys' clubs (190 members), men's American football (143 members), and the rho clubs (142 members), all intended for the young men and women of the camp. The largest all-age social groups were the Red Cross and the United Service Organizations.

In the church groups' category, various Christian denominations had slightly more named members than the Buddhist groups, but this gives a false impression, as about two thirds of all Heart Mountain inmates were Buddhists. In this social network, however, Buddhists' share is much lower, at 38 percent. We can only venture guesses as to the reason for the dominance of Christian groups, but it might be possible that the Christian parishes reached out for volunteers more than the Buddhists. Scholars like Stephen S. Fugita and Marilyn Fernandez have claimed that the WRA discouraged Buddhist churches or that Buddhist priests were kept interned and allowed in camps only later, but at least at Heart Mountain, Buddhist services and events were organized and publicized weekly from the beginning of the *Sentinel*'s circulation.[20] Therefore, the administration's possible favoring of one religion over the other does not seem to explain the difference. Nevertheless, the *Sentinel* reporters were predominantly Nisei and typically associated with Christianity. The number of self-proclaimed Christians among the paper's employees was significantly larger than that of Buddhists.[21] Thus, there may be a preferential bias in the reporting, although events as such were equally publicized.

Most of the social groups are clustered together, meaning that at least one shared member connects the groups. There are three groups without outside links: the officers of the Catholic church, the Seventh Day Adventists, and the country club had no other known connections within the social sphere, though all these groups did connect to the full camp network through at least one member. Otherwise, the groups are positioned predictably: sports clubs are close to each other, indicating many shared members, as are the different Buddhist groups. One community formed around the USO, which shared many members with all the girls' clubs and the Student Y club. The USO and the girls' clubs, especially, were natural companions, because the USO—an organization oriented toward young soldiers—relied on young women to organize much of its activities.

Other communities were more fragmented and consisted of smaller and less similar organizations. Instead of searching for cohesion, however, one could also interpret the lack of large communities in other parts of the graph as showing a higher degree of mobility on the parts of these individuals. They made more extensive affiliations with different types of organizations instead of associating with closely tied groups. As an example, Hisa Hirashiki, one of the powerful women in the social network, was active in four organizations that belonged to four different communities. Thus, her affiliations were more varied than those of another power woman, Sophie Toriumi, whose five connections were in only two communities.

Looking at the social network with all individuals included, the Fair Play Committee appears as its own community. It is not isolated, in that a considerable number of its members are connected to other groups; but in proportion, it has enough otherwise unconnected members to make it a separate community. For that reason, too, it will be important to treat the group on its own in more detail.

The social network consists overwhelmingly of American citizens. Based on this result alone, it appears that the Issei did not actively participate in the formal social life of the community. What the WRA called "Japanese type of entertainment" was discouraged and more closely monitored than "American sports and entertainments," but many sources state that the Issei were eager to participate in hobby courses and classes offered in the center.[22] The finding that Issei were missing in the social network probably has to do with organizational structures; the Issei participated in more formal activities that the camp authorities organized, such as the night school (and thus did not invite volunteers or board members), while members themselves governed the most popular organizations among the Nisei. Moreover, the WRA encouraged Nisei leadership in general, and this undoubtedly extended to social activities.

There were exceptions to the rule, however. All the officials of the Judo Club and the Fishing Club were Issei, although the *Heart Mountain Sentinel* frequently reported the former as having dozens of young Nisei members.[23] Other groups with significant Issei membership were the Buddhist and Christian churches, the mess hall workers' club, the golf Club, and, somewhat surprisingly, the Red Cross. The Red Cross membership is surprising; why would the Issei want to join an organization that was inseparably linked to the American war effort? Indeed, the Heart Mountain Red Cross chapter had in late 1943 struggled with a fundraising campaign, because the national organization had captioned the campaign materials as the "War Fund Drive." This upset the Issei who considered it an attack against the Japanese. According to social welfare counselor Virgil Payne, however, inclusive leadership brought the unit back to its feet and saw an increase in members.[24] Going beyond the assumption that the Issei would not support the war effort, it made sense for non-citizen Japanese to want to contribute through the Red Cross—for example, for the wellbeing of their sons serving in the army. Many parents also felt the need to prove their loyalty to the United States to their own children, who had come to resent their Japanese roots during the war. Finally, there was a practical justification for the popularity of the organization: it distributed messages between Japan and the United States, enabling at least some contact among relatives in the warring countries. For example, though Eiichi Sakauye was not a Red Cross official, he named the Red Cross as having contributed to his ability to correspond with his future wife, who had been studying in Japan when the war broke out and got stranded in the country for its duration.[25]

The Red Cross offers an opportunity to zoom in on a diverse set of examples of the relationship between education and connectedness. The organization attracted a membership of both sexes and all ages, which is reflected in the education levels of the group members, ranging from no schooling to postgraduate studies. While a low education level did not prevent activity or connectedness, it is evident that those with a larger number of overall connections tended to have a higher education level. This is true of the social network overall, despite the fact that most of the social actors were very young: eight of the ten most common birth years were in the 1920s, followed by 1919 and 1918.

The high education level, in turn, can indicate at least two characteristics of individuals and the network alike. First, we may assume that people with a higher education level had *more desire* to be active in general and that they were part of a diverse selection of institutions. This may be linked with assimilationist aspirations (proving one's Americanness) or with a sense of duty that may have come with education. Second, the rest of the camp community may have valued the individuals with a higher level of education and either elected them as leaders of social organizations or more indirectly endorsed their participation in multiple activities.

While the Red Cross had more female than male members, the social network overall had more men. This is mostly due to the very large Fair Play Committee, but, additionally, the men's sports teams and the senior boys' clubs had more active members than similar women's clubs. This lack of women may be a result of women's family responsibilities or women's activities may have been structured less formally, as I suggested in the Issei case. Yet the individual with by far the most social group memberships was a woman, Toshiye Nagata. She was listed as being active in the Buddhist church, the Young Buddhists' Association, girls' clubs and rho clubs, the USO, her block club, and, finally, both the Young Women's Buddhist Association and the YWCA. In addition to these organizational affiliations, she participated in organizing at least two events connected to the

Buddhist church. Her position as an adult volunteer (or possibly an employed leader) in the girls' clubs makes her a key individual in the social network, especially as a representative of youth and young adults. Aside from participating in an abundance of social activities, though, she did not appear in other contexts. Her affiliation with the girls' clubs suggests that she was employed in that sector, most likely in community activities.

Individuals with more than one social group membership were spread out across the network, but a denser group of people was located around men's football. Most of these men had connections to other sports groups and the boys' clubs. A handful of people had at least five links, while only four had at least six. These four, one of them Toshiye Nagata, were located in slightly different parts of the network but were nevertheless all directly linked to each other, although not through a single organization. Nagata shared two memberships with Yoshio Robert Kodama (USO and girls' clubs) and one with Chitoshi Akizuki and Texie Watanabe (Young Buddhists' Association). Akizuki and Watanabe connected to each other through the Young Buddhists, several sports clubs and boys' clubs, and both also connected to Kodama through the senior boys' clubs.

For the purpose of focusing on the spread of ideas (like the FPC or resettlement), it is fruitful to identify individuals who were active in many different types of organizations. Solely from that viewpoint, Chitoshi Akizuki, for example, is a less interesting individual despite his large number of connections to heavily populated groups. His companions probably already shared many of his interests, like sports, and were in the same situation in life. In comparison, Minoru Horino, who was a member of the FPC, as well as a block club, senior boys' clubs, and two sports clubs, was both a broker (a linking person between two or more groups) and a hub (a well-connected individual). Another individual in a similar position was Tamio Miyahara, a member of the FPC, a block club, two Buddhist groups, and boys' clubs. Many members of the boys' clubs, sports teams, and Buddhist groups joined the FPC, and as young citizen males, they belonged to the obvious target group. For that reason, it is difficult to assess solely through network analysis whether any of the above-mentioned individuals were influential in recruiting FPC members or whether members were more instinctively drawn toward the organization. This is a topic of further discussion in chapter 8.

New Connections: Marriage at Heart Mountain

In Japan, three generations often lived under one roof. The *ie*, meaning household, was also a political and religious unit in which each person was financially, physically, and psychologically responsible for everyone else. The family hierarchy was based on gender, age, and birth in the household. Women had no public position or authority, but because the bond between mother and son was so important, women could exert hidden power. In the United States, the *ie* became much smaller. Few Japanese American families at first included multiple generations or extended kin. As a result, some Issei couples informally adopted single men into their households to create a kin network.[26]

An abrupt event, like the exclusion of Japanese Americans from the West Coast, necessarily strains family life. For the most part, and regardless of place of residence, authorities let Japanese Americans register as family groups that extended well beyond the American concept of family to include grandparents, adult siblings with their families, and even friends and neighbors. Some families with members living outside the exclusion area, however, were split upon registration. Some individuals who feared that their families would be broken up, registered as "voluntary evacuees." They would have been exempt from incarceration either due to place of residence (for example, children going to college outside the West Coast) or due to their race (spouses and children considered White), but they voluntarily entered incarceration camps to stay with their families. At Heart Mountain, there were seventeen individuals classified as non-Japanese and twenty-four as multiracial Japanese.

One of the White voluntary inmates was Estelle Ishigo. An artist, she had met her future husband, the aspiring actor Arthur Ishigo, through a circle of mostly Asian American artists in Los Angeles. The miscegenation laws of the time prevented them from marrying in California; they traveled to Mexico for their wedding. At Heart Mountain, the WRA hired Estelle Ishigo to document the camp life through her drawings.[27]

From the *Heart Mountain Sentinel*, I gathered the data for 245 marriages (490 individuals) ranging in date from October 1942 to August 1945. Seventy-six of the marriages were formed between a Heart Mountaineer and someone from another camp or outside the incarceration area altogether.[28] News of marriage was probably submitted to the paper in the same way that it was shared with newspapers on the outside: the persons in question chose what (or whether) to disclose their wedding. Among the four announcements on Saturday, January 9, 1943, for example, was the wedding announcement of "a popular Santa Clara valley couple, Haru Okuda and Albert Mamiya." The paper went on to state that the Reverend J. Clyde Keegan read the ceremony, which was followed by a reception at one of the recreation halls.[29]

In some cases, information included elaborate details about the bride's dress, number of guests, and honeymoon plans, while in other instances, only the names of the members of the couple were listed. Most often, however, details also included the names of their parents and the wedding date. For my marriage network, I included the names of the rest of the wedding party when a person was specifically labeled as "attendant," "maid of honor," "bridesmaid," "best man," or similar, except in cases where these titles were given to the couple's parents. Siblings were included. With such criteria, fifty-nine marriages included at least one attendant.

Furthermore, forty-six marriages listed baishakunins, sometimes in addition to attendants. The baishakunin can be translated as a "go-between," or even a "matchmaker." They were typically older Issei couples (sometimes older Nisei couples in my data) who participated in arranging the marriage of a young couple. Before the war, most Nisei marriages were not arranged, at least in cities. Indeed, one survey reported that some Nisei selected baishakunins only after they had privately agreed to marry.[30] Regardless of the purpose of the baishakunins, their presence in the wedding announcements shows reverence for Japanese culture, or at least for the couple's Japanese parents. In the Heart Mountain network, eighty-one of the 109 baishakunins were Buddhist, as were the couples listing one, making the tradition appear more religious than cultural. However, there were several examples of Buddhist baishakunins assisting Christian couples, as well as Buddhist couples naming Christian baishakunins.

Baishakunins were first mentioned in the *Sentinel* in June of 1943—in the eightieth announcement of the paper's life cycle. It is unlikely that this was the first time a Heart Mountain wedding featured baishakunins. Rather, it appears to be a case of either WRA, editorial, or inmate censorship. We can only speculate about the reason for the sudden appearance of baishakunins in the *Sentinel*. If this were a case of WRA censorship, did the editors decide to allow more references to Japanese culture in the paper? If they initially took a different stand, why did they change their minds? At this point, Bill Hosokawa was the paper's editor. Both he and editor-in-chief Haruo Imura were Christian Nisei, and thus perhaps inclined to overlook something they saw as overtly Japanese, such as adhering to traditional wedding practices. Yet, these dynamics do not explain a change in policy. And if it was the inmates who changed their publicizing strategy, was it a sign of an opening culture or a sign of no longer caring what the authorities thought? No full study on the change in marriage patterns among the Nisei exists.

An overwhelming 75 percent of the marriages occurred between spouses who did not share a prewar place of residence. Considering that so many camp activities were centered around previous residence (such as football clubs that organized based on the players' hometown), this result is staggering. Even taking into account couples where hometown data was missing for at least one of the spouses, we come to 59 percent of non–hometown-based marriages.

Since so many spouses did not share a prewar hometown, I presumed that meaningful shared experiences occurred within camp. Ted Hamachi, for example, felt that the camp had a positive impact on the young people's relationships, at least as he observed his sisters. His sister Kazuko got married in camp, and Ted implies that incarceration enabled her to select her partner more freely: "Where if she stayed, there was no war, maybe my oldest sister might have gotten married by intermediary, baishakunin . . . but she found her mate there in camp. And so that sort of helped. My other sister that became a nurse had a boyfriend."[31] However, as often as members of this camp marriage subset appeared in the social and employment networks (although some individuals were also present in the political network), few of the couples seem to have been united through a shared interest or workplace. This holds true even for the church and young people's groups, which could have been expected to unite young couples. The remaining possibility is that people found their spouses through block residence, but this is difficult to measure.

Sometimes, of course, meeting a significant other might be a matter of coincidence. Toshiko Nagamori Ito met her husband, James Ito, when she applied for a leave to study in Kansas City, Missouri. He worked in the leaves office and assisted her in filling out the applications. "And the day I left, Jim came down to see [me and my friend], going to college . . . and then when I came back the first summer, he came over to see how college life was, and then we started to date," Toshiko Nagamori Ito described.[32]

As happened to Toshiko Nagamori Ito and James Ito, many relationships became long-distance following resettlement and service in the army. Many inmates were in their prime and anxious to leave the camp. I discovered that employment at the camp hospital and the *Sentinel*, especially, forecasted early resettlement.

Employed on the outside

Employment clearly prompted earlier resettlement decisions for some people, and it appears in general that those who were the most connected in the employment and social networks left slightly earlier than those with weaker ties. On the other hand, across departments, the highest-ranking employees tended to leave late: council chairman Minejiro Hayashida departed in late August 1945, while police chief Ryozo "Rosie" Matsui and community activities assistant director

David Yamakawa only left at the end of October, just days before the last trains. The very last departees included many employees of community activities, the fire department, and the motor pool.

In general, however, leave dates were evenly distributed, with the exception of the *Sentinel*, which had a higher concentration of early departees. Employment in camp reportedly affected many later educational and career choices. Especially young women employed in the schools and hospitals in all camps reported pursuing careers in education or nursing, respectively. The Heart Mountain Welfare Department reported that many inmates had expressed their satisfaction regarding the job training they had received in camp, preparing them for work on the outside.[33]

One example of a person whose camp work experience carried into later life is Marjorie Matsushita Sperling, who was twenty years old when she was first incarcerated at the Portland Assembly Center before relocating to Heart Mountain. She was a Girl Scout prior to incarceration, helped set up the recreation department at Portland and Heart Mountain, and had a full career in running recreational services ranging from children's playgrounds to an air force base. Similarly, Sachi (Tamaki) Kaneshiro, who helped establish the social work and employment offices at the Poston camp in Arizona before transferring to Heart Mountain, described the deep impact the experience had on her future. Describing what she learned, she said, "I don't think anybody was as privileged as I was because (they were) two top social workers. They [Kaneshiro's coworkers] were leaders in their field and, and they just shared so much with me. It even made me choose social work as a profession when I got out of camp."[34]

Nevertheless, leaving camp even with the promise of a job was not a decision to be made lightly. Tetsuko Okida Zaima considered leaving camp among the early resettlers to be "gutsy" because what little work experience she had was from camp. She did not encounter difficulties in finding jobs, however, and having "new friends who were in the same boat" made life easier.[35]

Although Zaima, like many others, described moving from one job and city to another, she benefitted from her prewar status: she had three years of college education. Almost a fifth of the early resettlers had at least a year of college upon their departure. This indicates that highly educated people were willing and able to leave the camp; they may have been financially prepared to venture to new cities and had suitable backgrounds for the jobs that were available. Although many inmates praised the training and work experience they received at Heart Mountain, employers outside of camp seem to have considered a wider array of characteristics, such as language skills and prewar merit, in their employment decisions. Based on available information, most well-educated people found jobs that fit their education level, regardless of whether they had been employed or otherwise highly connected in camp. This was true especially of the Nisei, who had an advantage over many of the Issei in language skills.

The Nisei, of course, spoke English. Their true asset on the outside, though, was their ability to speak Japanese, although officially, Japanese language school attendance in the United States among these early resettlers was low.[36] Half of them did have at least spoken Japanese skills, which increased their desirability on the job market—even outside the incarceration camps as Japanese language teachers and interpreters for the army. One of the biggest known employers of the resettlers was the Japanese language school at the University of Colorado, Boulder, which recruited at least nine Heart Mountaineers. There was also a language school at the Camp Savage military base in Minnesota.[37] In addition to direct civilian recruits from camps, Camp Savage Language School enlisted draftees. At least nineteen language teachers were drafted out of Heart Mountain.

While the most common leave type was indefinite leave for employment, the single most common "job" title on the outside was student.[38] Students were one of the earliest and largest groups to depart all camps. The Japanese American Student Relocation Council worked hard to enable them to continue their disrupted studies outside the West Coast or to start completely new degrees.[39] The largest intake university from Heart Mountain was the University of Wyoming–Laramie, with nineteen students. Of this group, eleven had started their studies before incarceration. They came from diverse backgrounds but not from exceptionally highly educated families.

Katsumi Hirooka, for example, had been intent on studying journalism when she came to Heart Mountain. At Heart Mountain High School, she had been a good student and an aspiring writer, earning her the position of managing editor of the school paper as well as reporter for the *Heart Mountain Sentinel*. As a high school senior in 1944, the Student Relocation Council contacted her. Two years in an incarceration camp had made her reluctant to leave her family, though. A friend "kept telling me that there's no future in camp. You have to start college." So she did, enrolling at the University of Wisconsin. Although Hirooka's primary reason for resettling was to pursue higher education, she funded her studies as a "schoolgirl"—performing household duties such as cooking and cleaning in the home of a White family.[40]

In fact, the second most common job title was domestic. It was typical for White families from across the country to post advertisements in the camp newspapers requesting to employ a domestic helper.[41] Not only young women but also older Issei, both men and women, did this work. In some cases, older couples found employment with the same family and resettled together. These instances probably entailed outdoor "handyman" work for the man and more typical housework for the woman. Although many Issei found opportunities as domestic workers, some did not consider it appropriate work for them, saying that such jobs would lower the status of the Japanese overall. The Heart Mountain community council took a similar, if slightly more lenient, view, saying that the Issei were too old for domestic and hotel service. They envisioned the Issei as establishing their own farms or other companies and requested the WRA's help facilitating those opportunities. In general, financial insecurity and old age were by far the most common reasons cited for reluctance to relocate. Other issues preventing resettlement were the draft, reluctance to leave, discrimination, business that could not be established elsewhere, the availability of only an unsuitable job opportunity, and housing shortages.[42]

The defense industry offered a special kind of employment following security checks to determine the applicant's integrity to work in the sensitive field of defense. One prominent example is the Tooele Ordnance Depot in Tooele, Utah. The town was the first destination of fifty-four persons, of whom at least thirteen became employed in the depot. The ordnance depot was a community in its own right, with on-site housing, recreation facilities, and basic services. The job advertisement in the Sentinel Supplement concluded with three statements from community leaders Howard Otamura (block manager), Eiichi Sakauye (block manager), and Jutaro Yokoi (Methodist reverend). Sakauye praised the "splendid opportunity" for Nisei to relocate and "to do our part on the home front for the war effort," while Otamura noted that defense employment gave the Nisei a chance to "gain a foothold for post-war plans." Yokoi, an Issei, lamented the disqualification of the Issei to apply but admitted the opportunity was "excellent" for Nisei.[43]

Defense employment had an added appeal: it gave draft-age men deferment from the draft for six months at a time. Miyo (Nakae) Uratsu's family moved to Tooele for this precise reason, she claimed. Uratsu said her mother needed her eldest son available and unharmed to run the family ranch.[44]

The above individual stories speak volumes about the various motivations and realities of resettlement. Some were courageous and just wanted out; some were ambitious and wanted to pursue education like Katsumi Hirooka; others saw employment as a way to keep the family together, like the Nakae Uratsus.

CHAPTER 6

Individuals of Power and Power Families

JUST AS THERE ARE many ways to measure power in society, power in a network takes different forms.[1] If we look only at a person's number of memberships in organizations (the outdegree), the most powerful person at Heart Mountain was Hidenobu George Nakaki. He appeared in connection to sixteen organizations. But looking at outdegree does not tell us whether his groups were big or small. If we examine interpersonal links, Minoru Horino has the highest degree at 621, twice that of Nakaki's. He participated in much larger organizations than Nakaki. And these numbers still do not tell us what a person's position in the network was, and thus what kind of power they had. Who had access to different parts of the network? Who had the ability to connect people?

Nakaki and Horino were both politically powerful. Here, I expand the definition of power and consider other segments of the network. I explored and evaluated my network findings in comparison with powerful inmates named in research literature, allowing us to see that influence as perceived by the WRA was not necessarily the same as the centrality of an individual within the formal networks.

Political Power

Three men stand out in the political network: Hidenobu George Nakaki, Minejiro Hayashida, and Minokichi Tsunokai. Nakaki was a Nisei who was born in Washington in 1908 and arrived at Heart Mountain from California. He had a bachelor's degree in engineering and some graduate education. Nakaki was a member of six political groups: the Relocation Planning Commission, the Relocation Coordination Committee, the Scholarship Fund, the Manpower Commission, the Space and Coordinating Committee of the Community Activities Board (hereafter Space and Coordinating Committee), the West Coast Study Committee, and the War Savings Committee. In addition, he was in the first community council, did not run in the February election of 1943, returned for the second council of 1943, and then served in the rest of the councils until his departure in September 1945; he served six terms in all.

Minejiro Hayashida was an Issei with American college-level education who came to Heart Mountain from Los Angeles, where he had worked as a real estate agent. He was elected to six community councils, missing only the second council of 1943, and served as chairman of the council in 1942, 1943, and 1945.[2] He was elected to the last council in August 1945 but left the camp at the end of that month. In addition, he was a member of the Scholarship Committee, the Relocation Coordination Committee, the Judicial Committee, and the West Coast Study Committee. Community analyst Asael T. Hansen characterized Hayashida as a "smooth politician, compromiser. . . . As Issei go, quite Americanized." Based on Hansen's report, Hayashida was a controversial figure in camp politics: "Not *inu*, just too aggressive and too smooth, or slick." The *inu* referenced here literally means "dog" and was used by other inmates to refer to inmates who were too close to the government. Some of the controversy around Hayashida may have arisen from the fact that his wife, a voluntary evacuee, was a White Englishwoman.[3] Since US antimiscegenation laws prevented multiracial marriages legally and Japanese cultural norms hindered them socially, most Japanese-White couples were, at the very least, noteworthy in the Japanese American community. Because these couples broke the norm, it was more difficult to them to enjoy a neutral status, despite the fact that many White spouses voluntarily went into incarceration to remain with their families.

The third leader, measured by degree, was Minokichi Tsunokai, who had five political group and six council memberships. He was born in Japan in 1874 and had gone to college there before coming to the United States but worked as a gardener in prewar Los Angeles. Tsunokai was on the West Coast Study Committee, the Relocation Coordination Committee, the Judicial Committee, the Scholarship Committee, and the Space and Coordinating Committee. He was a member of all six councils preceding his departure in June 1945.

In addition to their prominence as council politicians, the three men shared memberships on several committees: the two relocation groups, the Scholarship Committee, and the West Coast Study Committee. This means they were in constant contact with each other and held top positions of political power at Heart Mountain.

Community leaders like these men were important to both the inmates and the WRA. Whereas the inmate community was looking for leadership, the WRA's interest was practical—administrators wanted to identify leaders who could either obstruct or support WRA policies. The names mentioned as

FIGURE 6. Community council, July 1944. Kumezo Hatchimonji is in the back row to the extreme left. Other members are not identified. Women in the front row are probably clerks. *Community Council at Heart Mountain Concentration Camp* (ddr-densho-242-13). Courtesy of Densho Digital Repository, the Ike Hatchimonji Collection.

influential in WRA documents are not always the same as those that emerge through network analysis. For example, Samuel Nagata often appeared in the WRA reports in the early months of incarceration, but he was formally connected to only one political group, the Relocation Coordination Committee. Assistant Project Director Douglas M. Todd relied on Nagata's insights in selecting the first block managers, and the community council called him a "co-worker." Cooperating with the WRA, especially, earned him a conflicting reputation, and some Issei considered him *inu*, a spy of the administration. In contradiction, the House Un-American Activities Committee (usually known as the Dies Committee after its chair, Martin Dies, Jr.), which investigated the alleged "coddling" of inmates at Heart Mountain, named Nagata as the *de facto* leader of the camp in lieu of the project director.[4] The Dies Committee thus elevated Nagata to an imaginary position that was not only influential among inmates but also carried power over the top administration.

Another man whom the WRA esteemed but who had a contradictory status in inmates' eyes was Ryoichi Fujii, a member of the Relocation Committee. He was considered valuable enough to the WRA to warrant a long report regarding his thoughts on incarceration and how his positive outlook on resettlement might benefit WRA resettlement policy. He was an evidently Americanized young Issei in his late thirties who advocated vocally for the resettlement of the Issei through a newsletter he published and sent to subscribers. His opponents considered him "too pro-American. To be pro-American is all right, but it is claimed that he carries it so far that . . . he is anti-Japanese. When a Nisei is anti-Japanese, it is understandable and forgivable. But Fujii is an Issei. Therefore . . . he is little better than a traitor."[5] Interestingly, Fujii was also a member of the Communist Party before the war, a fact that the WRA either did not know or did not care about, since his overall stance toward the resettlement policy was favorable. For a period of time before his resettlement in Chicago, Fujii always had a friend accompany him for fear of physical violence. His case is an excellent example of the spectrum of sentiment at Heart Mountain. There were extremely Americanized Issei who were perceived as betraying Japan for expressing views that were better suited for Nisei. There was no single behavior that was expected of or allowed for everyone. Of course, those who were openly antagonistic toward Fujii and other Issei seen as anti-Japanese occupied an extreme position. Others, Hansen wrote, "view him with tolerant disregard."[6] Most people were not agitated by the views of a single individual.

A third man of interest for the WRA not arising in the network model was Rikio Tomo, a Hawaiian Nisei block manager. Contrary to Nagata and Fujii, whom the WRA considered assets, Tomo was seen as a potential troublemaker. Project attorney Jerry W. Housel went as far as to say that Tomo was "a leader in the campaign against any form of evacuee government in the center."[7] Housel's views are not supported by any evidence that I have seen, and Tomo definitely does not occupy a place in the network where he could direct such a campaign. Heart Mountain WRA administrators described him as a "tough, direct bargainer," embittered by incarceration and prepared to sue the government.[8] In any case, these disputes with the WRA led Tomo to resign his position as the chairman of block managers. In his letter of resignation, Tomo said he had tried to "honestly interpret and transmit the wishes and thoughts of the residents" but felt that the WRA and assistant project director Douglas M. Todd, in particular, had made all disagreements personal. In Tomo's final statement, he may have revealed the true cause of his discontent: "This Center has not followed the WRA instructions pertaining to [only American] citizens being the temporary council [before setting up the more permanent community government structure]. The rights of American Citizens have been almost entirely ignored in this respect."[9] He was angry at the Heart

Mountain WRA administration for allowing Issei to become councilmembers during a time when the national WRA had instructed otherwise.

Contrary to the WRA point of view, none of these men appeared to be particularly powerful in the formal networks. Their participation and reach were nowhere near those of Minejiro Hayashida, Hidenobu George Nakaki, and Minokichi Tsunokai. Nevertheless, we cannot deny their influence in the community. Their networks appear to have been informal rather than formal, but in many cases, this may have increased their power. This interplay between formal and informal power and involvement is key to understanding the social networks.

Interpersonal Power

Another way to look at connectivity is to detect interpersonal connections that have a strong weight, which indicates that two individuals connect through several organizations. Person-to-person networks are in many ways less multifaceted than multimode networks because they do not automatically take into account *how* people are connected, but they make certain interpretations easier. When all the Heart Mountain formal networks were converted into an individual-to-individual network, the 2,881 individuals had 172,192 edges, with an average degree—the number of links an average person has—of 119. The network is highly segmented in the sense that there are many social spheres in which the members have strong connections among each other. At the same time, the average path length—the number of individuals through whom one must connect to reach any other person in the network—is 2.5, about the same as in the smallest political network, but this interpersonal network is eight times as large, thus making the relative path length shorter. Coupled with the high segmentation, the shorter paths demonstrate that, although there were several subcommunities, there were also central people connecting the communities.

In this type of a projection, most nodes have a relatively high degree: if a person is a member of a group with twenty other members, she will have twenty connections. Some of the groups in this graph are so large that if a person is, for example, a member of the men's football team and the senior boys' club, he will already have 233 connections. Measured by degree only, the most powerful person in this network is Minoru Horino, whose degree is 621. Naturally, anyone on the Fair Play Committee, like Horino, appears very well connected due to the size of the organization.

A large overall number of contacts, however, does not indicate strong relationships. Three pairs of people have particularly strong connections to another person. One of these pairs is Dick Fujioka and Donald Toriumi, both of whom, as we shall later learn, were significant men in the networks. They were connected through the USO, the Student Y, the YMCA, the Relocation Planning Commission, the Scholarship Fund, and the Relocation Committee. However, they lack a linkage in the employment network. The other strong pairs only connect within one network, thus further strengthening the bond between Fujioka and Toriumi. Fujioka is also one of the pairs in several other strong interpersonal relationships, which further adds to his power.

Another way to consider the reach across the network is to look at access to other network actors. The individuals in the formal camp network were about 2.5 steps from each other, which is a high number for a fairly small network. This is due to the fact that so many people were only connected to one organization, making it more difficult to find a connecting link. The significance of the bridges (or brokers) becomes pronounced because so many Heart Mountain people were on the fringes of the community. From the men named above as significant, either due to their number of contacts or to their value to the WRA, only Minejiro Hayashida was a bridge in network terms.

Bridges and Brokers

As I noted previously, simply measuring the number of connections of an individual—or even the strength of those connections—does not always yield sufficient information about the distribution of power in a network. The concept of betweenness is particularly useful in this context. The betweenness centrality value of any network actor shows how often that actor is on a path connecting any two actors. An actor with a high betweenness score is a bridge, or a broker, that can bring together parts of a network that would otherwise remain unconnected. A bridge could, for example, introduce two people who previously did not know each other, or they could relay information from one faction to another.

There are several potential bridges in the Heart Mountain network. In order to account for changes in the camp population, I looked at three snapshots in time: the beginnings of the camp in the fall of 1942, the network at its largest in the winter of 1944, and the situation toward camp closure in the summer of 1945.

A snapshot of the full network in the fall of 1942 shows that Heart Mountaineers did not waste time in getting their community organized. Within the first four months of their incarceration, they had established nine political groups, seven social groups, and four events in addition to the WRA workplaces. Altogether, 840 people were part of these early efforts.

The highest betweenness score belongs to Minejiro Hayashida, as does the highest degree. Hayashida is a bridge between the political network, the Adult Education Department, and the mess hall workers' club. The latter should especially benefit from Hayashida's participation because its members were generally less connected. The Adult Education Department, meanwhile, has several bridges, giving it connections to the hospital as well as men's sports groups.

Yoshio Robert Kodama also demonstrated high bridging capabilities, bridging community activities and political organizations. Kodama is not part of any specific modularity community (groups or communities, where linkages within the group are stronger than to other parts of the network), whereas Hayashida is in the political group. In other words, Hayashida has an obvious attachment to the political network, but not so much to the other networks. Meanwhile, Kodama has about the same number of connections to all of the different networks. In the social network, too, he appeared as a person that was not necessarily committed to a single organization or clique. He truly seems to have navigated different kinds of environments and contexts. This can be a valuable attribute for someone looking to increase their influence, but it can also come across as an inability to settle down. Indeed, as we shall see below, Kodama had a conflicting role in the community. Paul Nakadate, the third significant bridge, is also in the political segment in this snapshot. He bridges men's sports, political groups, and the night school. Nakadate later became known as one of the leaders of the Fair Play Committee, but it seems his influence in the community dates to the beginning of incarceration. Although his position on the Fair Play Committee network did not seem to indicate particular recruiting power, he obviously knew many people and was thus able to exert his influence.

Meanwhile, a snapshot from the network's peak moment in the winter of 1944 reveals another power dynamic. First, the average member of the network at this time had significantly more connections than in the first months of incarceration. Second, the communities were fewer and larger than in the first months of incarceration. In other words, there was more segmentation: the same people associated with each other through multiple organizations. Yoshio Robert Kodama, who was the second strongest broker in the 1942 snapshot, is the clear winner in this second portrayal. He truly had connections spanning in all directions, which is not evident when we look only at his organizational connections.

Kodama was a twenty-five-year-old Nisei at the start of incarceration and had worked as an office manager in Los Angeles. While his camp job was never explicitly stated, he was probably employed by the boys' clubs or the Scouts. In any case, Heart Mountain residents seem to have known Kodama as the organizer of various types of social activities and events. In addition to social activities, Kodama was a member of the first community council in 1942 and three community political committees, as well as being an active of the Christian parish. In these capacities, he was able to connect people in the male-dominated part of the network with those in the female-dominated part (and, likewise, he could connect people in the political networks with those in the social networks). Kodama, however, probably had a conflicting position in the community: the FBI listed him as a source of information in the early stages of the Fair Play Committee.[10] Willingness to report to the authorities about the "un-American" (draft-resisting) activities of fellow Nisei suggests that he was a member of the patriotic Japanese American Citizens League, which was sometimes harshly criticized for extending too much accommodation to the policies of the US government.

The next two bridges, though far from Kodama, are Kiyoshi Fujiwara and Eiichi Sakauye. They are located in the same community, probably because they were both listed as members of the Fair Play Committee. Kiyoshi Fujiwara draws our attention to the dissemination of information and indirect power. He was a Japan-educated (Kibei) FPC member, connected to Buddhist organizations but also part of the employment network (through the night school, where he taught Japanese) and the political network (through the Judicial Committee). The fact that he was a member of the Judicial Committee makes him important in camp politics. The committee had power in local trials concerning smaller misdemeanors that did not have to be tried on the state level.[11] That he was also a member of the FPC—and that he was sent to internment in Santa Fe in late 1945—suggests that he had power that previous research has entirely missed.

By the third snapshot, the summer of 1945, the network had again diminished. The number of connections was less than half of that in 1944, and the number of communities had increased. Unlike in the fall of 1942, when several people shared the bridging power, by 1945, one individual stands out. That person is Yukio Abe, who worked for the Community Activities Group Activities Department, was a member of the senior boys' clubs—and was also a member of the Fair Play Committee.

Minejiro Hayashida, who was central at the early stages of community building, makes a return to influence. He left the camp in late August of 1945, thus continuing to bridge the political and employment networks almost throughout the camp's existence. After August, the formal camp network dissolved almost completely. In the final weeks, it no longer resembled a web, but was rather a collection of cliques without links between groups.

In the more restricted employment network, Chieko Otsuki, a thirty-year-old Issei doctor at the hospital and teacher at the night school, appeared to be a relatively important bridge (especially in the context of the Issei). She had a high degree because she was employed by two large institutions, and in addition to being a broker, she was also close to other members of the network. She was able to bridge a more professional part of the network (the hospital) to a more social section (the night school). Thus, she certainly appeared a significant person in terms of reach and reachability, although little is known about her life in camp or afterwards. To move beyond an individual's influence in a network, I will next investigate the opportunities brought by strong family involvement.

Power Families

Studying key individuals in the political network shows that some people might have indirect power in addition to their direct linkages. With a spouse or other family members in the network, an individual could expand their indirect reach significantly. Although there were differences between the network layers in that especially the employment and social networks had power families of their own, these two networks overlapped for the most part.

Family connections within the political network were limited and specialized, and few families had exceptional power. Two families had three family members in the political network, and while their reaches were quite different, neither family appeared to have significant influence. Furthermore, only one of the individuals with the highest outdegree had family members in the network. Hidenobu George Nakaki, the councilman with the highest outdegree (twelve), had a father in the network who served as a member of the Judicial Committee. We could speculate that the father and son pair may have influenced each other and had access to practically all key institutions in camp. Because many of the family's connections arose from the son's network, they cannot be considered a power family in a broad sense. However, one of the two families discovered at this first stage built up its family power throughout all the different network contexts, becoming a camp-wide power family: the Fujiokas.

In the political network, they were represented by an Issei mother and two children in their later twenties. Chiyo Fujioka, born in 1884 in Japan, had studied in college before coming to the United States. From the prewar years, however, no occupational data is listed. She was a member of the Judicial Committee, which was one of the elected bodies of the camp. Children Dick and Peggy, born in 1913 and 1914, were both members of the Relocation Committee and the Relocation Planning Commission, and Dick was also a member of the Scholarship Fund. Both emerged as prominent individuals in various networks, contributing to their family's power.

Though the Fujiokas were not particularly powerful to start out, their power grew over time. With five siblings in the employment network—Dick, Peter, Peggy, Setsuko, and Ted (Teruo)—the Fujiokas reached a wide section of the network, spanning to its periphery. Dick and Peggy had the most connections in the family. Dick was supervisor of the Community Activities Section and the only individual in the five power families to leave the camp in 1945. He had been born in Washington in 1913 but was among inmates arriving from California. He only had a high school education and was recorded as a retail manager upon entering camp.

Peggy Fujioka emerged as a well-connected woman in the political network and increased her power through employment connections. With a bachelor's degree in social sciences and mathematics, she began working in the camp's Ceramic Project in 1943, participating in the making of tableware and other ceramics, then as a secretary for the Office of Design Coordination, and finally as a social welfare counselor. Of the three other siblings in the network, two, Setsuko and Peter, had attended college, Peter finishing a degree in biology. He had been in the military but was supposedly discharged after Pearl Harbor. At Heart Mountain, he worked as a supervisor in the post office. The oldest daughter of the family, Setsuko, was a supervisor of the milk station in the camp hospital. Ted, who was still in high school when the war broke out, worked in an unnamed position at the *Heart Mountain Sentinel*.

The secondary connections of the Fujioka siblings—in other words, all the individuals and organizations they reached through the people they knew by virtue of their memberships—spread in almost all directions of the employment network. While a single individual would not be able to retain all these connections, the family was very powerful in terms of access to people. The Fujiokas' education levels also appeared to give them power; three of the five had a college degree and one had some college education. Two of the five were in supervisor positions, while Peggy, a social welfare counselor, also served an important role in the community.

Finally, the Fujiokas participated in the social network with seven family members. Dick, Peggy, and Ted, who were in the employment network, and Chiyo (the mother), who was in the political network, were present in the social network. New family members were Ayako (daughter), Yoshiro (son), and Doris (Peter's wife). While family members other than Dick and Doris did not have more than one or two organizational connections, family memberships in the senior boys' clubs, men's football, and the rho clubs meant that the family had an extensive combined network. Not all the connections occurred simultaneously; Chiyo Fujioka joined the USO Parents in the spring of 1944, after Ted Fujioka had volunteered for the United States Armed Forces. Ted Fujioka was something of a celebrity among the Heart Mountain youth. He was popular in high school and was overwhelmingly elected as the student body president.[12] In 1943, he volunteered for the army, was sent to Europe, and fell in France in November 1944. According to classmate and fellow reporter George Yoshinaga, "When he was killed it was really something, more than any other person from Heart Mountain that lost their life in the war."[13]

The family member missing in these networks turned out upon further inspection of sources to be the one with perhaps the most hidden power. The head of the family, Shiro Fujioka, was a prolific newspaperman and served as the executive secretary of the Central Japanese Association, Southern California branch, before incarceration. Having been interned alongside other community leaders, he was transferred to Santa Anita Assembly Center along with his family due to poor health. Although he recovered, his illness was probably the reason that he was missing from the formal networks.[14]

The second largest family measured by the number of family members—and one that was not prominent in any of the one-layer networks—was the Tanouye family. It was complex in composition, including teenage and adult children, adopted children, and spouses. The family had thirteen members at Heart Mountain (with two children or grandchildren born in camp) and eight members in the integrated network. One member worked at the Salvation Army, two as officers of the block 23 Nisei club, one in the fields, one in the supply section, one in the sewing project, and one in the hospital. One was a member of the Young Buddhists' Association, despite all members of the family having registered themselves as Christian. Their combined reach, compared to the Fujiokas, is low. Since each family member was only connected to one institution, their reach was not very wide, although the employed family members reached a relatively diverse range of institutions. The Tanouyes present an interesting example of a family with many members in the integrated network, but that nevertheless did not seem to have much influence beyond its numbers; the family is large, but its reach does not extend to the political network.

The third family, the Sakauyes, is a very different example. In the employment-only network, it had six members and included one new spouse, yet its reach was very modest. This was because all five family members worked in small units. The oldest sibling, Eiichi Sakauye, however, was the assistant

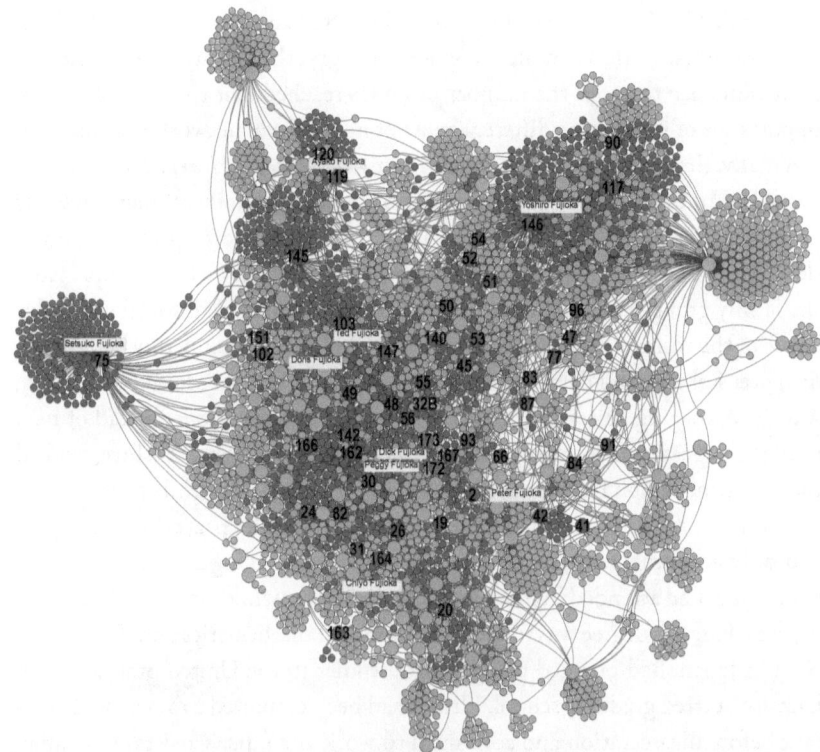

FIGURE 7. Reach of the Fujioka family. Darker nodes are individuals and organizations reached directly or through one intermediary by members of the family. Family members are placed approximately in the neighborhoods of their densest connections. Most of the unreached nodes are at the bottom right with predominantly political organizations.

superintendent of the Agricultural Section, so we can assume a wider reach outside the strictly administrative agricultural section and into the more practical departments, such as farm work and fieldwork. Without his additional engagement in block management, the family's reach would be inconsequential. Other family members in the employment network included Kimiko (who worked in the Property Control Office), Isao (timekeeper's office), Ayako (social welfare), and Isao's wife, Kiyoko (Statistics Section). All four Sakauyes had attended college, but education information was not available for Kiyoko Naito Sakauye.

In the Sakauye case, the change in reach from the employment network to the full-network model is remarkable. While the family's reach, including seventeen institutions, was concentrated on a smaller area than the Fujiokas', the total number of nodes that it reached grew manifold. This is due to Eiichi's membership in the Fair Play Committee and Kiyoko Naito Sakauye's in the rho clubs, both very large organizations. In the integrated network, the Sakauyes thus increased their influence through the number of nodes reached, but they also show the importance of integrating different types of networks in network research.

Finally, three power families shared a connection to the *Heart Mountain Sentinel*. The Imura family is an interesting example of a family that sustained its prominence in network terms despite having a more narrow variety of connections. In the employment network, it scored the highest with six people from the family group but had few additional connections through social networks. Three of the women in the family group worked in the hospital: mother Hisaye, daughter Kikuye, and daughter-in-law Masako. Son Haruo, Masako's husband, was the managing editor of the *Heart Mountain Sentinel* from the fall of 1943 until the paper was discontinued in July 1945. Another daughter, Yoshiye, worked for the Mimeograph Department and the Reports Division, while her husband, Tom Okuda, was an English teacher at the night school. Hisaye, born in Japan, had only an elementary school education; the three younger women, born in California, had attended high school. The men, meanwhile, both had bachelor's degrees. Haruo's degree was in social sciences and mathematics and Tom, while born in Japan, had pursued postgraduate studies in the United States. Haruo had also started graduate school. Hisaye had been employed as a personal assistant before incarceration and continued to work as a nurse's assistant in camp. Kikuye, Masako, and Yoshiye had worked as maids before camp, while Haruo worked for Japanese American newspapers in San Fransisco.[15]

The father of the family, Sakanosuke Imura, was a member of the Judicial Committee. With this connection, and with the membership of Haruo Imura in the Cooperative Education Committee, the family reached toward the political part of the network, but otherwise its reach was limited. Though Sakanosuke Imura's formal connections at Heart Mountain appear scant, he had made a name for himself as the owner of a popular San Francisco hotel. And while he was not a member of the last community councils known for their resistance to the closing of the camps, Imura participated in the campaign, successfully petitioning the secretary of war, Henry Stimson, for a later departure date for his wife and himself.[16] In addition to the employment connections, the family had social links to the Buddhist Gyotoku Kai club through a daughter-in-law; and to the USO through Sakanosuke Imura. These did not stand out in the investigation of social connections, demonstrating the importance of both layered and integrated analyses of the networks.

The Masuda family had a much more modest reach in terms of number of organizations and individuals connected. This family consisted of siblings James, Kikue, Masako, and Sueko Masuda; and James's wife, Nobu Bessho Masuda. James worked in the Statistics Section of the Administrative Management Division. His wife, meanwhile, worked for the *Heart Mountain Sentinel* advertising department. James's sister Kikue also worked at the *Sentinel*, and Masako was a secretary to Vaughn Mechau, the reports officer in charge of *Sentinel* operations, among other things. Finally, Sueko was a secretary at the hospital dental clinic. Kikue resettled in 1943 and the rest of the family members left Heart Mountain in the spring and early summer of 1944, making them some of the early departees. When we add Nobu's three employed siblings to the selection, the family's reach increases, although it still occupies the same niche of the network. Nobu's sister Takako likewise worked in advertising at the *Sentinel* and in the Mimeograph Department, while her brothers Tatsu and Kei both worked for the Community Activities Group Activities Department.

James was the oldest of the Masuda family, age twenty-seven upon the start of incarceration. He had attended college but had not completed a degree. His prewar occupation was listed as stock clerk and upon his entry into Heart Mountain, he had listed accountant as a potential occupation, suggesting he had education or experience in that field. Based on the scant available employment details, his job at the Statistics Section probably suited his education and experience. Nobu, two years younger, had also attended some college, as had Masako, while the rest of the family members had high school diplomas.

The third *Sentinel* family, the Satos, occupied a section of the network similar to that occupied by the Masudas, both in terms of size and organizations reached. The Satos are another interesting example of new networks, as this group of five included Jack Sato and his new wife, Mary; Jack's sister's new husband, Harry Hashimoto; and two apparently adopted brothers of Jack, Tom, and Fred Yamamoto Sato. Tom's new father-in-law could also be included, but his addition would not expand the size of the network as such because he worked in the same workplace as his son-in-law. Tom Yamamoto Sato worked at the hospital as a dental technician, although in the entry database he was listed as "skilled carpenter." Fred Yamamoto Sato, meanwhile, had some college education and was a reporter at the *Sentinel*. Jack Sato, who had some college education, worked as an accountant in the Education Section administrative office, and his wife, also a college student, worked at the hospital. All of the Satos, like the Masudas, left Heart Mountain during the indefinite leave period.

When looking at the integrated network, Fred Yamamoto Sato increased the family's connections—he had five social institution memberships. He had more connections in the social network than the average inmate, although not enough to appear in the examination of powerful individuals. While the Satos were not a remarkably large family, nor did they have an exceptional reach, they present an extremely valuable example of extended networks. In the employment network, the extended family included three brothers, one of their wives, one brother-in-law (the Satos' sister's husband), and one father-in-law. The integrated network also brought in Kiyo Sato Hashimoto (whose husband was in the employment network) with her social connections, her sister-in-law, as well as Jack Sato's father-in-law. Because of the father-in-law's work as a member of the Mess Hall Advisory Board, the family network added a political dimension.

During the process of searching for power families and reading inmate oral histories, it became evident that the concept of family was not straightforward. As noted in chapter 5's discussion of marriages in camp, the old Japanese concept of *ie*, the extended family or household, was part of the culture at Heart Mountain. During data collection, I discovered the same family number assigned to as many as thirty-eight individuals, who had multiple last names and block addresses. I determined that they were not part of the same family unit. I call them "registered family groups" to emphasize that they had chosen to register together even though they may have had loose, if any, kinship relations.

In the camp networks, some of these registered groups became power families. The largest of them was the Hayashima-Kawamoto-Kimoto-Kow-Mohri-Nishimoto-Shinohara group, with eleven network actors. Compared to the number of family members, the group's combined reach is small. It has members in thirteen institutions, although the scope of connections increases due to the fact that only two of those were shared by several members of the group. On the other hand, the group's strong presence (five members) in the Buddhist congregation suggests strong influence in that group. Indeed, two of them, Reichi Mohri and Daitetsu Hayashima, were reverends of the congregation.

Meanwhile, the Endo-Otera-Sashihara group, with eight members, reached twenty-seven institutions in all of the networks. The only organization this group shares is the Adult Education Department, where Allen Otera was a dance teacher and Jacob Otera taught tailoring. Thus, their contacts span practically all parts of the network. Remarkably, neither of these powerful registered family groups had contacts in the hospital or the *Heart Mountain Sentinel*—the two organizations that almost without a fail were key to the extensive contacts of the other power families.

It is difficult to know why the *Heart Mountain Sentinel* and the hospital were such prominent employers among most of the highest-scoring families. Simply looking at degree, the large employers understandably score highly, and, to a certain extent, it makes sense that families with many members in the employment network also had people in the largest workplaces. The fact that four out of five families had (sometimes several) members working in the hospital seems extraordinary. Similarly, the *Sentinel* was part of four out of five power families' networks.

Notably, the workplaces that employed the most people were the most gender-balanced workplaces. Consequently, both men and women had to work in camp for their family to rise to a power family position. Only the Sato family had a stark discrepancy between the number of female and male family members (one to five).

In addition to the hospital and the *Sentinel*, the boys' and girls' clubs and the sports clubs were present in varying combinations in each of the family networks. Notably, only one family had a member on the FPC, although it was the largest organization in the network. The absence of power families on the FPC demonstrates that while FPC members on average belonged to the mainstream Heart Mountain community, the sons of the most active and well-connected families were less active in that organization. I see the near absence of power families' members on the Fair Play Committee as a proof that the very elite of the Heart Mountain network exhibited pro-WRA behavior by avoiding membership in a controversial organization like the FPC.

Although I began my power family investigation by looking at numbers (by choosing to analyze family groups with the largest numbers of members in the network), it became evident that a high education level was, on average, a prerequisite for becoming a power family. The numbers show that the WRA favored well-educated inmates in its employee searches—and that well-educated inmates wanted to work. Looking at the networks these families created, we can imagine the family members' ability to influence the people with whom they associated.

When we combine the reach of the four most powerful families, most of the network is covered. In other words, knowing somebody in all four families would get one access to almost any organization in camp. But there are also organizations that could not have been reached through these power families.

Although we have found before that political power was concentrated in the hands of a group of Issei and a few Nisei, their families are not featured in the networks. Therefore, there is a significant lack of connections to political organizations through these otherwise powerful families. Moreover, only the Satos had direct linkages to the Red Cross and none of the families had access to the Adult Education Department, although the night school is on the list of reached organizations. Interestingly, links are also missing to Christian groups, the Girl Scouts (although links do exist to the Coordinating Council of Girls' Clubs and Scouts), and the Boy Scouts.

CHAPTER 7

Women of Heart Mountain

MARY OYAMA MITTWER IS one of Heart Mountain's most well-known women. A college-educated journalist, she wrote an etiquette and advice column for a Japanese American newspaper in the 1930s, informed mainstream American newspapers about the plight of the Japanese Americans during the war, left the camp in early 1943, and continued to write to various publications. We know of her because she left a paper trail but she did not emerge in any of the networks.[1]

Similarly, we know of Ruth Hashimoto. She was mentioned regularly as a block manager in the camp newspaper as well as the official camp documents, and she donated her papers to the Heart Mountain Wyoming Foundation. In addition, she is prominent in the network model.

Katie Koga Uchiyama was a twenty-three-year-old mother of a newborn baby when she arrived at Heart Mountain in late August of 1942.[2] Her main memory of wartime and incarceration was of monotony: "I never went anywhere," she said.[3] She represents the countless women who were not present in the formal networks. However, she shared her story in several oral history interviews.

Finally, Toshiye Nagata did not feature in newspaper articles, nor did she leave personal records or oral histories. The network model, however, shows her as the most active woman at Heart Mountain and the most active social networker out of everyone, including men, in camp.

Women's histories continue to be marginalized and it is crucial to bring out their experiences. When discussing Japanese American incarceration, scholars' focus was long on the experiences of men: as internees, soldiers, even draft resisters. Even more recently, few volumes have focused on the women's perspective.[4] As is often the case with historical documents, sources to reconstruct women's networks were more difficult to find than those about men's networks. For one thing, women often participated in informal rather than formal networks:

instead of joining the political committees that received attention in the newspaper and camp documents, they associated with their neighbors. That said, the *Sentinel* did not omit mention of women's activities; rather, it reported on private get-togethers and female-only events, such as the graduation of a large class of nurse's assistants.[5] Women were also well represented in the employment network, and this chapter focuses in part on women's employment opportunities both in camp and afterward.

The Connected Women

The women's network (see figure 8) consisted of 1,078 individuals, seventy workplaces, forty-four social groups, twelve events, and eight administrative groups. The women's network was at its largest slightly later than the overall camp network. At its peak, it included 544 women with 764 connections, so it was generally quite sparse. Throughout the camp's existence, 1,674 edges were formed between a total of 1,206 nodes.

The fact that the number of women was about the same in both the employment and social layers is surprising. The small number of women in the networks overall suggests that women were more involved in informal networks, tending to associate with their friends and neighbors rather than taking part in formal activities. Consequently, I expected the leading women to concentrate in the social network, which had a looser and more informal structure. Their equal distribution between the employment and social networks, nevertheless, demonstrates that those women who participated at all did so in a wider range of settings than expected.

Several large communities formed around the biggest organizations. The largest community was around the hospital, and the rho clubs were almost equally large. Other communities had several central organizations, one forming around the USO and the *Sentinel* for example. Among the otherwise large organizations is the Christian congregation, but it is not a community hub. This means that its members participated in a diverse number of other organizations rather than concentrating in similar groups.

As in the larger integrated network, although the average number of memberships was low (1.39), there was a fair number of women with many connections. The highest outdegree was eleven, and twenty-five women had an outdegree of at least five. The five women with the highest degrees were Toshiye Nagata, Ruth Hashimoto, Hisa Hirashiki, Amy Nose, and Louise Suski. While they were all

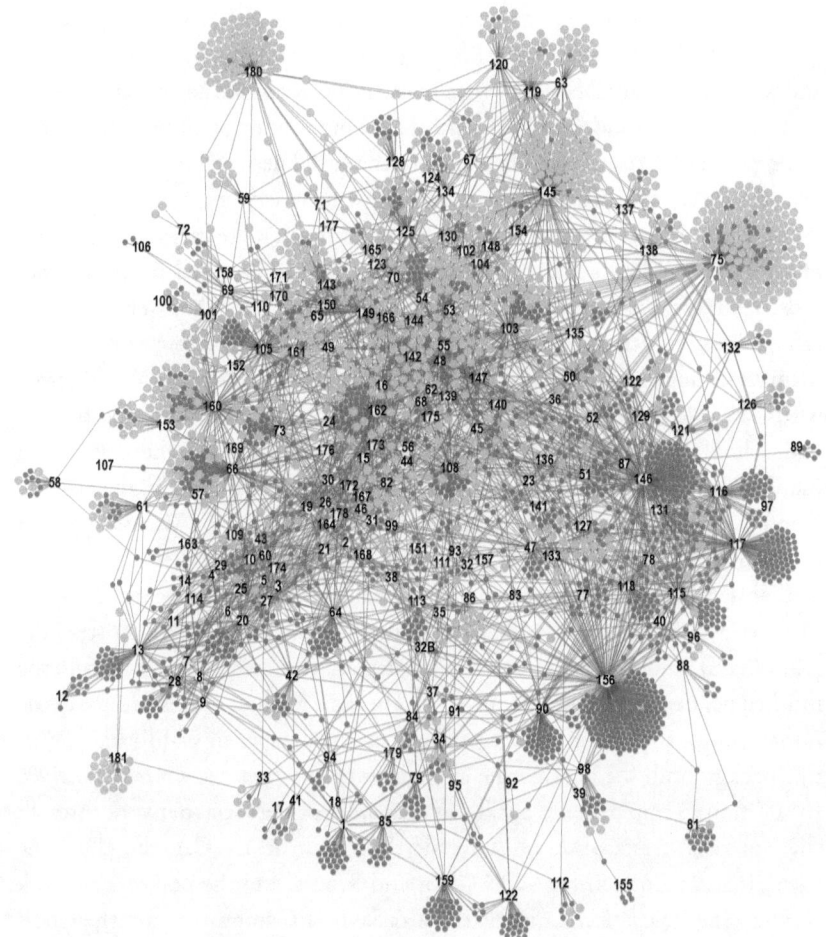

FIGURE 8. Division of the full network by gender. Women are represented as lighter and larger nodes. Organizations are numbered. Created by author.

Nisei, they were old by Nisei standards, born between 1905 and 1917. Their age makes them quite interesting; was this what made them prominent in the network? Many Nisei women were too preoccupied with family and childrearing to actively participate in camp politics. Of these five highly connected women, only two (Ruth Hashimoto and Amy Nose) were married when coming to Heart Mountain and none of them married in camp. Hashimoto had small children but Nose was childless. Overall, only a third of the women in the network were married. Therefore, these women prove the difficulty of combining active participation in politics or the working life with that of motherhood. Married women and women with small children were in the minority in the network.

Toshiye Nagata and Hisa Hirashiki are not quite as interesting as a few of the other women because they only appear in the social network and in the closely related segment of club employees in the employment network. Meanwhile, Ruth Hashimoto, Amy Nose, and Louise Suski show much more varied engagement. Hashimoto, the lone female block manager, will be discussed in more detail shortly, but Nose and Suski warrant more exploration here. They were especially prominent considering the short time they spent at Heart Mountain, both of them relocating in the early summer of 1943. Amy Nose was born in Washington, where she also lived upon eviction. She did not have formal education beyond high school, but at Heart Mountain, she worked for the girls' clubs and was a founding member of the YWCA as well as taking an active role in the Student Y and USO clubs. In the political realm, she participated in the War Savings and the Relocation Committees and was an advocate for early resettlement.[6]

Louise Suski, meanwhile, came from a family of highly educated inmates. Her father, P. M. Suski, was a doctor and surgeon, and Louise and her sister Julia (Kuwahara) and brother Joe attended college in the United States. Before she finished her degree, however, Louise Suski became the first English editor of the *Rafu Shimpo*, the oldest and largest Japanese newspaper in California.[7] With this background, she became the city editor of the *Heart Mountain Sentinel*. In addition to employment, Suski was a member of the social network through the American Association of University Women, the YWCA, the USO, the Coordinating Council for Girls' Clubs and Scouts, and the political network through the Relocation Committee, War Savings Committee, and the Coordinating Council for the Prevention and Disposition of Juvenile Delinquency. These memberships show a diverse knowledge about the Japanese American community in both professional and private life.

Amy Nose and Toshiye Nagata also had the strongest interpersonal link in the women's network. Both active in the social networks, they also shared a workplace at the Community Activities Clubs and Organizations Department. Amy Nose and Mary Lucy Nakamura shared an equally strong connection, five shared organizations. Nakamura, likewise, was employed at the same place as Nose and Nagata. Compared to the full network, where several strong links existed between pairs of men who connected through several organizations, the women's network is sparser and more segmented. The strong pairs that emerge mostly connect through social organizations.

From this individual-to-individual point of view, Nagata remains a central character, although others emerge as well. If we look at the number of connections only, a woman named May Shirao Muranaka appears at the center of the network. She was employed in two of the largest camp institutions: the hospital (in the obstetrics ward, her general skills listed her as a stenographer/typist) and the Community Activities Clubs and Organizations Department (as YWCA correlator), alongside Nose, Nagata, and Nakamura. In the social realm, she also participated in the rho clubs, which brought her a significant number of contacts.

Looking at the networks of these most-connected women, we see that while women had a solid presence in the employment network, they made their strongest connections doing social activities. There were, nevertheless, several women also in the political network.

Women in Politics

Women remained a rarity in community politics throughout the camp's existence. The reason is probably both cultural and related to women's life situations. Issei women were not used to participating in community affairs but it is difficult to estimate why Nisei women did not take up political positions more eagerly. Considering their age, a good portion of them probably had small children, while another large group of single women left the camp early to study or work in the eastern United States. More importantly, though, women rarely participated in political life, as described by community analyst Asael T. Hansen's report on the fall 1944 coal shortage: "The crowd [at the block meeting] was almost twice as large as usual, even some women attended."[8]

None of the seventeen women in the political clique were on the community councils. There was, however, one woman each on the Judicial Committee and the War Savings Committee, which both dealt with matters typically in the male realm. The Relocation Committee had many female members, five out of twelve. The committee was selected from officials and employees of various other institutions, such as the girls' clubs and the Red Cross, which contributed to its more balanced gender distribution.

The women represented a broad age range, with birth years varying between 1884 and 1925. Only three of them were Issei. Chiyo Fujioka, member of the Judicial Committee, was born in 1884 and had received a college-level education in Japan. In addition to being on the Judicial Committee, she was a member of the Heart Mountain Scholarship Fund, which gave small grants to Heart Mountain students. Another scholarship fund member, Yayoi Inoshita, was ten years younger but had also received a college education and teacher's credentials from Japan. Her other institutional network connection was to the YWCA. The third Issei, Chiyo Sashihara, came to the United States as a small child and received a degree in education there. Sashihara was a member of the Coordinating Council for the Prevention and Disposition of Juvenile Delinquency, one of the earliest camp committees, which sought to prevent the formation of gangs. In addition to her political connections, Sashihara was also active in the social networks (through the YWCA, Coordinating Council for Girls' Clubs and Scouts, and block twenty-five's elementary school PTA), as well as employed in the camp public library. Although the Sashihara family did not emerge as an actual power family, Chiyo Sashihara and her husband Thomas seem to have been a true power couple, with fourteen organizational memberships between them. Adding to their reach, none of these memberships were shared, so they had an impressive array of connections. They were also part of one of the biggest "registered family" groups (groups of families that registered under the same family number) in camp.

Like the three Issei, the rest of the women in the political network were highly educated. Eleven of them (65 percent) had studied in college (with five listed as having completed a degree), while the remaining six had at least some high school education. This means that the women were much more highly educated than the men in the political group, and also much more highly educated than the average women in camp. Of the entire Heart Mountain female population, 60 percent had attended at least high school, and of those, 15 percent had at least some college education. Although the women politicians were exceptionally highly educated, the education level of Heart Mountain's residents was overall quite high, with 11 percent having at least started college.[9] Nevertheless, it seems that for a woman to gain a position in the political network, a high education level was even more important than for a man.

In January 1943, the *Sentinel* published a story about Ruth Hashimoto as an exception in the male-dominated political world of Heart Mountain. She was the block manager for block six in 1943. Hashimoto (b. 1913) was a Seattle-born Nisei who had come to Heart Mountain from California. She had received a high school diploma and worked as an interpreter at the Provost Marshal General's Office before Pearl Harbor.[10] Her two children were under school age when they arrived at camp. In addition to having block manager duties, she was a candidate for the first community council in 1942 and active in many social organizations.

As a block manager, Hashimoto participated in many initiatives to improve the quality of life at camp. In the spring of 1943, Heart Mountain block managers conducted a dietetic survey that sought to improve the quality of food served in the mess halls. The group found that the food was too greasy and heavy on starch and that, overall, the food needed more variation to be wholesome. In apparent connection to the survey, Hashimoto kept a list of residents of her block who were unable to eat the provided foods. Their reasons ranged from "lack of teeth" to "food doesn't agree."[11] This extensive study was fruitful, as a month later the block managers announced that each block was to have two "block mothers" in charge of dietary matters in consultation with the hospital. The *Sentinel* later reported about the "diet kitchens," which also helped respond to dietary needs by preparing special meals for the inmates.[12]

Women's Employment

As demonstrated in the examples above, the Japanese valued education. While Issei women's education and careers often stopped at immigration, Nisei women were encouraged to educate themselves. However, Nisei women's own inclinations and aptitudes were not necessarily the starting point in the selection of a career; rather, decisions were made based on parents' assumptions about employability. The focus of much writing on picture brides has obscured the fact that Japanese immigrant women, both picture brides and independent migrants, were often very highly educated. One such example comes from Toshi Nagamori Ito, whose mother, Kei Hiraoka Nagamori, studied at an American missionary college in Japan and was subsequently invited to be the director of the Jane Couch Home, a shelter for picture brides in Los Angeles. Kei Hiraoka Nagamori thus broke the female immigrant pattern: she came to the United States by herself, she spoke English, and she had converted to Christianity before arrival. Later, she taught at a Japanese school.[13] At Heart Mountain, Kei Hiraoka Nagamori became involved in the YWCA and worked at the social welfare department, befitting her educational, social, and employment background.

Hiraoka Nagamori may have been the exception as an Issei woman in that she was able to pursue her occupation after marriage. Many other Issei women were more restricted. If they did not experience discrimination in their community, they were often kept at home for the simple reason that their husbands operated farms far away from places where their wives could find outside employment. Consequently, many Nisei women said their mothers encouraged, or even demanded, that they focus on their studies. Miyo (Nakae) Uratsu shared that her mother believed in the permanence of education: "She said, 'You put it in your brain and no one can take it away from you,'" which became an especially valuable lesson when most of their physical possessions were lost in the war.[14]

Prewar Japanese American society, however, did not look favorably on women leading independent working lives after graduation. As Haru Ichishita later recalled, "When a girl finished her education, she was supposed to get married.... [Otherwise,] you'd be an old maid." But she kept her head, moving to San Francisco after finding employment at a Japanese American company. There, she met her future husband and eventually quit work after her first child was born, but in the prewar years, this excursion beyond one's expected life trajectory was exceptional.[15]

Although many women did find new opportunities to work while incarcerated and afterward, this old cultural expectation is visible in the Heart Mountain network. Out of the 597 women in the employment network, only a third were married. The bias in reporting about employment—such as the fact that most mess hall workers remained unnamed unless they otherwise contributed to the community—means that the numbers are indicative rather than absolute. I trust, nevertheless, that the shares of Issei and Nisei individuals and married and single individuals reflect real-life circumstances.

Women worked in almost all departments, but there were concentrations of women in certain sections. Most hospital employees were nurses and nurse's assistants, and following the customs of the time, they were all women. The Community Government Section of the Community Management Division was the only larger workplace with an all-female workforce. All employees in this section were block clerks—again, a job seen as suitable for women. In the incarceration camp, the clerks were all young Nisei, with nineteen of the thirty clerks born between 1921 and 1925. Likewise, the education section had many female workers and the kindergartens, for example, had only women as teachers. The elementary school had just one male teacher and the camp public library system employed seventeen women and two men. Quite surprisingly, all workers listed in the field worker category were women. This gives the impression that many men had traveled further away for agricultural jobs, leaving field labor in camp to inmate women. On the other hand, there was only one woman (who was a supervisor) in the farms department, a unit separate from the fields department. The lack of women might be a more cultural question of the division of labor. Japanese women were accustomed to working in the fields and orchards, but perhaps other farming, such as tending to livestock, was not as familiar.

The women's employment network was not very dense, as was the case for the full employment network. Rather, it was characterized by cliques with occasional bridging individuals. The average path length, however, was significantly shorter than it was for the full employment graph, 1.8. In other words, the women could reach each other more easily in their restricted network than in the one with men. This may be due to the smaller size of the women's network or the fact that their workplaces were smaller, more tightly knit units. In that sense, women's relationships become increasingly significant. The lower their numbers, the more important it became not to get disconnected from the network. At the same time, it was theoretically easier to maintain connections in a smaller network, since the path to traverse was shorter.

One person rose above all others in terms of bridging otherwise unconnected parts of the network. Mary Homma worked as a teacher of flower arrangement in the Adult Education Department and then as a club advisor toward the camp's closure. As in the full employment network, people working in the hospital and some other organization (most often one of the departments of the community activities) were other important go-betweens.

One of the most balanced workplaces, in terms of gender demographics and the positions available for women, was the *Heart Mountain Sentinel*. Although both the editor in chief and the managing editor of the paper were men, there were many women in significant positions in the organization. Thirty-seven of the seventy-eight *Sentinel* employees were women. Thirteen women did not have specific job titles, but eleven women were either reporters or editors involved in the core work of the paper. The Japanese edition employed at least three women as translators or users of the special Japanese typewriter. Advertising was a big operation with six employees, five of whom were women. Most of the women (and *Sentinel* employees overall) had not completed any higher education; one had a bachelor's degree in social sciences and one in engineering. Thirteen women had started college before being incarcerated. Three had previous reporting or editing experience, although only one of them was listed as a reporter for the *Sentinel*, since the two others were in the paper's business and advertising departments. Five had been stenographers or typists prior to their employment in camp. One of them had the same job title at the *Sentinel*, while four others were unspecified.

Many women (159 in this network) also worked at the hospital, but their status there did not seem as equitable as at the newspaper. At the same time, the hospital was a valuable learning environment for women in different stages of life. Many employees were young professionals advancing their careers. Their job titles included professions like dietician, registered nurse, and supervisor. The WRA also created opportunities for those who lacked formal education. In June 1943, twenty-four women graduated as nurse's assistants and became hospital employees. Other trainee positions included diet aide and dental assistant.

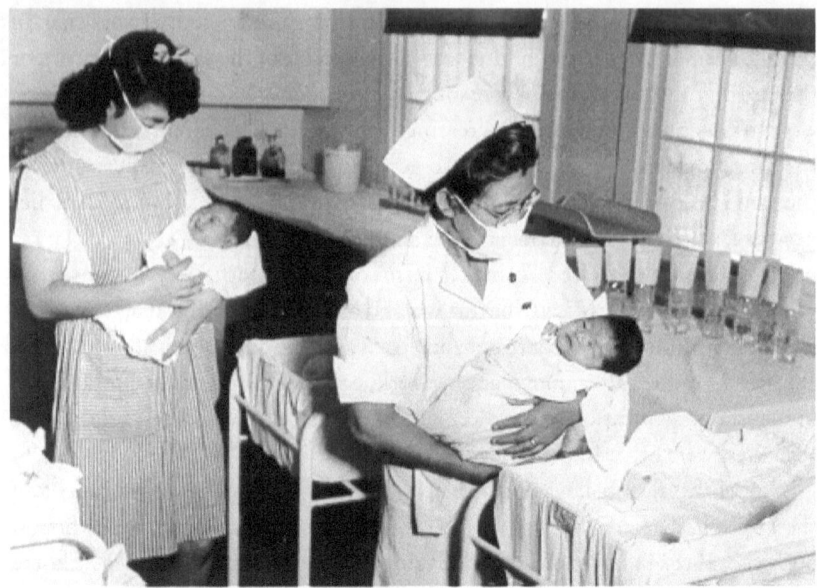

FIGURE 9. The hospital was one of the biggest workplaces at Heart Mountain and employed as well as trained many women. Original caption: Mrs. Ai Hanfrisaka, nurse, and Toshiko Honda, nurse aide, hold new babies. Photograph by unknown photographer. Courtesy of the Ethel Ryan Collection, John T. Hinckley Library, Northwest College, Powell, Wyoming.

Although these are conventionally viewed as women's jobs, they nevertheless improved women's opportunities to find employment after the war. And while most of the nurse's assistants were Nisei, older Issei women were also included.[16]

As exemplified by the job titles at the *Sentinel* and the hospital, camp life presented many new work opportunities for women. Although women usually found themselves subordinate to men in workplaces, they were not limited to menial tasks, and as the historian Valerie Matsumoto has pointed out, women and men received equal pay.[17]

One discussion about salaries took place between Girl Scouts director Tsuji Nako and assistant director of community activities David Yamakawa. Nako approached Yamakawa to request the highest salary category (nineteen dollars a month) be applied to two Girl Scout employees, Misao Hirohata and Chiyo Sashihara. According to Nako, the two women deserved to be in the highest salary rate due to "their education, experience and the many present duties." Hirohata was a college-educated Nisei with thirteen years of experience as an insurance agent, while Sashihara, an Issei with an American college degree, had worked for fifteen years in bookkeeping and two years as a teacher. Yamakawa "heartily agreed" but reported that the WRA was looking to cut its inmate staff in the highest salary category.[18] This exchange of letters shows two kinds of solidarity: of Tsuji Nako toward her female coworkers and of David Yamakawa toward fellow inmates.

As was the case everywhere except the political network, Issei were in the minority in the women's employment network. The fact that Nisei women so strongly overpowered Issei women is probably both a cultural and language competence matter. Issei women appeared most notably in the Adult Education Department as teachers of classes like sewing and flower arrangement and at the hospital as nurse's assistants, jobs for which they had received training at Heart Mountain. The lack of Issei women probably stems from various circumstances: they were not accustomed to working outside the home or farm, and while they were often well-educated, they spoke, on average, less English than their spouses. It was probably easiest for them to get jobs in education and at the hospital.

But adult education was about more than just easy employment. Sure enough, the department arranged training for both Issei and Nisei, men and women, in various fields and occupations. One of the key functions of the department, nevertheless, was to offer social activities.

Women's Social Networks

In the entangled employment-social network, the departments under community activities were a key player. While the hospital was the biggest single employer, at least 141 women were employed in the branch of community activities. If it were not for their work, many of the formal social networks would not have been realized.

In the Heart Mountain social network, women accounted for slightly over a third of all actors. By far the largest organizations in terms of membership throughout the camp's lifetime were the young women's rho clubs, followed by the Red Cross, women's basketball, and the United Service Organizations. In addition to being large, the rho clubs—along with the YWCA, Girl Scouts, and women's sports teams—were important for their exclusively female memberships. At the same time, prominence in only these organizations meant a lack of connections to the overall social network. Many of the nodes that were characterized in the network data as "events" also had to do with the social life of the camp, and they had predominantly female participants. This further emphasizes the social nature of the women's involvement in the Heart Mountain networks, as well as the importance of including one-off events to show the extent of women's participation.

Women's social affairs, like their employment, were the realm of the young and the single. Only a quarter of the women participating in the formal social network were married, and the most common birth year was 1922. This means that these organizations were led by young women, not that married or older women could not participate. Often, though, the young married women with children were too busy to participate. Katie Koga Uchiyama felt like there were not many activities in which to participate: "Even if there was some, there wasn't much for me to do. We'd just visit with our neighbors. I think that's what we did most of the time."[19]

For some, this lack of pressure to be involved and productive was a relief. Susie Emi described the incarceration camp as the "perfect place to have a baby." There was no push to work, no need to cook, and most women had at least some family in the same camp. Contrary to many parents of teenagers, Atsuko Abe, whose children were infants, felt like the years in camp brought the family closer together instead of driving them apart. There was more time to engage with the children. Katie Koga Uchiyama and Ada Otera Endo, meanwhile, felt like they had little life beyond childcare. Endo missed her husband, who was mostly out of the camp on seasonal leaves. One way for the young mothers to network was going to the "well baby clinic," which offered guidance and healthcare for mothers and small children. The hospital also had a "milk station," which delivered baby formula to the barracks—there were no refrigerators where parents could store such necessities.[20]

Childless young women, of course, had a different experience. As Katie Koga Hironaka recalled, she was a young mother for her time and most of her friends were not even married yet. They would regularly attend social activities, such as movies and dances, in the mess halls.[21] These activities were an integral part of daily life and gave opportunities for young people to socialize and gain leadership skills through the organizations in charge of the events. The leadership training was not just a byproduct of participation; it was formally organized. Girl Scout leaders were allowed to travel out of the camp for training, which they then passed on to other Scouts. Similarly, community activities organized leadership events for the youth in the block clubs. The purpose of the training was to prevent children from loitering, especially around latrines and laundry rooms.[22]

Nisei women's participation in leadership positions in the social network did not appear out of nowhere, however. As Valerie Matsumoto has shown, clubs like the YWCA and women's sports teams allowed at least the urban Nisei to acquire leadership and organizational skills before incarceration.[23] In the camp context, the significance of these skills was amplified, as the Nisei had a unique opportunity to serve as organization leaders without racial discrimination.

The share of Issei in the social network is about the same as in the employment network: about 10 percent. Issei women were most strongly present in the Red Cross, but even in the Buddhist congregation, their number is a meager three out of nineteen women. Even in the elementary school parent-teacher associations, where one would expect the older generation to dominate, the Nisei were in the majority.

Hana Okada was an example of a woman whose education and language skills brought her prestige in the community. She was older for a Nisei (thirty-five years old when she arrived at Heart Mountain) and had a college education. Because she also spoke Japanese, she became a liaison in the community, and was quickly selected as the president of the parent-teacher association of her block area.[24]

In the employment network context, I argued that the Issei women did not work due to cultural and language competence reasons. In the social world of the camp, they appear to have confined themselves to the informal networks, rarely participating in the more formal organizations. It seems that Issei women stayed or were left outside the formal camp community. Since Issei women were often not accustomed to working outside the home, they tended not to be comfortable taking public positions in the social world. The Nisei women, having been brought up by their parents and by the public school system to be more American, more readily adopted official roles.

To say that the Issei women were not in formal or leadership positions is not to claim that they did not participate. Miyuki (Yabe) Yasui pointed out that her mother "had time now on her hands to do some of the things that she was always interested in because she no longer had to worry about feeding the kids and herself." As an example, her mother and her neighbors, like hundreds of inmates at Heart Mountain, planted "victory gardens," small plots of land where they cultivated vegetables.[25]

Dorothy Zaima recalled her mother going to different classes at the night school. According to Zaima, the courses "gave them something to do, and for the first time, you know, they were go[ing] to a class. They didn't have to stay home or anything like that." Having somewhere to go was, in general, a new experience for some of the Issei women who had only ever taken care of their homes before incarceration. Having a sense of purpose was important not only in times of incarceration but more widely. "It was communication and getting together with other people and probably laughing and getting acquainted with people from different areas, not just hometown people," related Zaima.²⁶

Similarly, as Kunio Otani later reported, some women simply enjoyed the opportunity of associating with other Japanese women in general. His mother had spent years in the United States without contacts to other Japanese women, whereas in camp she was suddenly surrounded by women who spoke her language and shared many of her experiences.²⁷

Thus, while the Issei women were mostly absent from the formal networks, the camp experience changed them. While their husbands often experienced acute loss—of physical property and livelihood but also of purpose—some Issei women found themselves liberated and independent for the first time in their adult lives. Sachi Kaneshiro described the change in her mother: "When she no longer depended on him she became a different person herself. . . . It was like she was emancipated. She was free to do whatever she wanted. . . . She was much bolder about discussing her feelings or telling us about what had happened to her." After decades of control by her husband, after incarceration, "To the end she was the matriarch. . . . She was in charge."²⁸

Female Power Families

The discovery of power families was central to the creation of the Heart Mountain networks. It was, therefore, only natural to look for families of power in the female context. There were several families with multiple women participating in the networks. This is surprising considering the relative lack of women in most of the networks. At the same time, given that participation in the networks accumulated (we saw the same people emerge repeatedly), it also makes sense that participation could amass within a family: when one person in a family was active, they brought their family members along. In the women-only network, two families had five participating women and six families had four. I will introduce those that have significance for the structure of the network.

The biggest family is the Nakamoto family, with five women (four sisters and their sister-in-law) in the formal networks. Family members not present in this network included their parents and five more siblings. Thanks to the sister-in-law, Dixie Honda Nakamoto, this family linked to another female power family, the Hondas, which had four women in the network. The Honda women included four sisters, two of whom married at Heart Mountain. Thanks to the family's participation in big social organizations and the employment of Dixie Honda Nakamoto at the hospital, the Nakamoto women had a wide reach in the women's network. While they only directly connected to five organizations, their collective number of connections was several hundred individuals. The Hondas, meanwhile, only connected to one social group and the hospital, leaving their collective reach much lower. Because both families mostly had memberships in the same places, their combined reach is not remarkably different, only adding a handful of women from block 27 Nisei club.

The Fujiokas, similarly, were by many measures the most powerful family in camp in terms of number of direct connections and types of contacts. The significance of the Fujiokas was that they had direct contacts in most of the organizations. Their only gap is their lack of involvement in community enterprises. The lack of this connection is surprising, considering how important the community enterprises were for both social life and employment in camp. At the same time, of course, the organizing the structure and services of the community enterprises were the cause of the biggest arguments in camp, so its absence in the family networks may be a conscious choice. Otherwise, the Fujiokas demonstrated striking connectedness.

In addition to these two families of five women, there were several with four members. A few of them are worth noting due to the different types of networks they represented. The Munekiyos, with three sisters and one sister-in-law in the network, differed from the Nakamotos and the Fujiokas. While they had memberships in the social groups—most notably in the rho clubs—their other connections came from very different parts of the network. Helen, the sister-in-law, was a member of the American Association of University Women, while Teruko was a block clerk and Asa worked for the Community Activities office. These two workplaces provided some of the "better" jobs in camp, usually involving tasks that aligned with women's education levels. Block clerk was a position that many valued, especially in the older generation. A Nisei clerk for the community analyst explained that "parents consider it an honor to have a daughter work as [block] clerk." Especially as the camp was closing, the clerks helped the non-English-speaking generation to organize matters relating to departure and resettlement, explaining procedures and filling out forms for them.[29]

Asa Munekiyo had a college degree and teacher's credentials from Japan despite being a Nisei of only twenty-six years upon incarceration. Her camp employment did not match her education but at least seemed compatible with what she did before the war; her prewar occupation was listed as stenographer-typist. Her competence was rewarded in postcamp employment, as in 1944 she was listed as "special instructor" for the Japanese language course at the University of Michigan.[30] The Munekiyos' large number of direct connections are a rare example of high connectedness without a link to the hospital.

The Masudas, the fourth family, emerged in the full camp model as well. The four women of the family (sisters Masako, Kikue, and Sueko, and sister-in-law Nobu Bessho Masuda) were members in some of the largest social organizations of the camp, and one of them worked at the hospital, bringing their total connections to eight organizations and hundreds of individuals. The Masuda network reach organizations that might appear appealing to different, even opposing, segments of the camp population. Masako Masuda had a fairly ambivalent combination of affiliations with the reports division and the rho clubs—she did camp administrative tasks and was involved in a WRA-supported youth organization. Similarly, Kikue Masuda was connected to the *Sentinel* and two WRA-friendly social groups, the tau clubs and the block 6 Nisei club. Nobu Masuda further strengthened this engagement with her involvement with the *Sentinel* and the tau clubs, and she added a connection to the USO. Finally, Sueko amplified both the number and type of connections for the family. She worked at the hospital, was a member of the rho clubs, and, as the only Buddhist member of the family, she was also member of a third large—and different—organization, the Young Buddhists' Association. She diversified the family networks in this case. The addition of Nobu Masuda's sister did not change the appearance of those networks, since she shared her sister's connections from the *Sentinel* and the USO.

Most of these power families were among the indefinite leave resettlers. None of the families had a female majority among those staying in camp; all the women in several families were among the early departees. As is well known, resettling family members influenced the rest of the family. They were able to scout for jobs and places to live, and since destinations were often not the same for all resettling family members, they obviously also had an exemplary effect in influencing their families' resettlement decisions.

Women on the Move

In the spring of 1943, the Heart Mountain YWCA sponsored a panel discussion entitled "Our Next Move," where panelists included officials (both men and women) from the outside as well as from Heart Mountain. According to the meeting memo, about sixty people between ages eighteen and thirty attended, "almost all women."[31] The discussion focused on the practicalities of resettlement, such as finding jobs and housing, but women had also been interested in the disruptive effect of incarceration on forming marriages. Furthermore, many women were concerned about the correct etiquette on the outside in relation to White Americans and soldiers especially. The panelists advised the audience not to "gang together" and that the appropriate limit was no more than three Japanese together at any one time.³²

Despite this interest in the resettlement process, the resettlement rate—especially that of young women—remained a pressing concern for the WRA more than a year later. A November 1944 *Sentinel* supplement encouraged women to "eliminate fears" preventing them from relocating. In the supplement article, the New England relocation officer Rose A. Reynolds placed part of the blame on (Issei) mothers, calling them "too conscientious" about their daughters' welfare to see what was best for them: "These girls should be out NOW so later in life they will not blame the parents for lack of opportunity." Reynolds further argued that the girls needed to learn about housekeeping on their own in order to become good wives.

The story went on to describe "little Tomiko," a girl whose mother allowed her to relocate from an incarceration camp. She made (White) friends in her new hometown in the East, found a job with a wealthy family, and thus became "financially wealthy" enough to continue her studies in college and also "wealthy having gained such friends." The article, further trying to persuade the parents of young women, asserted that the New England area was home to a Nisei social group that only accepted "well-bred" new members, meeting in church, concerts, and lectures. What the area did not have, according to Reynolds, were public dance halls, further adding to New England's allure.³³

Yoneko Watanabe was one young woman that accepted an offer from the East. Watanabe was born in Japan in 1917, apparently during her mother's interim stay in the country. Her mother, Hama Watanabe, is shown as having first migrated to the United States in 1912. At some point, as many did if they had the means, she returned to Japan and had her daughter there. Both mother and daughter were recorded as being born in the "urban prefectures" of either Kiyoto, Osaka, or Tokyo, which was rare for Japanese immigrants, who often hailed from the more rural prefectures. Mother and daughter returned to the United States in 1924, where a brother, Fran, was born in 1926. By the time they were at Heart Mountain, Hama Watanabe was a widow, and the WRA records do not include information on her husband.

Yoneko graduated from Los Angeles City College before incarceration. No employment data at Heart Mountain was available, but she was active in various operations of the Christian congregation. In September 1943, she relocated first through Cleveland, Ohio, and then moved with a friend to Philadelphia. There, she was employed as a medical secretary at the Women's Homeopathic Hospital. According to a *Sentinel* relocation article, she was happy in Philadelphia, and in

October 1945, her mother and brother followed her. In addition, she was part of a relocation film that was shown to inmates in order to encourage them to resettle.[34] Yoneko was a valuable showcase for WRA propaganda: a successfully resettled woman and a non-citizen at that.

Perhaps a more traditional story was that of Katsumi Hirooka Kunitsugu, whose path to university studies was described in chapter 5. After graduating from the University of Wisconsin, Kunitsugu tried to find a job in journalism but was not successful. She felt that her lack of success was not due to being Japanese but to being a woman. Eventually, she got a position at an English-language Japanese American newspaper in Los Angeles. Although attitudes toward working women were changing in those years, Hirooka Kunitsugu, too, stayed home for years after her children were born, though she eventually returned to writing. While she felt that "unquestionably ... the bad out-balanced whatever good occurred," she maintained that if it was not for incarceration, she and many other Nisei would not have received a college education. "We simply wouldn't have been encouraged or helped to go to college," she said.[35] This statement somewhat contradicts Nisei who said that their parents encouraged education. Hirooka Kunitsugu's parents were not highly educated—her father had gone to high school and mother only to elementary school. The family had infant children in addition to the grown Katsumi. All of these factors may have affected their outlook on higher education. On the other hand, her father was a member of two of the community enterprises committees, meaning that he was fairly well integrated in camp political life, at least.

Overall, women were quite eager to resettle. Among the indefinite leave resettlers, 59 percent were male and 41 percent female. People left for different reasons. Figure 10, below, offers a breakdown of the different leave types within the indefinite leave category. Although the women's employment rate seems high, the men's is remarkably higher. Women joined their husbands (or sometimes adult children) three times more often than men joined their resettled wives. Considering that the men joining the armed forces were young, some of them might have entered educational institutions, but most of them probably would have hiked the share of employed men even higher. It is thus evident that while women were well represented among those leaving the camp for work, a working woman was still not the norm among Japanese Americans.

The majority of the population was, of course, far from the model set by Yoneko Watanabe or Katsumi Hirooka Kunitsugu. Decades after incarceration Katie Koga Uchiyama sounded somewhat institutionalized when she described her sentiments about life in an incarceration camp: "No one even talked about things like ... what's going to happen to us. .. the people that I lived around,

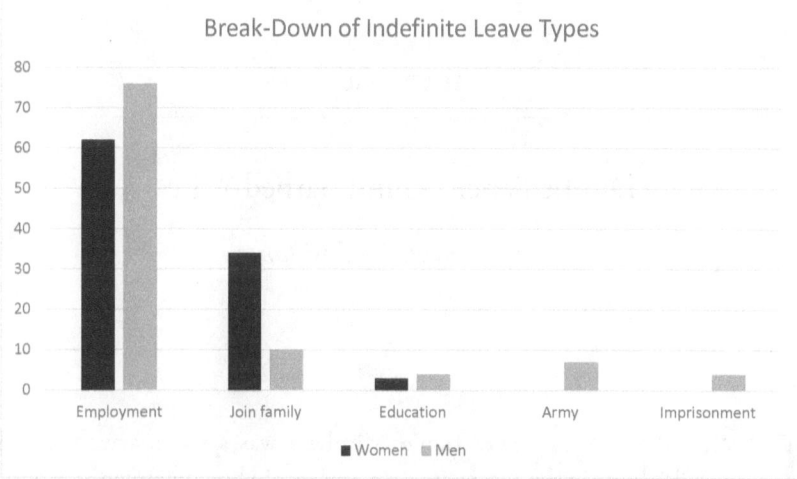

FIGURE 10. Breakdown of indefinite leave types. The employment category includes both those who left camp with job offers and those who were invited to look for jobs. It is likely that most of them found jobs; therefore, they are in the same category here.

they were all . . . accepting it [being incarcerated and not knowing when they were getting out]."[36] Uchiyama, who spent an "uneventful" incarceration rearing her child, was among the last to leave the camp. At the end of October 1945, she moved to Mountain View, California, another big transition from her prewar home in the village of Reedley, California.

Of the other women introduced at the beginning of this chapter, Mary Oyama Mittwer resettled very quickly, in February 1943. Settling in Denver for the war years, she returned to Los Angeles and remained active in fighting racism.[37] Ruth Hashimoto was offered a language-teaching position at the Military Intelligence Service Language School in the fall of 1943. She accepted but not without hesitation; most notably, her husband was opposed to relocation. Toshiye Nagata moved to Chicago in February 1945. She was among the first of her family members to leave the camp. Based on leave records alone, her family seems to have dispersed: her parents went to Long Beach, California; her siblings spread out to New York, Utah, and Colorado; and she ended up in Illinois.

These four women represent the diversity of women's camp experiences and the value of network analysis in rediscovering them. Ranging from having a complete lack of formal ties, like Katie Koga Uchiyama, to expansive network involvement with no remaining documentation, like Toshiye Nagata, they present a powerful case for considering women's networks as a sphere of its own.

CHAPTER 8

Disobedience behind Barbed Wire

Passive and Active Resistance

In the spring of 1942, Tamio Miyahara was a twenty-two-year-old farmer, doubling in the wintertime as a gardener in his hometown of Mountain View, California. With the exclusion of all people of Japanese descent from the West Coast, Tamio and his parents were first held at the Santa Anita Assembly Center and subsequently sent to the Heart Mountain Relocation Center in Wyoming. Unlike many others who had never been to a place as cold as Wyoming, the Miyahara parents knew the state: their only child, Tamio, was born in Sheridan, Wyoming, in 1920.[1] Records do not state whether Tamio or his parents worked during their incarceration at Heart Mountain, but in the spring and summer of 1943, Tamio was making trips in and out of Heart Mountain "to look over farm prospects," "[to] interview for prospective work," and "[to prepare] for relocation."[2] Whether he was successful in his relocation endeavors is not known, but for some reason on March 29, 1944, he failed to appear at his pre-induction physical examination in Cheyenne, Wyoming. He became one of the first at Heart Mountain to refuse military service, bringing the Nisei draft issue to a new level in the camp.

The above is just one example of resistance. A few Japanese American individuals, like Gordon Hirabayashi and Mitsuye Endo, became famous before the camps were set up for their acts of resistance. Others woke up to resistance only later. Some of the forms of disobedience were active, like refusing the draft, while others were more passive, like accepting segregation to keep families together. The subtlest form of resistance was probably informal disobedience, often displayed in daily intercourse. Women's resistance especially falls under this category.

Women's resistance to incarceration usually came in the form of protecting the family: women resisted orders about things to take to camp, bringing along items like baby cribs; requested private rooms for their families; and demanded to serve their children better food. Issei mothers in Minidoka, Topaz, and Amache petitioned against the their sons' drafting from incarceration camps. In an interview with Susan McKay, Aiko Horikoshi of Heart Mountain recalled stepping up to a Caucasian registered nurse who had requested all Japanese hospital employees to bow to her.[3] A larger community event at Heart Mountain was some three hundred women's protest at the project director's office against the closure of their block's latrine and laundry room toward the end of camp's existence. Their previous petitions had been to no avail and once the doors were closed, the women offered a compromise: they would organize volunteer labor to keep the facilities open.[4] This type of disobedience went unnoticed more often than the typically more formal resistance performed by men.

The Fair Play Committee (FPC) resisters, long labeled as disloyal or unpatriotic, have in recent years become heroes defending the constitution, and rightfully so. I want to draw attention to the fact that the "no-noes," citizenship renunciants and others who committed acts of disobedience, deserve this recognition as well. Their resistance was more passive and more seldom articulated, but it was nevertheless an act of defiance to their incarcerators.[5]

The Issue with Loyalty

The entire process of incarceration was, of course, entangled with the question of loyalty—of an individual's presumed sympathy toward either the United States or Japan. To evaluate loyalty, the War Relocation Authority (WRA) kept an "evacuee case file" for each inmate, consisting of relevant documents pertaining to the individual. Information included camp employment and wage payment records, seasonal leave applications and permits, school reports, and medical histories. Among the recorded matters were memberships in pro-American organizations, such as the Reserve Officers' Training Corps, the JACL, and the Boy or Girl Scouts. Positive points were also given for having relatives in the United States military service, being a member in a Christian congregation, and canceling a Japanese birth record. Internment of father, immediate relatives in Japan, and employment by a Japanese government agency brought negative points.[6]

The loyalty questionnaire was the single most divisive action by the WRA during incarceration. Although the WRA did not intend the questionnaire to directly recruit soldiers, question twenty-seven, which inquired about inmates' willingness to serve in the military, caused many inmates to draw the equation. Similarly, question twenty-eight, on loyalty, seemed impossible to answer—Nisei did not see how they could be anything but loyal to the United States, while the Issei feared they would become stateless if they forswore allegiance to Japan, should the United States decide to deport them. In his autobiography, WRA director Dillon S. Myer acknowledged that the WRA made "a bad mistake" with the loyalty questionnaire, particularly the question requesting unqualified allegiance to the United States. He stated that the question had been drafted for the Nisei before it was decided that the Issei would also fill out the questionnaire. In fact, the question's original wording was changed after four days to "Will you swear to abide by the laws of the United States and to take no action which would in any way interfere with the war effort of the United States?" According to Myer, however, most of the damage had already been done before the new wording reached the inmates.[7]

In many ways, Heart Mountaineers reacted more mildly than Japanese Americans on average: about 7 percent of all adults responded "no-no," compared to sixteen percent across all camps. Below the surface, however, they protested. Eventually, Heart Mountain had the highest draft resister rate of all camps. Almost three hundred men paid the FPC membership fee and eighty-five men were sentenced and imprisoned under the Selective Service Act. Heart Mountain was the only camp where resistance was organized and had a formal leadership. Five leaders of the organization received sentences for conspiracy, and two that were considered both leaders and resisters were convicted on both counts. Groups of resisters also emerged at Granada (Colorado), Minidoka (Idaho), Poston (Arizona), and Tule Lake (California), but these were not organized. For example, at Minidoka, those failing to report for induction were said to have acted on an individual basis.[8]

The issue of draft resistance has remained controversial and burdened by misinformation ever since, with Japanese Americans, the general public, and the research community neglecting to distinguish between different forms of resistance. "No-no boys," military resisters (Japanese Americans who were in the military when the war broke out and refused to go into active duty), and other types of draft resisters have often all been labeled as draft resisters or as disloyal. For example, the political scientist Shirley Castelnuovo talks about the FPC members as draft resisters, as does the historian Roger Daniels. Daniels, however, distinguished in *Concentration Camps USA* (1971) between what he called "left resistance" by loyal Japanese Americans and "right resistance" by those with pro-Japan sympathies. A later edited volume by Mike Mackey, Daniels, William Hohri, and Eric L. Muller further separates the FPC from draft evasion (such as fleeing the country to avoid the draft, something that the Nisei naturally could not do), "confused if principled opposition," pacifism, and pro-Japan sympathies. John Okada's 1957 novel *No-No Boy* has added to the confusion of terminology: its protagonist, Ichiro, returns to his hometown of Seattle after imprisonment for draft evasion, and as the title suggests, he is referred to as a no-no boy.[9] I propose a new category, characterizing the FPC as an organization of civil rights resistance. The members were engaged in active resistance to the United States, but their motivations were very American: to uphold their constitutional rights as citizens.

When the army began to recruit volunteers during the winter of 1943, a group of men organized in resistance to military service. Frank Inouye ignited the movement. He wanted to get people together to discuss the eligibility of Nisei for service and other pressing issues, organizing the Heart Mountain Congress of American Citizens in February 1943. Inouye was chair of the group, Paul Nakadate was its secretary, and other key members included Kiyoshi Okamoto and Frank S. Emi, later leaders of the FPC. They opposed volunteering for service and they met this goal with only thirty-eight men volunteering from Heart Mountain during the campaign period ending on March 6, 1943. They also persuaded the army to change its policy to allow conditional responses to the controversial loyalty questions.[10] Conditional responses could include statements like "I will serve the United States Army in the event that the government reintroduces the draft," instead of requiring an unqualified "yes" under any condition. Frank S. Emi recalled writing, "Under the present conditions and circumstances, I cannot answer these questions," and he encouraged everyone to respond along the same lines.[11]

In fact, even though volunteering for the army was not officially part of the questionnaire and the draft was still almost a year in the future for the Nisei, the inclination toward draft resistance can be inferred from the imprisoned FPC members' responses to the loyalty questionnaire. Hardly any of the seventy-seven men for whom evacuee case files were available had responded "yes-yes" to the questionnaire. They had all sworn unqualified allegiance to the United States, but their reactions to the question about military service varied from an unconditional "no," to claiming they could be of better service on the home front, to a conditioned response of "until civil rights are clarified." Tamio Miyahara, for example, belonged in this third category with his response: "[Not] until my citizenship status is cleared and my immediate family is relocated." Some, like Tom Oki, said they had made up their minds about refusing to serve on constitutional grounds before incarceration.[12] Thus, the men who were eventually imprisoned for draft evasion already shared the FPC's values before the draft question became a reality.

Fair Play Committee Is Formed

In September 1943—around the same time that the first trains of segregated inmates departed for Tule Lake—the Fair Play Committee began to form around Kiyoshi Okamoto and take a more determined form. Okamoto was cited as a "charismatic figure" and had been a critic of the WRA policy and incarceration throughout the war.[13] When the loyalty questionnaires were being circulated and information sessions held, Okamoto was a vocal opponent of registering "loyalty," although as an older man (born in 1888 in Hawaii), he was not in danger of being drafted. Okamoto first called himself a "Fair Play Committee of One," but in late 1943, Emi, Nakadate and several other men joined him.[14]

When the government announced in January 1944 that the Nisei could be conscripted into a segregated army unit, the newly appointed community analyst Asael T. Hansen claimed that the announcement of the draft "did not produce a strong reaction of any kind" in the first few weeks.[15] In the background, however, the group under Okamoto's leadership began to organize more formally and call itself the Fair Play Committee. According to Emi, the meetings were at first "informational," and Okamoto talked about the Constitution and civil rights. The FPC organized mass meetings three to four times a week across the camp, and on any given night several hundred people attended. FPC members emphasized that they were not draft resisters or disloyal—as a distinction from the "no-no boys"—but they demanded the restoration of their legal rights as a condition for military service. Eventually, they formulated their goal as an outright refusal to participate in the pre-induction medical check-ups.[16]

At its largest, the Fair Play Committee had about 261 members who had paid the membership fee of two dollars. A third of the members were men who could not be drafted due to their older age, demonstrating that the draft was a significant issue for many—not just those directly affected by it. These backgrounds affirm the FPC founders' argument that it was a universally appealing organization dedicated to human rights, not a protest group for men with "Japanese sympathies."

Very quickly, during the spring of 1944, the FBI started questioning members, and those who had been called for check-ups but failed to show up were arrested. New cases surfaced almost every time a group was called for induction, and by June, sixty-three Heart Mountaineers were in jails in several Wyoming towns. The trial of the first sixty-three resisters, the "Heart Mountain Sixty-Three," was the largest mass trial in the history of Wyoming. It concluded on June 19, 1944, and the group was divided between the Leavenworth (Kansas) and McNeil Island (Washington) federal penitentiaries, depending on the age of the convict. Despite the sentences, resistance continued. The second group of twenty-two convicted members and the FPC leaders followed in late October and early November. Eighty-five draft-age resisters from Heart Mountain were sentenced to three years in prison, which they served.[17]

Before their eviction from the West Coast, the men who went on to join the Heart Mountain Fair Play Committee conformed to the portrait of the average Nisei man. Half of the members were born in or after 1919 and were under twenty-five years old in 1944, the year of the reinstitution of the draft. Twenty of the men had reached adulthood in camp. Despite their young age, many of the members were married, but among those imprisoned, single men were the majority.

Those who had graduated from high school before the incarceration were most often self-employed farmers or they were working in the agricultural sector for somebody else. Later, their family members almost unanimously described them as typical young men, interested in sports and friends, without delinquent habits other than smoking. At Heart Mountain, they held different camp jobs; carpenter and truck driver were among their most common jobs, especially in the early months of incarceration. Many, like Tamio Miyahara, had already left the camp on seasonal leaves to work on harvests in Wyoming and beyond.

A distinction should be drawn between the leadership, the lay members, and the imprisoned members. As stated above, the imprisoned men had almost unanimously protested in the loyalty questionnaire. Because they answered positively to the question on allegiance, they were not automatically transferred to Tule Lake. Most had been on seasonal leave and many had even had an indefinite leave granted before being detained. Thus, they were not among the so-called troublemakers, but most did not act on a whim, either. Although their leadership may have come from these older men who had yet to be tried, they believed in their case enough to push on.

While the general FPC membership attracted older and married men in addition to youngsters, those in the imprisoned group were closer in age: two thirds were twenty-five years old or under. Four out of five were single, but the vast majority of those who were married also had children. This, to me, is another proof of the strong conviction of these men—they were prepared to sit in prison for their beliefs, although they had families to raise. Likewise, becoming soldiers would have taken them away from their families, and going on active duty, of course, brought the possibility of death. In many cases, however, families could follow the soldiers to training locations within the United States, and military service always entailed a financial allowance for the family. Imprisonment, on the other hand, meant almost complete severance of ties, with extremely limited meeting rights, the permission to correspond with only two outside people, and no ability to assist one's family financially.[18]

Many of the convicts later lived up to their statements that they would serve if their families were freed. Teruo Matsumoto, for example, served twice in the late 1940s and early 1950s. There was no reason to object to the draft once all the civilian incarceration camps were closed.[19]

Fair Play Committee Characteristics

According to leader Frank S. Emi, only Nisei could become members, although one of the founding members, Guntaro Kubota, was Issei. Kubota denied his official role and active participation in the organization, but he was imprisoned with the rest of the leadership.[20] Emi also stated that women attended the meetings, although the membership roster does not include any women. In the background, though, Sylvia Toshiyuki is a rare example of a woman influencer. She was a White American woman married to a Heart Mountain inmate and voluntarily stayed in the camp for her little son. James Omura, the Denver reporter who was tried with the FPC leadership, later recalled that Toshiyuki had visited him in Denver after her release from Heart Mountain, describing her close friendship with Kiyoshi Okamoto and calling him a genius. This was, according to Omura, the first time he heard about the Fair Play Committee.[21] Issei leader Guntaro Kubota's Nisei wife, Gloria Kubota, said she helped her husband type some of the organization's statements, although she personally did not participate in the meetings. Gloria Kubota's understanding was that elder Issei women, especially, donated to the organization: "It was really cute how some of these old people followed him [Guntaro Kubota] around. And that's what they had to have, was the Issei ladies to help raise the money for this trial [because they Nisei were young and unable to donate for the support of their peers]."[22]

What really made the FPC stand out among other Heart Mountain organizations, however, was the large number of Kibei, or Nisei educated in Japan for at least one year. In my investigation of the Heart Mountain networks, I found a total of 12 percent Kibei, but most of them were not active in the institutions that formed the core of the networks. At the FPC, their share is 17 percent, so this organization stands apart from the rest of the social network and the Nisei networks in general. The Kibei were in their time and later in research literature portrayed as "rebellious" and sometimes as un-American, and their large number in the FPC certainly seems to support those views.²³ At the same time, the Kibei were considered less American than the fully American-educated Nisei, and the Kibei and the Nisei did not typically associate with each other. On the one hand, these characterizations are simplified: the Kibei were not as homogeneous a group as they are often portrayed. Some were intentionally sent to Japan on their own to live with relatives; others stayed for a short period of time with their parents; and yet others became stranded in the country for multiple reasons, such as personal or family illness.

Katsumi Hirooka Kunitsugu, a young high school student at Heart Mountain, would have been perceived as Kibei since she had lived in Japan for four years. However, she disagreed with her designation as Kibei:

> I do read, write and speak Japanese fluently, but I don't think Japanese enough, and it's not my native tongue either, so that strictly speaking, I think Kibei were Nisei who were sent to Japan at an early age, probably stayed there longer than ten years and then returned to the United States to live the rest of their lives here, but their native language is Japanese and they think Japanese probably.²⁴

In Kunitsugu's definition, a few years was not enough to make her a Kibei. Men who had taken a short-term visit to Japan, though, were in the minority on the Fair Play Committee. Only four members had received between one and five years of schooling, ten had received more than ten years, and thirty-one had received between six and nine years. If we draw the line at ten years of schooling like Kunitsugu, only 4 percent of FPC members as well as members of the entire camp network were Kibei. In other words, most Nisei classified as Kibei spent more than five years but less than ten years in Japan.

The high share of Kibei on the Fair Play Committee can be interpreted in two ways. On the one hand, their involvement could show that they were, in fact, very Americanized and wanted to fight for their civil rights even more vigorously than the other Nisei. On the other hand, one could argue that, despite their American citizenship, they identified with Japan so strongly that they wanted to avoid fighting against the country. By the time the Fair Play Committee was up and running, the "disloyals" had already been sent to Tule Lake, and a good number of American citizens had even requested repatriation to Japan. Thus, any Kibei would already have had his chance to demonstrate so-called disloyalty. In fact, if anything, the Kibei reinforced the roots of the FPC as an ideological organization fighting for the rights of US citizens, not one for "disloyals."

Although none of the FPC leaders were Kibei, the large number of Kibei members did not go unnoticed among Heart Mountaineers. *Sentinel* associate editor Nobu Kawai—known for his opposition to the Fair Play Committee—said in his interview with camp and FBI investigators that he was "apprehensive . . . that the Fair Play Committee may be taken over by the Kibei." Kawai went on to say that "from his past experience with Kibei this will not be a pleasant situation."[25] These statements enforce the idea that the Nisei—especially the JACL Nisei—were on poor terms with the Kibei.

Thirteen percent of the imprisoned men were Kibei, so compared to all members, their share slightly decreased. Twenty-seven of the listed FPC members went on to take their physical examinations despite their original interest in the organization. Only one of them was a Kibei. This suggests that the Kibei were not inducted for one reason or another, most likely because half of the FPC Kibei were over twenty-five years old. From the authorities' point of view, the Kibei did not appear to be different from the other imprisoned members. There were few special remarks in their case files, although one person, Kenroku Sumida, was singled out because all of his immediate family members lived in Japan. Sumida's circumstances support the notion of the Kibei's loyalty to the United States, because he had not chosen to be repatriated despite his family connections but went on to fight for his civil rights.[26] That said, the Kibei were not a homogeneous group, and, like any other group of people, they had various motivations. But based on network data, they formed a significant segment within the Fair Play Committee.

The second characteristic that sets the FPC apart from other Heart Mountain social organizations is the members' religious affiliation. Sixty-six percent characterized themselves as Buddhists, and while this is consistent with the religious affiliation of the entire camp population, it is markedly higher than in the social network context, where only 38 percent self-identified as Buddhists. The founding members and leaders of the organization, however, demonstrated a more diverse range of backgrounds, again supporting the notion of a multitude of incarceration experiences. Of the seven leaders, two were Buddhists, three Christians, and two in the category "none, undecided, atheist, or agnostic."[27]

Based on the large numbers of Buddhists and Kibei in the FPC, I would have expected to see a high percentage of people attending Japanese language school, yet another marker of assumed "Japaneseness." The records show attendance for only twenty FPC men, 8 percent. This is interesting, because both contemporary Whites as well as the Japanese themselves claimed that all Nisei attended language schools.[28] Both parties viewed the language school as an example of attachment to Japan and as an integral part of Japanese American culture. However, in the entry dataset, only 597 (6.5 percent) of the 9,156 Nisei were listed as having attended language school. This figure is drastically lower than the already comparably low figure stated by Noriko Asato in her research: she found that, in 1920, 42 percent of California and 30 percent of Washington school-age Nisei were attending language school.[29] It seems that the dataset is not entirely reliable in this regard, but it is difficult to determine the reason. The original questionnaire form does not have an explicit question about language school attendance, but in some cases, attendance was recorded in the "additional information" field. This may have prompted respondents not to state their participation for fear of difficulties in camp, or the Japanese American interviewers who helped with filling out the forms did not always remember or want to include this addition. Frank S. Emi, for example, was listed in the entry dataset as not having attended Japanese language school, although he was one of those who reminisced about "everybody" attending. In the entry data, there is much geographical variation, but it often contradicts Asato's research. Overall, recorded attendance was higher in the Pacific Northwest (23 percent of Nisei) and especially Seattle, Washington (34 percent), and less than 1 percent in Los Angeles. The entry data, however, also asked people for their language skills. In this column, only seven FPC members were listed as English-speaking only. All others reported that they had at least some Japanese skills.

As shown above, the Fair Play Committee was a diverse group of men brought together by their support of civil rights. What about their network connections? How were they placed at Heart Mountain?

FPC Connected and Unconnected

Network analysis brings additional dimensions and depth to the spread and influence of the FPC at Heart Mountain. Although the number of direct links of FPC members to other groups at Heart Mountain is relatively low on the whole, those connections span a large part of the network. It is no surprise that the young men of the Fair Play Committee participated in the activities of the Nisei block clubs, boys' clubs, and men's sports teams. There are also six men who were active in the Buddhist church and/or the Young Buddhists' Association. Tamio Miyahara was one of them. He was among the founding members of the YBA and active in the Buddhist congregation, but also a leader of the Boy Scouts and his block's Nisei club. With these connections, he is also the most connected (tied with Minoru Horino) of the imprisoned men.

Neither of the two can compete for number of connections with Eiichi Sakauye and Kiyoshi Fujiwara, who were members of the FPC but were never inducted. The types of connections and the backgrounds of these men are very different from each other, demonstrating the appeal of the FPC to people across the spectrum of incarceration experiences. Eiichi Sakauye can be considered a member of the camp elite. He is fairly well covered in research literature and was known among the Japanese American community. Kiyoshi Fujiwara was one of the most potentially influential people at Heart Mountain despite having gone unnoticed by researchers.

Eiichi Sakauye was one of the older Nisei, born in California in 1912. He had attended college, which, coupled with his relative seniority, led the administration to pick him as a block manager. He also worked as the assistant superintendent of the Agriculture Section of the Operations Division and served on five committees, including the Relocation Planning Committee. His participation on a committee that was organized by the WRA, or at least driven by its ideals of resettlement and dispersal, shows the conflicting roles of incarcerated Japanese Americans. At one end of the continuum was the desire to be a compliant, onward-looking American citizen, and at the other, the urge to protest against the incarcerating government.

In a later reflection, however, Sakauye did not acknowledge his membership, instead claiming that despite agreeing with many of the FPC's demands, he "did not feel the climate in the country was right for their approach." He further said that, as block manager, he "publicly announced that each person would have to act according to their private convictions and [I] was kept from active duty only because I failed the army physical examination."[30] Sakauye's statement speaks to the FPC's loose organization: many might have paid the membership fee to support the cause but there was no obligation to act one way or the other. Two of Sakauye's brothers were also on the membership roster, neither of them among the imprisoned. This extensive family engagement with the FPC further emphasizes that some members agreed with the principles of the organization even though they would have chosen to act differently if inducted.

Kiyoshi Fujiwara, meanwhile, corresponds more closely with the image of the rebellious draft resister (although he never resisted in practice, only through his membership). Born in 1917, he had received more than ten years of his basic schooling in Japan but returned to the United States to attend college, from which he had not graduated before incarceration. He was connected to several Buddhist organizations and was also part of the employment network and the political network (through the Judicial Committee). His membership in an elected position on the Judicial Committee demonstrates his power and, to some extent, popularity among inmates. Although he was not imprisoned as draft resister, his wife's family connected him to two other members, one of whom was among the convicts.

These extended connections—and their implications—show what network analysis can add to our understanding of the Fair Play Committee. We should consider not only the *number* of connections an individual has, but also the *quality* of those connections. In the context of the incarceration networks in general and the Fair Play Committee in particular, it is valuable to find out which individuals may have had an impact on the decisions of large numbers of people.

In this vein, the Fair Play Committee's "key characters" look quite different. In the context of the full social network and especially the camp-wide network of the final months of incarceration, FPC member Yukio Abe appeared central. His attributes—at least what could be known of him based on written information—do not reveal him as an important character in a story. He was not a member of any political groups and there is no record that he worked in camp, but through his social group memberships, he knew a large number of people. He was a member of the USO, his block club, the senior boys' clubs, and the Fair Play Committee. A certain level of caution must be applied when analyzing the position of the average Fair Play Club member. Emi said that, apart from its seven-man leadership, the organization was rather loose; he did not personally know most of the men who were imprisoned, let alone the entire membership.[31] Paying the membership fee indicated interest in the organization but not necessarily active participation in organizing or governing the group. Assuming that all the FPC members were connected poses some risks to the network analysis. At the same time, Yukio Abe's position, for example, suggests that he had access to a lot of people. We know he was a member of the FPC, so he probably went to the meetings, and if he chose to speak, he would have received a large audience. More importantly, his participation in the other organizations made him a potential broker.

The main hub was not a person but the senior boys' clubs. The organization connected people who otherwise had few things—like housing block or employment—in common. Theoretically, a person who wanted to directly or indirectly reach as many people as possible should have done so through the boys' clubs. It is thus no wonder that the two main individual bridges were both active in the senior boys' clubs: Tadao Kitamura and Tamio Miyahara. Otherwise, their lives took very different paths, as we will later see.

On the graph, they occupy opposite sides. In addition to being in the boys' clubs, Tadao Kitamura, a native of Toppenish, Washington, was a member of the Mess Hall Advisory Board, although no camp employment information for him was available. He acts in the network as a link between those who took an active role in the senior boys' clubs and those who participated in the political or working life—to generalize, segments of younger and older members. Kitamura's younger brother George was also an FPC member but his lack of connections made him obscure in the network.

Tamio Miyahara, as we saw earlier, was active in the Buddhist church in addition to the senior boys' clubs and his block club. While Tadao Kitamura bridged older and younger parts of the network, Miyahara could be seen as a broker between the social and religious segments, although age seems relevant here as well, with other Buddhists representing an older age group than Miyahara. His activity in his block Nisei club (Club 23) suggests that he was well known to his neighbors.

Overall, block 23 had the largest number of members in the FPC, and at one point the WRA authorities claimed that "every family except one has a son in jail."[32] The exact accuracy of the claim is difficult to ascertain, but it is true that the largest number of convicts came from block 23—as did the fiercest opposition to the community enterprises cooperative plans. It seems that members of this block spearheaded of Heart Mountain resistance to incarceration across generations. In relation to the total number of FPC members, the block stands out with just under half of the members imprisoned, when the imprisonment rate overall was about 33 percent. Block 23 was, however, not unique, as nine out of the twenty blocks with members had an imprisonment rate of 45 percent or more. It is, in that sense, more relevant to look at the shares of imprisonment in blocks with FPC leaders.

The seven leaders of the Fair Play Committee emerged from six blocks, with only Frank S. Emi and Ben Wakaye residing in the same block. The imprisonment rate in the leaders' blocks varies from below the average to an astonishing 100 percent, but the latter is a block for which only four members were recorded. Block 22 is noteworthy, as it had a below-average imprisonment rate; this block was home to the main FPC leader, Kiyoshi Okamoto. Okamoto was known as a controversial figure, but it seems possible that after his imprisonment, interest in the organization dwindled. All four imprisoned men from this block were arrested after Okamoto, suggesting that they were committed to Okamoto despite his disappearance from the scene.

Block 21 is also noteworthy; there, no FPC members ended up in prison and several accepted induction. One explanation for this may be that more members in this block belonged in the older age segment. Members of block 21 also appear to have had a stronger than average sentiment regarding the other camp-wide debate about cooperatives management of the community enterprises. Where there was a lot of division and heated discussion in block 23, block 21 displayed a clearer preference for the cooperative model. Perhaps compliance with the WRA-promoted model indicates similar sentiment toward the draft in that block, guiding the block's FPC members in their final decisions. Finally, block 21 was the home of Tadao Kitamura, the 23-year-old man whom I previously identified as a key bridge between different parts of the network. Might he have impacted the decisions in his block? Another bridge, Tamio Miyahara, meanwhile, came from block 23. It would likewise seem that he may have recruited his friends and block mates to stick with opposing the draft.

The network model does not reveal the leaders of the organization. None of the seven tried and convicted leaders had enough connections to suggest that they were influential in the organization or the larger camp networks. To understand their position, we need to look to traditional historical sources.

FPC Men in Charge

Seven men were recognized as leaders of the FPC, although only three had named positions. They were Frank S. Emi (publicity chairman), Sam Horino (publicity chairman), Guntaro Kubota, Paul Nakadate, Kiyoshi Okamoto, Minoru Tamesa, and Ben Wakaye (treasurer). Of these, the authorities showed particular concern for Emi, Horino, Nakadate, and Okamoto. Although all seven were eventually convicted, Kubota, Tamesa, and Wakaye seem to have been more operational officials than driving forces in the organization, and although tried as leaders, Tamesa and Wakaye were first convicted of draft evasion for failing to show up for their pre-induction physicals. Frank S. Emi's brother, Arthur Emi, while never arrested as a leader or resister, had a major background role in the organization, especially after the imprisonment of the seven.

Frank S. Emi has become one of the most well-known members because he lived long enough to see increasing interest in the draft resistance movement toward the end of the twentieth century and because he was willing to share his story. In one oral history interview in 1994, he stated, "Everybody was concerned with the injustice of being drafted out of these camps, even if they did not resist." In 1944, Heart Mountain community analyst Hansen shared this sentiment, saying in an FBI report that although some people thought the FPC too extreme, the "opposition to the draft was much wider than this organized manifestation." [33]

Although Kiyoshi Okamoto did not have a named position, he was obviously one of the main leaders of the organization. The WRA had identified him as a potential troublemaker from early on, and where other evacuee case files consisted of at most a few dozen pages, Okamoto's file is almost three hundred pages long. In December 1943, Heart Mountain director Guy Robertson explained his opposition to granting leave clearance to Okamoto in a letter to Myer: "He has endeavored to thwart any effort by WRA to assist the evacuees in peaceful relocation. He does not have the respect of a large majority of Japanese and Japanese Americans who want to be loyal to the U.S.A."[34] Later, Hansen described him as an "economically incompetent intellectual hobo," showing that much of the administration's opposition to Okamoto was personal and not only related to perceived disloyalty or conspiracy.[35]

Okamoto was not shy in his demands. In addition to opposing the draft, he was vocal in requesting better health care and more private living quarters. He gives the impression of a man who was, if not a troublemaker, at least a very principled and pedantic person, whose desire to advance those principles could in an incarceration camp lead to a troublemaker reputation. In addition to containing information about his concerns over incarceration, his file also includes a long correspondence with various recipients on a wrecked car, another case where he seems to have persisted in his views more out of principle than any potential personal gain.[36]

As an orator, Okamoto was also the Fair Play Committee's voice to the outside. In the spring of 1944, he contacted the ACLU for support to the organization. The ACLU refused, famously arguing that the FPC had "a strong moral case but no legal case at all." Eventually, the ACLU-affiliated Samuel Menin and A. L. Wirin agreed to defend the resisters but they did so as private attorneys. Similarly, Okamoto communicated with James Omura of the *Rocky Shimpo* newspaper and, although Omura began writing his anti-draft editorials before learning about the Fair Play Committee, the two were inextricably linked, and Omura was tried with the FPC leadership. *Rocky Shimpo* was the most widely read newspaper at Heart Mountain, and during the height of the FPC movement, its camp circulation rose by 20 percent. Whether the rise in circulation speaks to the support of the Fair Play Committee or curiosity about the rising conflict in general is irrelevant—Heart Mountaineers knew what was happening, even if only a small contingent took concrete action.[37]

Despite being known by the authorities as the publicity chairman of the FPC, Frank S. Emi was viewed more favorably. Like many of the young men, Emi had applied for leave clearance before the draft issue escalated and he was arrested.

In a letter regarding leave clearance, WRA solicitor Philip M. Glick stated that Emi was "obviously Americanized," and had a "very clean" record besides his conditional response to the loyalty questionnaire. Glick further gave his assessment that "Emi is a young man who feels strongly that his civil rights have been wrongfully taken from him and who has concluded that until they are restored he has a grievance which morally justifies a refusal to serve in the armed forces."[38]

Authorities saw Paul Nakadate, as they did Emi, as a "confused" and harmless young man.[39] At the same time, however, it was clear that Nakadate was considered more dangerous than Emi. The Heart Mountain officials even suspected Nakadate of communist sympathies and characterized him as being on bad terms with the JACL, one of the Japanese American organizations the WRA had chosen as an ally.[40] Some of these suspicions may have stemmed from the fact that Nakadate's parents were influential among the older Japanese and were related to high-level Japanese officials. As the secretary of the Japanese Association of San Diego, his father had been interned at Santa Fe before coming to Heart Mountain, and he was also known to have donated money to two Japanese organizations.[41] Neither parent, however, appears as prominent in the network model. The fact that he had three brothers and a brother-in-law in the United States Army seemed to be of less importance to the authorities.

Among the leadership, Minoru Tamesa did not catch the attention of the authorities but has an intriguing personal history and is an example of a person whose Issei father became involved in the cause. Minoru Tamesa was more than thirty years old—the age above which the Wyoming draft board typically did not recruit soldiers— but among the earliest group of men called for induction. Upon refusal, he was arrested and convicted of draft evasion. While he was serving his first sentence at Leavenworth in Kansas, he was tried for his leadership role and convicted of conspiracy. An argument could be made that Tamesa's individual history shows the FPC as a patriotic, not rebellious, organization. Minoru and his father had been incarcerated at Tule Lake, but when that camp was designated as the segregation center for the so-called disloyals, both Tamesa men swore allegiance to the United States and transferred to Heart Mountain. Hailing from Seattle, they do not seem to have had preincarceration connections to the rest of the leaders, who all came from California. They formed an intergenerational friendship with Frank S. Emi and his brother Arthur, however, and Min's father, Uhachi, was in frequent contact with Arthur Emi throughout the conflict and beyond, although Uhachi Tamesa was not a member of the organization.

Finally, Ben Wakaye, who worked as an insurance agent before the war, was a surprise candidate for a leadership position. Described as a "shy and reserved" intellectual by his sister Kiyono, he had not been interested in social or political activities in general or leadership positions in particular.[42] He also was not among the founding members of the FPC. As he said, there were already fifty members when he joined. The WRA officials seemed to think that he did not have "a clear picture of his position" in the FPC and perhaps was not prepared to bear the consequences of his actions. That said, his commitment and loyalty to his peers were so strong that, when pressed by project director Guy Robertson and relocation officer W. J. Carroll, he refused to publish a statement in the *Heart Mountain Sentinel* denying his participation in the FPC.[43]

These seven men followed diverse paths to FPC leadership. While they appear largely disconnected from the formal camp networks, they all must have had their unofficial networks—otherwise they would not have attracted a following. Different backgrounds and circumstances led men to join the Fair Play Committee and unite not only those who were incarcerated but also thousands of family members.

Fair Play Committee as a Family Affair

The Fair Play Committee influenced the lives of more than one thousand family members. The FPC members did not live in their own resistance bubble; their choices unavoidably affected those in their vicinity. Psychologist George Tsukuda's small-scale interview study indicated that Nisei veterans were raised in traditional, hierarchical Japanese families, while draft resisters grew up in more democratic, egalitarian homes. While this suggestion supports the view of the FPC as a civil rights organization, it is too straightforward a claim. As can be seen in FPC membership statistics, many markers of "tradition," such as Buddhism and Japanese language skills, were dominant in the organization.[44] It is important to look at not only the connections of the FPC members as individuals but also their family context.

Despite the FPC's appeal to inmates from a variety of backgrounds, its members or their families mostly were not among the "elite" at Heart Mountain in terms of connectedness. Many of the FPC members, in fact, could be viewed as unintegrated in the camp network. Only few had any other connections at all, and most connections were to social organizations, not to political or employment institutions. Perhaps this lack of connections was also one of the reasons that the community council refused to support the FPC case. In Frank S. Emi's opinion, the problem was not a lack of understanding on the councilmembers' part; rather, "a lot of them [councilmembers] were Issei or first-generation so they didn't want to make waves, so they more or less cooperated with the WRA administration."⁴⁵

An investigation of the family networks of the imprisoned men reveals that, in some families, all the young men joined the Fair Play Committee. The most noteworthy example is the Ishikawa family, in which all four sons were tried and imprisoned. Their extended family (consisting of spouses of several sons and daughters) had two more convicts and three untried members. All but one of the draft-age men in the extended family were members of the organization.

Whereas the loyalty questionnaire was marked by family decisions—especially parents influencing their children—the draft question became a matter of personal reflection. There were many families where all draft-age sons were FPC members but also families where one son went with the FPC while the other chose to serve the army. Ray Motonaga described one such example. While Ray refused the draft, his older brother, Masuo, volunteered for service and retained a life-long rift with his brother for their different choices. According to Ray Motonaga, these decisions reflect the two brothers' temperament. Masuo was one to "flow with the crowd," whereas Ray considered himself more of an individual thinker.⁴⁶

Another family history comes from Minoru Tamesa's father, Uhachi. He wrote to his son about his visit to a friend's apartment, where the mother worried about her son's health in prison. She said that her younger son had joined the army and worried that the imprisoned son's feelings would be hurt by the decision. Uhachi responded to this with "no such thing"—suggesting that the imprisoned son would join the army, too, as soon as his citizenship rights were returned and his parents treated like American Germans and Italians who were interned only on the basis of individual suspicion. Here, the parents' support of the FPC—and the fact that the issue focused on civil rights, not draft evasion—is clear. Other Issei parents were known to actively support the resisters, too. Satoru Tsuneishi even helped interpret FPC meetings into Japanese, although three of his own sons were in the military. He later wrote that he was proud of his sons' service, but at the same time, he understood the resistance "under such circumstances."⁴⁷ This seems to have been the sentiment of many inmates. Tayeko Matsuura, whose husband Frank was among the imprisoned, recalls that her fellow inmates treated her as cordially as ever despite the imprisonment. "They're all Japanese, so they all understand."⁴⁸

Tayeko Matsuura perhaps did not experience hatred or discrimination because of her husband's resistance. There was, however, an even larger group of people labeled as disloyals and troublemakers, or as "spoilage": those who responded "no-no" to the loyalty questionnaire and were sent to Tule Lake. The individuals segregated at Tule Lake may not only have been unjustly categorized; they may also have been on the outskirts of the camp network even at their first camp locations.[49]

A Different Kind of Migration: Segregation at Tule Lake

The segregation of "disloyal" inmates at Tule Lake was a tragedy in many ways. The separation of "loyals" and "disloyals" was, in the first place, artificial, and many negative responses to the loyalty questionnaire arose from misunderstandings among respondents and the fear that their families would be broken up. Thousands of underage children were affected by their parents' choices. Many adult children, too, made decisions to follow their parents due to family loyalty. Hitoshi Naito later described his decision as follows: "Family was the only thing I had left. And if you said 'no-no' then you may be able to go with your family and face the future together, so I said 'no-no.'"[50]

Although the WRA director Myer and other authorities consistently promoted an image of Japanese Americans as loyal citizens ("Japanese only by accident of ancestry") or harmless "aliens," the people held at Tule Lake were an exception. They were double segregates: people first forcibly removed from their homes on the West Coast, then segregated from their Japanese American community.[51] Tule Lake was designated as a segregation center for those who refused to swear allegiance to the United States and sever all ties with Japan because it had been a so-called political camp from the start. There, the mixing of urban Los Angelenos and rural Pacific Northwesterners created severe tensions that led first to a mass movement against responding to the loyalty questionnaire and later to a violent strike resulting in a military takeover of the camp in the late fall of 1943 for several months. The disproportionately large number of no-noes at Tule Lake was the cause for its designation as a segregation camp. There was also a large proportion of Tuleans who refused to leave their families and were allowed to remain in segregation while technically being considered loyal. Similarly, Heart Mountaineer Jimi Yamaichi described signing "yes-yes," expecting to go to Ohio to study, but being told by his father that he must follow the family to Tule Lake.[52]

Incarceration-era administrators and researchers like Dorothy Thomas categorized inmates' reactions to the loyalty questionnaire based on religion and former residence. They believed that Christians and Pacific Northwesterners left during the indefinite leave period, while Buddhists and Californians were among those most frequently responding "no-no" to the loyalty questionnaire and being segregated. As I will later demonstrate, the Pacific Northwesterners were, at best, marginally more eager to resettle from Heart Mountain. However, the reverse was true in the Heart Mountain segregate population: only forty of 995 were from outside California, and almost 68 percent were Buddhists.[53] Here, the characteristics align very well with the finding of community analysts who stated that prewar residence, occupational class, and religious preference determined responses to the loyalty questionnaire. Pacific Northwesterners (coming from a more tolerant region where Japanese Americans were better integrated into mainstream society and had more interaction with Whites) resettled and Californians (more ethnically concentrated and familiar with discrimination) went to Tule Lake. Those with cross-racial social relationships resettled more frequently than those who had been isolated.[54]

The division between those that were strongly integrated into the White society and those that led a more segregated life is probably all true for Heart Mountain, but the question about the number and strength of connections with Whites should especially be assessed.[55] On the one hand, residents of large cities were surrounded by White people but lived and associated within predominantly Japanese circles. At Heart Mountain, this group constituted about half of the population. The segregates amplified this pattern, with two thirds originating from a city. On the other hand, agricultural groups—whom the sociologist Dorothy Thomas has suggested had few White contacts—had little necessity or opportunity to assimilate. But in between these groups there seems to be a sizable group of people who lived completely immersed in a White (or multiracial) community, such as those living on Vashon Island, as depicted by Mary Matsuda, who described growing up as an equal among other island residents.[56]

Based strictly on the final roster data, 995 people from 357 family groups were transferred from Heart Mountain to Tule Lake to be segregated.[57] Of them, 678 were American citizens and 317 citizens of Japan. Close to a third were born in or after 1926 and were underage at the time of segregation. (In addition, transferees from Heart Mountain had twenty-three babies while at Tule Lake.) Japanese citizens made up 32 percent of the segregated population, as compared to 34 percent in the entire Heart Mountain population. This could be interpreted as a marker that the loyalty questionnaire struck the Nisei deeper, prompting them to answer "no." At the same time, as mentioned above, even adult children followed their parents' leads in their responses.

An analysis of the segregates' Heart Mountain networks demonstrates that, much like the Fair Play Committee resisters, the no-noes were more marginal than the members of the core networks. The segregates' place in the network model is scattered. There is employment information for only forty people at Heart Mountain. The Adult Education Department employed nine people, four of whom were teachers in the most popular Issei classes of judo and artificial flower making. Seven people were employed at the hospital, one as a dentist and others in supporting positions, such as nurse's assistants. In fact, the Heart Mountain chief nurse, Velma Kessel, later recalled that the hospital had a severe shortage of nurse's assistants following the segregation movement because so many of the assistants followed their parents to Tule Lake.[58] The fire department had seven workers that became segregates, one an assistant chief and two captains. Other workplaces did not have significant numbers of no-noes, but there were two, for example, in the camp police force.

Social relationships did not significantly alter the appearance of the network, although a small cluster emerged around the fire department, men's sports groups, and senior boys' clubs. Another cluster appeared around three Buddhist associations. Without a non-segregate bridge, this cluster would be disconnected from the core network. This bridge, Aimee Iwamoto, came from a prominent Heart Mountain family from which her older brother Koyo segregated; her parents and another older brother remained at Heart Mountain. Her father, Toragusu Iwamoto, was a member of many of the camp's most important political groups. The Iwamoto family experienced the Tule Lake controversy first-hand not only through their segregating family member, but also through Shyogo, the oldest son of the family. Shyogo was reported in the fall of 1945 as wanting to marry a girl at Tule Lake—if she was guaranteed to be released and not deported. Shyogo was among some of the last departees from Heart Mountain, as he was waiting to hear the fate of his bride.[59] He ended up relocating to Boston; the result of the romance is not known.

Political group and council positions only strengthened the existing, albeit small, cluster mentioned above. There was one person on the Agricultural Committee, three on the Mess Hall Advisory Board, and two on two different community councils.[60] The same few people were active in all types of organizations, while the majority remained in the background, probably utilizing services and voting in elections but not "making noise" themselves.

Adding residential blocks to the picture brings us additional camp geospatial considerations. Almost a third of all Tule Lake transfers hailed from blocks 27, 20, and 9. None hailed from blocks 22, 23, or 30, which is striking, considering that block 23 was the hub of FPC activity as well as the block with the most vocal opponents to the WRA-led cooperative project. Block 27 was the center of the cluster that included employees of the various mess halls, members of the mess hall workers' club, and the police department. The two other blocks with many no-noes did not show evidence of active participation in the networks, but another cluster formed around block 17 with stronger participation in the fire department and the senior boys' clubs.

Due to the scarcity of formal connections at Heart Mountain among the Tule Lake segregates, it is the most relevant to look at where we *do not* find them in the networks. Their numbers were low overall, but those who appeared in the networks concentrated in social groups, such as sports teams, Buddhist groups, and jobs requiring little training. The absence of segregates in the political and most of the social network is striking. While the segregates-to-be participated in sports, they were virtually nonexistent in the other organizations favored by the WRA: the boys' clubs, the Scouts, and jobs related to community activities, for example. It seems that, from the early days of the camp's existence, many were left outside its core social, employment, and political functions.

Whether this exclusion contributed to their later opposition to the loyalty questionnaire is more difficult to ascertain, but, as we saw in the employment and social networks, it looks like the WRA favored the more highly educated Nisei in its administrative practices. Those who ended up in Tule Lake were, on average, not among the "elite" when it came to education.

An exception to the rule that Tule Lake residents were less educated and probably one of the most famous segregates among Heart Mountaineers was Reichi Mohri, a reverend at the Heart Mountain Nishi Hongwanji Buddhist Church. Mohri was relatively young for an Issei, having been born in 1909. He had arrived in the United States in 1937, possibly to serve as a reverend. Despite his clergyman status, he avoided internment in the aftermath of Pearl Harbor thanks to a misspelling in an FBI file.[61] Mohri and his wife had three young children, and although at least two of them were born in the United States, it is likely that the family had not intended to stay in the United States in the first place but wanted to secure a return to Japan. The entire family was, eventually, among those repatriated.

While members of the Heart Mountain formal networks were, in general, exceptionally well-educated, the educational categories in the Tule Lake group were almost reversed. The most common education level in the entry data was elementary school completed in Japan which was given as a designation for a quarter of the people. In considering the high rates of the designations "no schooling" and "High School US," the large number of children must be kept in mind, as they bring down the highest completed education level. Adults with no schooling or only a US elementary school education added up to 3 percent. Even when leaving out underage children, education levels remained lower than for the general Heart Mountain population.

The number of Kibei was also significantly larger than in the general population: over 30 percent of the Nisei segregates were in reality Kibei. And, considering Katsumi Hirooka Kunitsugu's characterization that a "true" Kibei had spent at least ten years in Japan, they represent a larger share in this contingent than in any other subsection of the Heart Mountain population. The large share of Kibei certainly supports the argument that the Kibei were bitterer and had more trouble resettling in both Japanese and American society. The Kibei, however, contributed to raising the general education level of the Tule Lake group: over 60 percent of them had studied at the high school level.

The larger cluster of the formally networked Tule Lake people had an especially low level of education. Meanwhile, the second, smaller cluster—around the Buddhist organizations—had a higher education level, almost exclusively from schooling in Japan. In all, only thirty-six people had college-level education (twenty-seven from the United States and nine from Japan), and only ten of them were connected in any way at all. It seems that within the Tule Lake–bound faction, other values were more important than education.

The difference in education level between those who stayed at Heart Mountain (and especially those who resettled) and those who were segregated can be interpreted from an assimilationist perspective. The less educated segregates were less integrated, did not "understand" the WRA and its policies, and thus were more prone to responding "no-no" to the loyalty questionnaire. Meanwhile, the more highly educated, more integrated inmates trusted the WRA in its promise that nobody would be forcefully resettled, agreed with the JACL stance of demonstrating loyalty through incarceration, and thus went along with the questionnaire as well. Connecting education with loyalty questionnaire responses supports the interpretation that most no-noes answered the questionnaire as they did out of fear of resettlement and family disbanding, not out of disloyalty or protest.

Hitoshi Naito, whose family responded "no-no" and applied for repatriation, described the loyalty questionnaire as the last straw for his normally quiet father. "That was the first time that he expressed his emotion. 'Why is this question posed to us now? Why wasn't this posed to us before the evacuation?' . . . If it wasn't for that I don't think he would have applied for repatriation." Naito's older brother was of draft age, and his father felt that volunteering for the army meant almost certain death in combat. As Naito explained, "In order to die for their country, you had to have some kind of . . . you know, feeling towards the country, affection towards the country, and how can you have affection towards a country when they treated you this way?"[62]

Although Hitoshi Naito's father expected his son to avoid the draft by signing "no-no," those who voluntarily segregated at Tule Lake were subject to the draft. Jimi Yamaichi, the Heart Mountain transferee who had responded "yes-yes" and wanted to study but had to comply with his father's orders, received his draft notice. Despite his "yes-yes" response, Yamaichi had made up his mind not to serve in the military in the early days of incarceration. As it happened, he was among the twenty-six Tule Lake resisters who were exonerated from charges of draft evasion.[63] Nobody in the Yamaichi family renounced their citizenship and they all stayed in the United States.

A "no-no" decision was easier for the Naitos due to their connections in Japan. Naito's father was the oldest son of a wealthy family, so he had some property and assets as well as a family network in Japan: "He knew something was in Japan. Where, on the other side of the coin, he didn't have anything in the US. It was all taken away."[64] In comparison, many others felt that their return to Japan would be impossible due to the struggle to make a living. Issei Marian Asao Kurasu, whose family moved to Heart Mountain from Tule Lake, pointed out that not all who returned to Japan were met with open arms. People were suffering after the war and were not happy about additional mouths to feed: "Of course if you are single, you might be able to survive. If you can find a job there. But if not, if you have a family, it is impossible."[65]

Family appears to have been the foremost concern for many no-noes. Only 116 immediate family members of no-noes chose to remain at Heart Mountain. They reaffirm the claim that many responded to the questionnaire in the negative to make sure they were not forcefully resettled: only ten from the group of 116 left before the terminal departure period, so they had little desire or means to resettle. Nevertheless, many of the rest were eventually forced to leave the camp—not for their previous homes but elsewhere. Seventy-nine had destinations outside the West Coast.

Moving on

The eighty-three FPC convicts were freed in the summer of 1946—months after their families were released from Heart Mountain. Many went wherever their families had gone. Takashi Hoshizaki was twenty-one years old when he was released from McNeil Island, Washington, and returned to his parents' house in Los Angeles. According to Hoshizaki, his imprisonment initially had an impact on his choice of career. Due to his background as a convicted draft resister and his fear of competition from the large number of students starting college soon after the war, he shied away from engineering and decided to study botany to help his father on his farm. Jack Tono, meanwhile, had decided at Heart Mountain that he wanted to start farming in Pennsylvania, "where the big market was." His family resettled there after camp and Tono followed them upon his release.[66] Consistent data on the prisoners is not available, but most of them probably went wherever their families were—and most of them returned to their prewar homes or at least home states.

Twenty-six one-time members of the Fair Play Committee went on to join the armed forces, most of them after having first resettled outside of Heart Mountain. Fifty-five others left during the indefinite leave period for destinations outside the West Coast states, and another thirty-seven found homes in new states during the terminal departure period. In other words, over a third of FPC members directly resettled to new parts of the country. Just over a quarter of them returned to their prewar hometowns, while a handful found homes in new cities in their old home states. If we interpret the places that people went during their army service as "new hometowns," the resettlement rate of FPC members is close to the average. The four most common destinations were Chicago (Illinois), Cleveland (Ohio), San Jose (California), and Los Angeles (California). The two California destinations were also the two biggest cities of origin among FPC members.

Leaving during the indefinite leave period was practically impossible for the Tule Lake segregates except for those who went on to be interned or imprisoned. Only two individuals, a married couple, left for outside employment during this period, both to Hawaii, the birth state of one of the spouses. Originally, most of the Tule Lake transfers had indicated a desire for repatriation or expatriation to Japan. Nationwide, more than four thousand inmates eventually repatriated or expatriated to Japan. This included only about fifteen hundred aliens, and almost two thousand Nisei, most of whom were underage.[67] In the end, only a quarter of the Heart Mountain population left Tule Lake directly for Japan. If all those recorded as leaving for internment camps were deported, the share rises to a third.

Despite its image as the halfway point to repatriation, the overwhelming majority of Tuleans remained in the United States and left under the regular terminal departure category, which enabled return to the West Coast from January 1945. They differed from their counterparts who remained at Heart Mountain by leave date: most of the leaves occurred between the final weeks of 1945 and March 1946, when Heart Mountain was already closed. Remarkable for the former Heart Mountaineers at Tule Lake is also the number of those who were moved to internment camps during the terminal departure period, close to 10 percent (116 men). It is also striking to note that most of these internees were from family groups that were repatriating, so Japan was probably their final destination as well. The internment of these men from Tule Lake appears to connect to the Justice Department's desire to get rid of the most "troublesome" individuals who had requested repatriation. It remains unclear why they were transferred to internment camps instead of being permitted to wait for repatriation with their families.

The 1945 surge in internment cases of young citizens had to do with the developing atmosphere at Tule Lake. The 1943 strike and military takeover at Tule Lake had resulted in a large faction that the WRA considered anti-administration and loyal to Japan. They were very vocal in their demands and even hostile toward fellow Tule Lake inmates that did not share their pro-Japan agenda. There were two major groups with this philosophy, the Sokuji Kikoku Hoshi-dan (usually called Hoshi-dan), consisting mostly of Issei, and the Hokoku Seinen-dan (Hokoku for short), with Nisei membership. They wanted complete removal of "pro-American" individuals from Tule Lake. Only those loyal to Japan would remain, and they would be allowed to express their views openly. Both were nationalistic and organized exercises related to the Japanese army, including marching and drilling, which sometimes terrified other residents.[68] Hitoshi Naito's father made him join the Hokoku in order to learn Japanese customs and to help him adjust to life in Japan. Naito later argued that the Hokoku members were not so much "anti-American" as they were disappointed with their home country: "We had to, at the time, express our dissatisfaction and the injustice, and so that was one way of showing the organized expression."[69] In other words, Naito, despite his personal reluctance to associate with the groups, understood its members' point of view and their urgency in trying to communicate it.

In late 1944, the Justice Department decided to remove the so-called troublemakers to the Fort Lincoln (Bismarck, North Dakota) and Santa Fe (New Mexico) internment camps. None of these leaders originated at Heart Mountain, although, as can be seen in the Tule Lake final roster, many former Heart Mountaineers appear to have belonged to the organizations and were among those interned. At least 1,370 of the 2,019 internees at Santa Fe in late 1945 repatriated, many of them on the same ships as those from Tule Lake.

Hitoshi Naito, barely eighteen years old at the time, was among those first interned at Bismarck. Not knowing when or where he might rejoin members of his family, he was overjoyed to find them on the same ship sailing to Japan. Upon arrival, he described his sentiments as:

> something different. . . . "Wait a minute, something, am I missing something?" And I looked around and opened the window. There was no barbed

wire, no tower, and it's been about four years to ever live in a place where there weren't any confinement. And my cousin was there, and I yelled out, "Freedom!" ... I feel so free. I'm so happy that I'm here, and how come I didn't feel this way, feel this way in the US?[70]

Although, like Naito, many Nisei felt temporarily liberated in Japan, most eventually wanted to return to the United States. The conditions in postwar Japan were difficult, and not everybody welcomed Japanese Americans with open arms. Those who had renounced their US citizenship were eventually given the chance to remain citizens. In court proceedings, the citizenship of over five thousand Nisei was restored.[71] Despite his expatriation, Histoshi Naito ended up working for the US occupation force in Japan, and this experience helped him regain his confidence in the United States. His work for the US government in Japan led to the restoration of his citizenship and his eventual service in the Air Force.

As Naito's example shows, members of the segregate group often settled at different final destinations than those freed at Heart Mountain. While most of the Heart Mountaineers leaving during terminal departure went to California, Oregon, and Washington, the five most common destinations for the segregates were Japan; Los Angeles; Bismarck, North Dakota; Santa Fe, New Mexico; and San Jose. Twenty-seven percent of those originally from Heart Mountain repatriated or expatriated from Tule Lake, while Bismarck and Santa Fe were locations of internment camps from which many if not most traveled onto Japan. Thus, the presumed ex-/repatriation rate among former Heart Mountaineers is over 30 percent. The two destinations within the "top 5" that did not relate to repatriation, Los Angeles and San Jose, drew a quarter of the Heart Mountain–Tule Lake population, although, as a number, the thirty-one individuals moving to San Jose were marginal.

When we study the destinations of Heart Mountain segregates, the WRA's policy of dispersing people becomes ever more evident. Of the ninety-three destinations, fifteen did not appear either as pre-evacuation or destination places in the Heart Mountain final roster. Significantly, there were fifty-six places with only one recorded mover. This does not necessarily mean that all those people left Tule Lake alone; they may have been joined by relatives from other camps. Nevertheless, when we locate on the map both the individuals and their family groups as they appeared in Tule Lake, it becomes clear that even the segregates leaving after the war's end were often separated from their families. While they may have made it possible for their families to remain intact by choosing segregation, the realities of postwar employment and housing may eventually have broken up families.

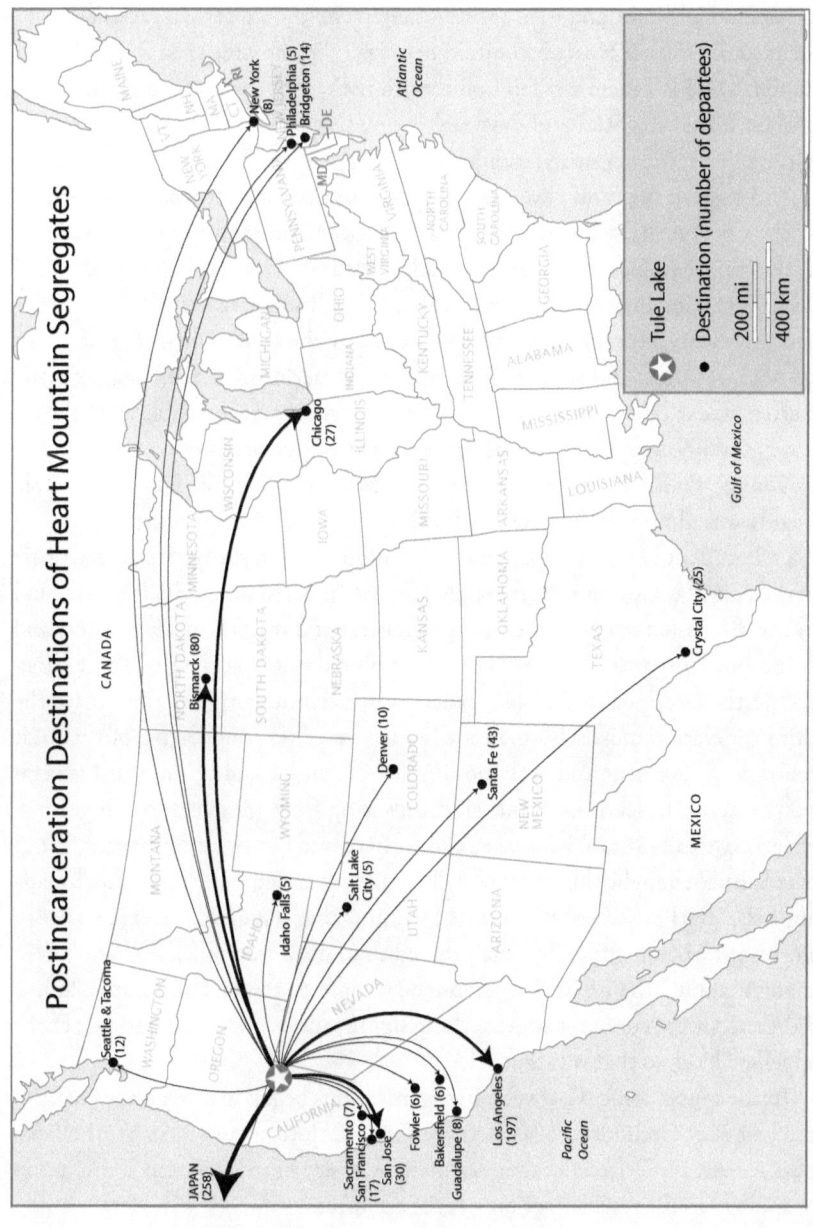

MAP 2. Postincarceration destinations of Heart Mountain segregates. The destinations include all cities and towns with six or more former Heart Mountaineers departing from Tule Lake. Map by Heli Rekiranta.

The Legacy of Tule Lake and the Fair Play Committee

What the Tule Lake and FPC resisters had in common was their lack of attachment to the formal Heart Mountain networks. By the time they were released, though, the FPC members fell in line with the rest of the Heart Mountaineers in their leave categories and destinations, while the Tuleans broke the pattern with their drastic ex/repatriation rate.

Throughout 1945 and 1946, the lives of former inmates returned to normal—or the new normal—but the Japanese American community found itself collectively in shambles. Most families had lost at least some of their property and livelihoods, and many had lost everything. In addition to material losses, people had experienced trauma that was heightened by the community's division into no-noes, resisters, and soldiers. The Japanese American Citizens League made matters worse by persisting with its ultra-American stance, renouncing the resisters and no-noes, and advocating for silence over incarceration overall.

Though Frank S. Emi stated that the substance of the Fair Play Committee agenda was almost unanimously appealing, its legacy was far more fraught. In 1947, President Harry Truman granted a full pardon to the convicted members of the Fair Play Committee. Nevertheless, the "pro-JACL" viewpoint took hold in the discussion over incarceration in general and over the draft resisters and no-no boys in particular. Emi, however, pointed out that the dislike of resisters mostly pertained to the Nisei generation. According to Emi, the Sansei, the third generation mostly born after the war, were "very supportive of the draft resistance movement and very inquisitive," as can be said of the third generation's interest in learning about and recovering from incarceration in general. Referring to a 1983 talk he gave at California State University, Emi said, "They [the Sansei] thought that everybody had just remained quiet and hadn't made any fuss, but they seemed very pleased to know that there had been resistance in the camps." Meanwhile, Emi maintained that, until that talk, he "hadn't even thought about" the FPC, not because he wanted to forget, but because "it just didn't occur to me that it was anything significant.... We won our case at the appellate level, so that was that."[72]

In the 1990s, some Nisei veteran organizations began to give public credit to the Fair Play Committee members for their patriotism, and in 2002, the Japanese American Citizens League adopted, by a very narrow margin, a resolution of apology to the resisters for decades of exclusion.

The JACL did not apologize to the no-noes until 2019. An apology to the Tuleans was an even more fraught topic. A potential apology was not only a matter of acknowledging passive resistance through non-compliance to the loyalty questionnaire or renouncing one's citizenship; it also prompted debate over whether to acknowledge those who had committed acts of violence against fellow Japanese Americans in conflicts related to the questionnaire.[73]

The tangible bitterness, even hostility, between different sides of these discussions almost eighty years after the events shows that incarceration left a deep mark on the inmates, resisters, segregates, and their descendants. It is also an effective reminder that, while most Japanese Americans of the time shared the incarceration experience, circumstances and attitudes varied, and people disagreed on many matters.

CHAPTER 9

Onward

Routes to Freedom

THE VERY LAST TRAIN left the Vocation, Wyoming depot on November 10, 1945, carrying about two hundred passengers. On board was Keen Yanagi, who was once among the most connected individuals of Heart Mountain. A shorthand teacher at the night school, an attendance recorder for the high school, and the executive secretary of the Community Activities administrative office, he was also a member of the Judicial Committee, the Red Cross, and the block 14 Nisei club. Now he was on his way to his native Hawaii with his wife, Irene, whom he had married at Heart Mountain.

On that last train was also Peter-Maria Suski, an Issei doctor and the father of some of the most prominent Nisei in camp. His daughter Louise, the former city editor of the *Sentinel*, had relocated to Chicago in 1943, and his son Joe, likewise an early resettler, had headed the Community Activities Athletic Department. Although only a handful of people from this last train went to destinations other than the West Coast or Hawaii, Suski had decided to resettle long ago and thus traveled to Denver, Colorado. His late departure was not due to reluctance but to his sense of duty to the hospital. So many other doctors had resettled earlier that he felt the need to stay.[1]

Much of the discussion in the previous chapters relating to departure from camp focused around resettlement—on *not* returning home. Resettlement was one of the WRA's central objectives, although it caused practical problems in the camps' ability to function: the (Nisei) community leaders that the WRA considered most desirable, tended to leave, and finding suitable replacements got increasingly difficult as time passed.[2]

I have suggested that being strongly involved in the camp's politics and social life delayed resettlement due to stronger practical and emotional attachments to the incarceration community. But in contrast, unconnected people left earlier. It is difficult to assess the individual factors that pulled some to stay and pushed some to leave. For many young people, camp life was unbearably controlled and lacked stimulation. Given the abundance of wartime jobs, they left as soon as they could. Others may have become institutionalized and unable to take the initiative to leave. Camp life was carefully organized around routines and inmates did not have to worry about maintaining very basic living conditions. The Issei, as has been stated, were fearful of yet another relocation.

The resettlers on indefinite leave were a deviation from the pattern: only 25 percent of the Heart Mountain population left on such a permit. Thus, those in the terminal departure category were more typical. They formed the backbone of the society, offering stability. Without people like Keen Yanagi and P. M. Suski, who deliberately chose to stay, closing the camps might have become even more chaotic, for they helped to sustain a sense of community for the large number of people who were unable to leave.

Nevertheless, resettlement was such a strongly promoted goal and the indefinite leave period dragged on for so long—over two years—that attention inevitably draws to those early departees. I initially chose to distinguish between the "indefinite leave resettlers" and the "terminal departure resettlers" and "returnees" under the assumption that earlier departure indicated compliance with the WRA and the United States government. This division of the inmates based on their time of departure also arose from placing the destinations on a map: the destinations for those in the indefinite leave category were different from those in the terminal departure category. While the early resettlers were forced to find new homes, the data shows that once the West Coast had reopened, fewer people wanted to go elsewhere. The return rate to the West Coast suggests that those who stayed in camp until 1945 were indeed those who had no desire to resettle in the first place. As a more detailed look at the destinations and routes will show, the path was not always straightforward, even for those who could return home. Similarly, being in the terminal departure category was not always a sign of inability or passivity. Many of the inmates who stayed until the very end described a sense of duty to the community. Like P. M. Suski, who wanted to serve his fellow inmates as a doctor, they made a conscious choice.

Leave Indefinitely?

The standard narrative about resettlement contains four premises: that typical resettlers were young, well-educated, Christian, and Pacific Northwesterners.[3] My analysis of the Heart Mountain inmates suggests that Pacific Northwesterners were, at most, only marginally more eager to resettle than Californians. There were 2,135 people from the Pacific Northwest (Oregon and Washington) in the dataset, constituting 15 percent of the entire camp population. Of them, 636 (30 percent) left during the indefinite leave period, representing 17 percent of all indefinite leave resettlers. This was not drastically over the total proportion of people in camp who took indefinite leave, 26 percent. Meanwhile, indefinite leave resettlers from California (2,973) constituted 27 percent of all Californians at Heart Mountain. Therefore, the claim that Pacific Northwesterners were more eager to resettle is to a large degree exaggerated, at least in the context of Heart Mountain.

The three other claims, in the meantime, were easy to affirm. The early resettlers were indeed young; 41 percent were between eighteen and twenty-five years old upon resettlement. Another 19 percent were between twenty-five and thirty years old. They were also predominantly (70 percent) single. Over half of them were Christian and a third were Buddhist.[4] Their education level was significantly higher (with 22 percent college educated) than for the camp overall.

The West Coast exclusion zone was upheld until January 1, 1945, effectively preventing the early departees from returning to their former homes.[5] While the WRA advocated dispersal, jobs were to be found in cities, and public opinion toward Japanese Americans dictated destination choices. Consequently, the largest destinations for indefinite leave resettlers were Chicago, Illinois; Denver, Colorado; Cleveland, Ohio; Minneapolis, Minnesota; Spokane, Washington; and New York City; all including their adjacent smaller towns. Many oral histories mention frequent movement from place to place, and some resettlers had moved several times before the camps were closed in late 1945.[6]

Only 188 people stayed in Wyoming during the indefinite leave period, although agricultural work was available. Some people are "invisible" in the data because of the previously mentioned seasonal leaves, but racism looms in the background: many people in Wyoming, and more officially the Wyoming policymakers that had welcomed the establishment of an incarceration camp, did not wish for inmates leaving the camp to stay in the state. Steps included the prevention of Japanese Americans from voting in state elections and of Issei from owning land.[7]

With this kind of persistent opposition toward Japanese Americans, it is little wonder that even many young, well-educated, independent Nisei were apprehensive about resettling. The WRA did try to portray the inmates in a favorable light. At Heart Mountain, assistant project director Douglas M. Todd became the president of the local Lions Club. This, the WRA hoped, would especially improve relations with the Cody businesspeople. Camp administrators also invited localBoy Scouts to visit the governor in order to help "dispel many rumors" that the inmates were being coddled.[8]

The WRA emphasized appropriate behavior in its communications to resettling inmates. Advice was perhaps implicit—from avoiding congregating with other Japanese Americans to making "a creditable record, scholastically and socially, not for himself alone, but for the benefit of other students or prospective students of Japanese ancestry."[9] The Nisei had internalized suspicions against themselves and wanted to make sure they did not draw negative attention. This is only natural, considering their prewar experiences and the fact that they had spent years physically locked outside the rest of society.

For the most part, however, resettlers reported a positive welcome. A letter sent from Colorado to community activities director David Yamakawa described how self-consciousness eased thanks to the "understanding" local residents, and another from Illinois mentioned smiling faces and new friends, both Caucasian and Japanese.[10] WRA officials probably did not originally envision associations among Japanese resettlers in their new hometowns. Nevertheless, in larger cities this became a reality. Tetsuko Okida Zaima described relying on friends she had met after resettling for comfort during a job search, and Katsumi Hirooka Kunitsugu described a First Baptist Church in Madison, Wisconsin where Japanese Americans got together. In fact, Kunitsugu recalled that White community leaders "encouraged [Japanese Americans] to socialize" with each other, although she admitted, "I guess we kind of sought each other out, too, just to support each other."[11]

As I have noted, families preferred to stay together, and the choices of one family member influenced other family members' decisions. One resettling family member was likely to try to get the rest of the family to resettle in the same location. It is also possible to study people's implicit values through their resettlement choices. The Hachiya family exemplifies family members' influence on each other's resettlement decisions. Their oldest son, George, left his family of five at Heart Mountain after only six weeks of incarceration to become one of the very first students to study at the University of Nebraska at Lincoln. His brother, Kay, followed in the winter of 1943 and their sister, Sachiko, arrived the following fall, after graduating high school. Their parents, Fusa and Toru, both Issei, left the camp in January 1944. From the WRA administration's point of view, the Hachiyas were a model family, eager to resettle. Their background data reveals a desire to resettle: the mother had attended college in Japan and worked as an editor or reporter in the United States but despite her former achievements was willing to take the job of a domestic. The father had received a high school education from Japan and had worked in a clerical or sales position, and similarly accepted domestic work.¹² Interestingly, none of the adult family members appeared to be connected to any of the social, political, or employment organizations at Heart Mountain. The youngest daughter, who left Heart Mountain after graduating high school, is an exception; she participated in both social and high school activities.¹³ The Hachiyas reaffirm the notion that unattached people found it easier to leave.

Despite some of the positive examples set by resettlers, the WRA continued to worry about the low resettlement rate. By the spring of 1945, the WRA emphasized that "any Nisei can expect rapid placement in a job commensurate with his skill," adding that the agency now advertised job listings for "young Nisei without work experience." The WRA also reminded the Nisei that nurseries were available to allow mothers of small children to work, and promised that resettlers would have opportunities to further educate themselves.¹⁴ The agency targeted prospective students with a "Student Relocation Handbook" tailored for each incarceration camp and listing inmates who had successfully left the camp for college. The Heart Mountain handbook did not offer direct behavioral instructions but was clear about the importance of education. In fact, the authors made a nod toward cultural pluralism in describing why the Nisei should seek college education: "As the American way of life becomes more complex, the importance of broader backgrounds of knowledge and information and the value of college training becomes more firmly established." This excerpt appears to promise that Japanese Americans' cultural and linguistic knowledge would be valuable to their home country in the future.¹⁵

These "success stories," or the "salvage," as defined by the sociologist Dorothy Swaine Thomas, represent the type of public image the WRA wanted to portray of the incarcerated Japanese Americans to Americans outside the camps. WRA director Dillon S. Myer branded the Nisei as "American as apple pie and a living proof of the strength and vitality of American educational institutions." Meanwhile, Thomas labeled the largest group of people as the "residue"—those who only left when the WRA announced the closing of the camps.¹⁶

Leave Terminally

The United States Department of War revoked the exclusion order on December 17, 1944, and the closure of all camps was to take place within the next year. Heart Mountain officials were hopeful that families with children would move quickly once the school year was over. But by July 1, 1945, Heart Mountain's population was still over six thousand. In addition to practical difficulties in leaving, rumors halted planning for many inmates. Whereas during the loyalty questionnaire period, rumors had focused on forced resettlement, they now focused on the closing dates of the camps. Some envisioned rapid closures; others were certain that the WRA would have to keep the camps running until the war ended and possibly beyond. There was another set of rumors about attacks against Japanese Americans returning to the West Coast. Incidents of arson took place and there were milder animosities, but the rumors describing attacks and murders were all eventually found false.[17] All these rumors reflect inmates' fears. Their future was uncertain.

Although camp closure was imminent from the winter of 1945 and the exact date was set in early summer, basic operations continued until the very end. Keen Yanagi, the executive secretary of the Community Activities Section wrote his last office letter on the day before his departure on the very last outbound train. The letter addressed to David Yamakawa described the packing of Yamakawa's office records and the attempts of the community activities staff to sell movie projectors. Closing the services must not have been an easy task: Yanagi concluded his letter by writing, "So help me I'll never again take the responsibility to clean up any such thing as this again."[18]

To accelerate the departure process, the WRA started closing schools and threatened the remaining inmates with eviction. Each person received a train ticket and twenty-five dollars to relocate.[19] Moving outside the former exclusion area was still encouraged, and from Heart Mountain, the resettlement rate during terminal departure was 36 percent.

There were 8,676 people in the terminal departure category. The gender division was exactly 50 percent women and 50 percent men.[20] If the early resettlers were young adults, those in the terminal departure category demonstrated what made leaving difficult: 35 percent were underage. Almost an equal share, 33 percent, were over forty-five years old. This age division demonstrates how difficult it was for families to resettle if they had young children. The WRA administrators acknowledged this challenge and repeatedly wrote in their reports that "only able-bodied unattached persons and families with ample resources can leave easily and readily whenever they decide to do so."[21] In comparison to the early resettlers, terminal departure departees had lower education levels. In the adult population, 43 percent had only an elementary school education and only 6 percent had attended college.

Although most who stayed until the camp started closing preferred to return to their prewar homes, resettlement still took place under the terminal departure category. One such person, who had prominence and social prestige, was Donald Toriumi. He was a Nisei, born in 1914 and in his late twenties during the war. He was a priest of the camp's Christian church and a man of influence not only by virtue of his direct memberships but also indirectly through various community service tasks. He had studied at the postgraduate level in the United States and, from Heart Mountain, he went to work for the Board of National Missions in Cleveland, Ohio. His wife, Sophie, was one of the most active women in the social networks and, through her husband's work, familiar to many others in the community. Sophie Toriumi had a bachelor's degree from the United States, so their late resettlement in July 1945 was not due to lack of education or opportunities. Having an infant daughter born in 1944 probably delayed their resettlement decision, but more importantly, it seems they felt committed to the incarceration community through religious service.

David Yamakawa also mentioned this community obligation as a major reason for not resettling. As the head of community activities, he had a vital role in keeping up inmates' spirits and giving them meaningful things to do. In addition to his commitment to the Heart Mountain community, he cited a lack of proper housing, saying he did not want his children to grow up in a slum "above saloons, gambling houses, and such environment in a strange town." Eventually, Yamakawa and his family resettled in October 1945, among the last of the inmates. Although they were able to return to their hometown of San Francisco, they had to start out by living in a government-sponsored hostel. According to Yamakawa, Heart Mountain project director Guy Robertson forced him out of Heart Mountain, refusing "to give me even a week extension to completely liquidate C.A. [community activities]."[22] As a result, the department's budget showed a deficit, which the inmates were left to sort out.

In addition to tight formal networks and duties slowing down resettlement, friendships also tied people to Heart Mountain. Some of the skilled employees even formed friendships with WRA administrators. Numerous oral histories describe trips to Cody and Powell with Caucasian friends, and some inmates maintained correspondences after their release. David Yamakawa and his wife, for example, corresponded with director of recreation Merlin T. Kurtz and his family, mentioning how they occasionally were "homesick for Wyoming." Yamakawa's personal archives also included references to his cordial relations with Kurtz's successor, T. J. O'Mara.[23]

Of course, the more likely friendships took place between inmates. Despite the fact that it was possible to mostly associate with people from one's previous hometown, those involved in camp administrative work made friends across geographical divides. Ricardo Ritchie, originally of and returning to Los Angeles, wrote to David Yamakawa, native of and returnee to San Francisco, hoping to go into business together: "You and I made a pretty good team at Ht. Mt. and it may be to our benefit to renew our association."[24]

Despite careful planning, the reality for many leaving camp was living in hostels and trailers. Even many who had been able to keep their houses were forced to wait for their tenants to leave before being able to return. In a letter to David Yamakawa, a friend described his experience of living in a hostel: "For the first week or so, it was really a torture; Heart Mountain was a paradise compared to here, but... now, we are somehow managing to stay sane."[25] In fact, many inmates who were children in camp described their release from incarceration as more traumatic than the incarceration as such. As Akira Yoshimura put it, the camp "was one big playground" that did not require many responsibilities, whereas the postwar era was characterized by hardship. In the words of Nobu Shimakoji, inmates were "dumped out." Shimakoji said, "It was a real dramatic experience."[26]

The lack of housing was especially pressing in Los Angeles, which was by far the largest destination in the terminal departure period, followed by San Jose and Chicago. According to the destinations list, only the four largest had more than five hundred Heart Mountain residents, while the "top 10" had more than three hundred people. The next ten cities evened out the distribution, as the last city—with more than one hundred Japanese residents from Heart Mountain (Sacramento, California)—was the twenty-first-largest destination. The WRA administration's vision of breaking up "enclaves" seems to have worked, at least in the context of Heart Mountain, through the dispersal of people in more locations than before the war. However, 104 of the 613 destination cities were in California and another sixty-three in Oregon and Washington, and overall, 64 percent of the late departees returned to those three states.[27]

There is, understandably, a concentration on the West Coast in the terminal departure destinations, as people were finally being allowed to return to their former homes. Nevertheless, the same midwestern and eastern cities that attracted people during indefinite leave continued to be central in the final months of incarceration. The sheer volume of people leaving in 1945 meant that their numbers surpassed the indefinite leave resettlers, even when the movement's concentration was on the West Coast.

Overall, those in the formal networks had different destinations than those in the general camp population. Chicago narrowly beat Los Angeles as the top destination, reflecting the earlier departure dates of those in the formal networks. Chicago was also popular among the later departees. The rest of the top

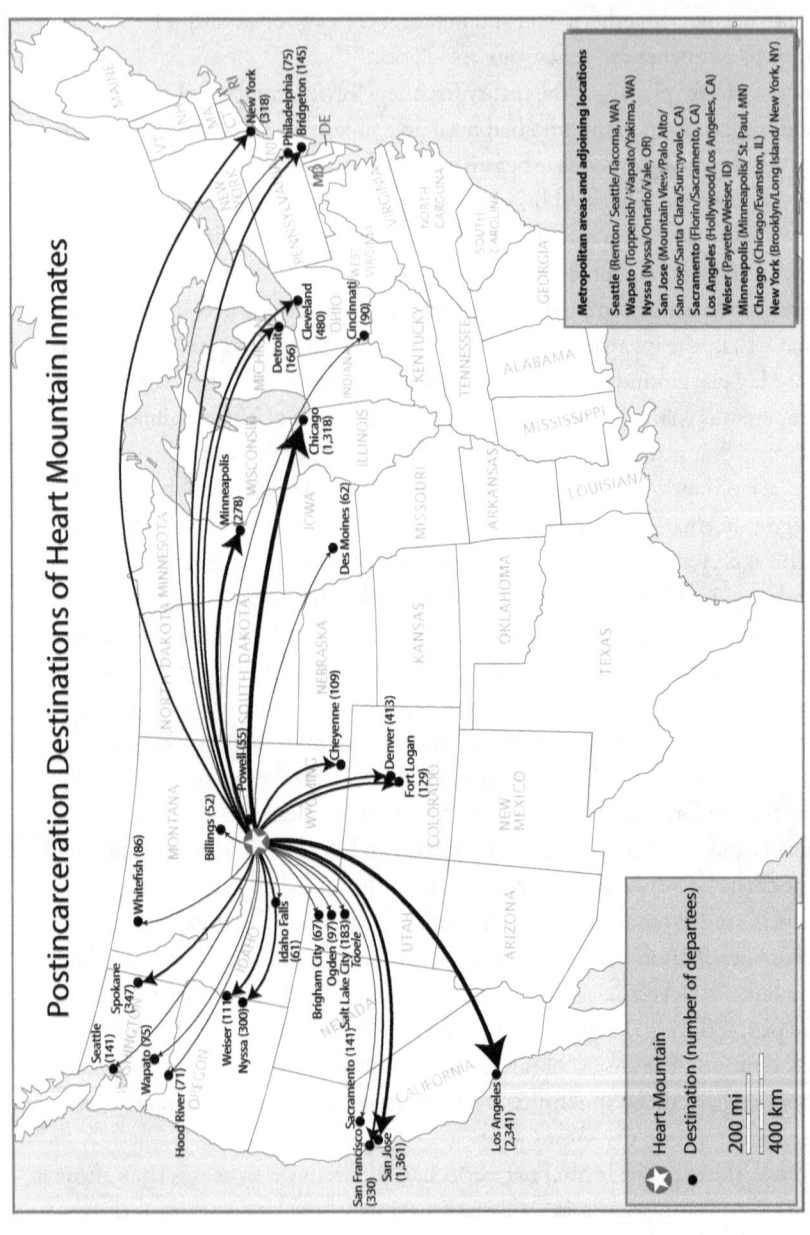

MAP 3. Postincarceration destinations of Heart Mountain inmates. The map shows the destinations where fifty or more inmates from Heart Mountain moved. Excluded are inmates who were transferred to other incarceration or internment camps or otherwise institutionalized. Map by Heli Rekiranta.

ten destinations (see map 3 for the most popular destinations throughout 1942–1945) were the same as for the entire camp population with the exception that the integrated network includes Cheyenne (as the "destination" of the Fair Play Committee convicts) and Fort Logan (for those entering the army). The order is also different: Cleveland, Ohio, and New York City precede San Jose.

Placing the People on the Map: Conclusions on the Final Destinations

If we turn our attention to movement on the state level, we get a very different view. Although Los Angeles and Chicago alone were such large destinations that they made California and Illinois the states with the largest number of migrants, Washington jumps to third place, passing Colorado by only two departees. In other words, the number of people moving to Washington and Colorado was large, but their populations were more spread out. Similarly, Utah, Oregon, Idaho, and Montana were among the top ten destinations, although Salt Lake City was the only top fifteen city destination among those states. Importantly, Heart Mountain inmates departed the camp for forty different states. The main gaps on the destination list, in addition to Alaska, were in the Southeast.

This finding leads us to consider what can be called a new place of living. Research has typically focused on the return rate to the West Coast states; that rate came to about 50 percent. However, only a quarter of all Heart Mountain inmates returned to the exact same place from which they departed. Los Angeles received 2,074 people from Heart Mountain. Of them, 1,430 had also departed Los Angeles. Thus, while the number of people going to the city from Heart Mountain dropped from the preincarceration 4,744, it gained 644 people who had previously lived elsewhere on the West Coast. The same is true for San Jose: 440 San Joseans returned home and it became the new home to 391 more people. In all, 15 percent of the people did not return to their former hometowns but to towns in their prewar home states. Another 6 percent found new homes in one of the following three states where they had not previously lived: California, Oregon, and Washington. In the Tule Lake population, 22 percent returned to their former hometowns and 30 percent to new addresses in their old home states. While the share of segregates returning to old hometowns was lower than in the full Heart Mountain population, a significantly greater number returned close to home rather than resettle to the Midwest. Meanwhile, out of those resettling in new states, only nineteen remained on the West Coast.

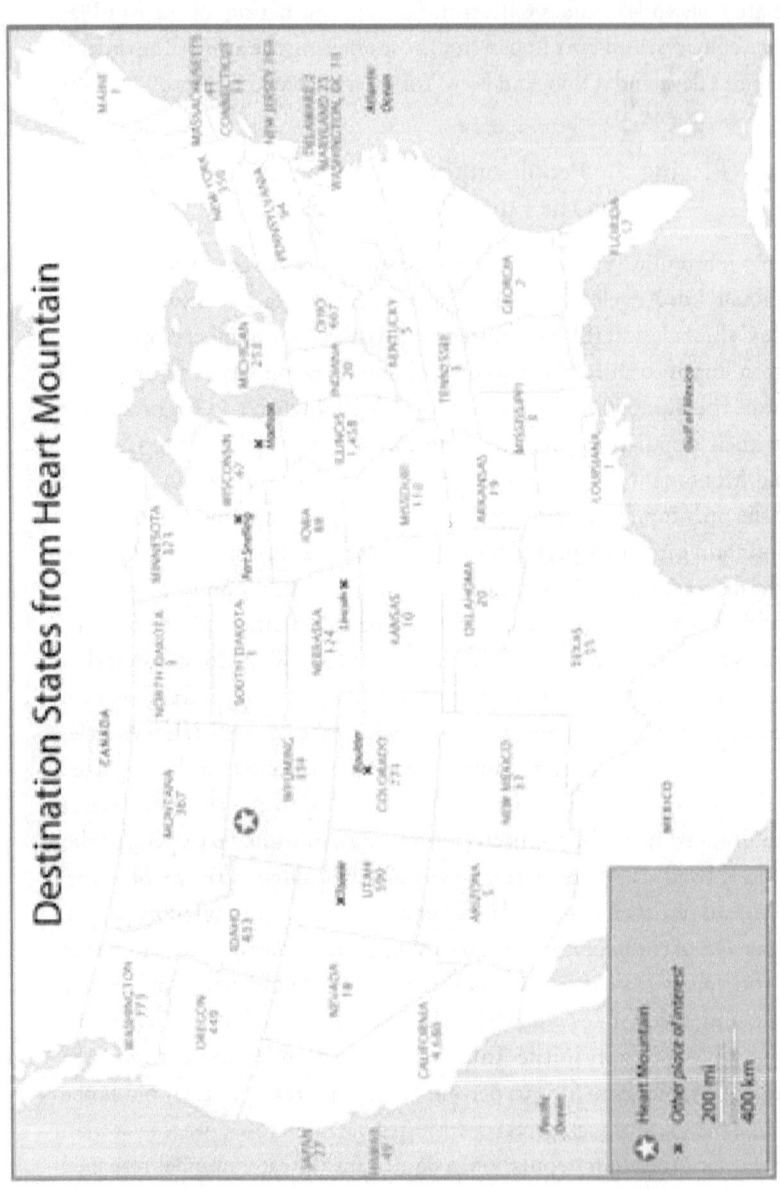

MAP 4. Destination states from Heart Mountain. Thickness of the line and size of the arrow reflect the volume of people entering that state. Each state includes the precise number of people moving to that state from Heart Mountain. Other places of interest reflect places that did not receive a large volume of departees but were significant otherwise. Tooele, Utah, for example, was the location of a defense plant, offering important employment opportunities for resettlers. Map by Heli Rekiranta.

Spokane, Washington, is an example of a city in the West Coast states with few Japanese Americans before the war that became a major destination (347 people from Heart Mountain). The 1940 census found only 362 people of Japanese origin in the city, but having been left just outside the exclusion area, it attracted several hundred settlers before incarceration. It was also available as a destination during the indefinite leave period. From Heart Mountain, a third of those heading to Spokane left on an indefinite leave permit. For its accessibility and proximity to the exclusion area, it was an appealing destination for people leaving the camps. The Spokane area had suitable jobs, especially for the Issei, in the agricultural and railroad industries. By the 1950 census, the Japanese population in Spokane had grown to 1,018 people.[28]

One Heart Mountain inmate resettling to Spokane was Amy Nose, who was among the most well-networked women—and, in fact, with eight memberships, she was among the top 1 percent of all inmates. Nose and her husband James were among those who went to Spokane during the indefinite leave period. Having been raised in the Yakima Valley, they were living in Seattle when the war broke out, and Spokane was not far from their original home. A significant share of those who went from Heart Mountain to Spokane were from the Yakima Valley. As so many Japanese Americans during the indefinite leave, though, the Noses ended up leaving Spokane after a year, moving to St. Paul, Minnesota. James Nose, despite being Kibei, had been in a clerical position before the war but was not able to find a suitable job in Spokane. After a few years in St. Paul, the couple returned to Washington, eventually settling in Moses Lake.[29]

Leaving camp among the last residents, the Nabata family made a permanent home in Spokane in 1945. Also hailing from the Yakima Valley, Kenichi Nabata established a pool hall, while Nami Nabata went to work on a local farm. Their oldest daughter was studying in Chicago and the two younger ones lived with their parents. Spokane's prewar Japanese American community was very tight knit, but the newcomers were well received. The influx of new community members meant the establishment of a new Buddhist church, for example, which helped in adjustment. These Japanese congregations were not only established due to discrimination but were also important sites of cultural preservation.[30]

Overall, the success of the relocation program from the administration's point of view was relative: about fifty-seven thousand Japanese Americans returned to the West Coast, while fifty thousand resettled in eastern states. Those who returned to the West Coast, especially, suffered from financial difficulties. They had missed the economic boom of the war years and had to settle for low-status employment. Many had lost their former homes and businesses. The Issei, who had already once built new lives in the United States, struggled to start all over.

The total losses of incarceration were estimated at four hundred million dollars, which would have come to over six billion dollars in 2021. According to one estimate, 76 percent of Japanese Americans removed from the West Coast lost *all* their property. Less than forty million dollars' worth of property was returned to Japanese Americans in the 1950s and '60s. When the change in the value of money is considered, these restitutions compared to less than ten cents on the 1942 dollar.[31]

The Nisei were in a better position: they were younger and began to build educations and careers. By the 1970s, Japanese American education and family income levels were above national average, and, along with members of several other Asian American ethnicities, they came to be seen as a model minority.[32] However, several scholars have disputed these educational and financial markers. A typical Japanese American household has several adult, working members. Thus, "household income" poorly reflects the economic leverage of a family with, for example, four adults, compared to a more traditional family of one or two employed adults.[33]

Despite the relative success of the Nisei in re-establishing themselves and despite some of the above-mentioned restitutions, incarceration became taboo in the Japanese American community, leading to a state of collective memory loss—or "social amnesia," as the sociologist Tetsuden Kashima called it.[34] The physical traces of the camps quickly disappeared. The barracks were sold and transported elsewhere. Previous owners, such as the Native Americans of the Poston and Gila River areas, reclaimed their lands. For the first few postwar years, the topic remained visible in books and films that touched on the subject. But once the Evacuation Claims Act of 1948 passed and the initial financial losses compensated, the subject disappeared both from the national and the Japanese American memory. Japanese Americans wanted to forget and focus on rebuilding their lives, and once the Issei were granted citizenship in 1952, Nisei organizations decreased their political activities. Between 1954 and 1967, there were no new book-length studies of incarceration. Former inmates mentioned "camps" to their children, but remained ambiguous about their nature. Many Sansei born after the war described their astonishment, sometimes as late as when they were in college, at discovering that their parents' references to "camp" did not mean happy days at summer camp.[35]

By rendering themselves invisible, the Japanese Americans regained the trust of members of the White mainstream, but doing so meant "a negation of identity and self."[36] This erasure of history shaped the identity of the Sansei, especially, and eventually made many of them want to dig up secrets of the past. Memories of racism and incarceration found their way back into Japanese American collective memory. With the rise of the Black Power movement, opposition to the Vietnam war, and the general advent of civil rights movements, the subject of incarceration reemerged. A new generation of academic books was published, also by former inmates. Many Japanese Americans no longer wanted to emphasize assimilation and conformity to government desires, instead becoming active in social movements.[37]

As a result of these efforts to receive proper compensation, the US Congress established the Commission on Wartime Relocation and Internment of Civilians (CWRIC) in 1980 to investigate incarceration. The commission went through government documents and contemporary writings and interviewed inmates. In 1982, its members concluded that, contrary to wartime claims, incarceration could not be justified by military necessity. Instead, the decision was motivated by "race prejudice, war hysteria and a failure of political leadership." By passing the Civil Rights Act of 1988, the government formally apologized for its violation of civil rights and awarded twenty thousand dollars to each surviving inmate, more than eighty thousand people.[38]

EPILOGUE

Networks of Power and the Power of Networks

THE HEART MOUNTAIN LEADERS we know today have mostly become known due to their own or their children's initiative as redress activists, pilgrimage organizers, and participants in oral history collections. Their contributions are invaluable as one piece in a historical puzzle, but if we want a more complete picture of power dynamics, network analysis is an excellent means to achieve that.

Looking at historical sources, we are left with the impression that Kumezo Hatchimonji, Frank Inouye, Bill Hosokawa, and Eiichi Sakauye were the most influential Heart Mountaineers. Thanks to the FPC, we know the names of Frank S. Emi, Kiyoshi Okamoto, and Paul Nakadate. Two young soldiers, Ted Fujioka and Stanley Hayami, both of whom lost their lives in battle, serve as the links to the youngest group of adults.

But there is much more to power than we are able to see through the life stories of the above men, as remarkable as they are. Through network analysis, we were able to get a glimpse into a very different kind of reality—one that includes women and countless men previously concealed from public consciousness. In addition to new people of power, we discovered that there are many kinds of power: the power of numbers (of memberships), bridging power, and family power. Nisei power was its own category, too, although the Issei seemingly had the highest inmate authority. We also learned that appearing integrated in one network could mean complete absence from another.

Some of the main individuals I hope will find new prominence in studies to come are Minejiro Hayashida, Hidenobu George Nakaki, and Toshiye Nagata, to name but a few. Their position in the networks is undisputed: they controlled camp political and social life, at least when it comes to numbers. They were the most active and thus had the most potential to influence, yet they have not appeared in previous literature at all. Power, especially in the political realm, also concentrated in the hands of relatively few people. Hayashida faced little competition as the chair of the council, and, similarly, there were other councilmembers who served in most if not all the councils during their incarceration. The fact that the same handful of people sat on a multitude of committees meant that political power was concentrated in the hands of a few individuals. Through them, the specific boards they occupied gained power as well.

The power of numbers also calls us to reassess the role of community government. The WRA tried to assist the Nisei to power, but their success was limited to block managership and the employment and social networks. In effect, Issei dominated all political bodies with elected members. Even the WRA acknowledged that the community government's role was "purely advisory," but the importance of these bodies went far beyond executive power. They provided self-worth, especially to the Issei who had been displaced from their homes and lost their livelihoods on the West Coast, and whom the WRA attempted to politically replace with the Nisei. The Heart Mountain councilmembers were also aware that they had achieved a higher status than those in other camps.[1]

The Issei would have been eager to collaborate with the Nisei, but the Nisei—and the Nisei block managers more specifically—were often not interested in sharing power. In some cases, they sought to protect the exclusive position that the WRA had tried to force upon them by excluding the Issei from councils. Although unsuccessful, the attempt left some Nisei clinging to their special status. Eiichi Sakauye elaborated on his preference to work with Nisei:

> They were in my age group and I can understand them. They have [the] same motive, and the trauma that we have gone through equivalent to my trauma there. Maybe their background might be different, but they have their same feeling; in other words, worried about draft and questionnaires and all that stuff.[2]

Leadership issues and the WRA's fear of the Issei also seeped into the management of the *Heart Mountain Sentinel* newspaper. WRA regulations allowed community enterprises a degree of influence in camp newspapers, perhaps with the original assumption that the Nisei would control the enterprises. When that did not happen at Heart Mountain, it prompted a WRA official to voice his concerns about the "editorial freedom" of the paper. Ironically, the *Sentinel* became known for its almost excessive Americanism, instead of as a voice of the Issei.[3]

When it comes to bridging power, the dynamics of the network change somewhat. Most of the individuals who enjoyed the power of numbers were not equally important when it came to their ability to connect people to each other. Minejiro Hayashida, though, had the strongest bridging power in the early and last months of incarceration, showing great persistence in his network participation. Where others left or gave up their assignments, Hayashida held onto power. Similarly, Paul Nakadate was a bridge in the early days of the network, which gave him an edge in the recruitment of FPC members. As a first arrival, he had established vital ties to the young men and, as a night-school teacher, also to Issei who had money to support the cause.

Apart from Nakadate, whose network power was limited to the early months of incarceration, none of the seven FPC leaders stood out in the camp networks. Based on this investigation, it seems that other men, like Tamio Miyahara, had more ability to influence draft resisters than the comparatively older official leaders. Although the FPC has gained much attention, more subtle forms of resistance were present at Heart Mountain. The no-noes portrayed a form of passive resistance by refusing to respond to the loyalty questionnaire as expected. Many inmates showed their resistance and agency by choosing when they left the camp: not pressured by the WRA but at their own pace.

None of the women of Heart Mountain made it quite to the level of the men in terms of numbers or bridging power. Toshiye Nagata, however, surpassed all the men in the restricted social network and was the lone woman among the ten most connected individuals overall. In general, the social network was of particular importance to the women, evidenced in the appearance of three women among the ten most connected members of the social network.

The institution with the highest bridging power was the United Service Organizations. It attracted a membership that came from different segments of the camp community and that participated in many other types of activities. When we take into account all its departments, the Community Activities Section was similarly prominent.

Group power leads us to consider the presence of what I have named "power families." In my original definition, these were simply families or family groups with several members in a given network. Upon further engagement with these family structures, I discovered that, in addition to family size, families had several possible ways of becoming influential. Some were connected to multiple different groups within one subnetwork (such as the Sakauyes in the employment network), others had a large combined number of connections through memberships in large organizations (such as the Nakamotos in the women's social network), and some (like the Fujiokas) emerged time and again in all subnetworks and the integrated network. While it was not within the scope of this study to investigate these families further, it can be assumed that they were, at the very minimum, well known to other residents. Whether or not they were *de facto* opinion leaders remains to be studied, but they certainly had many opportunities to spread whatever agenda they might have had, be it a desire to advance resettlement, recruit members for the FPC, or promote the *Sentinel* newspaper.

Women were in the minority in all of the networks except the employment network, where their share was very close to 50 percent. Most of the available roles were most suitable to single or childless women. Women who did participate in the formal structures of the camp, though, had more diverse connections than might have been expected. The women had an especially strong and versatile employment record. This indicates that the change taking place in women's roles during World War II applied to Japanese American women—and to incarcerated women.

Lack of participation in the formal networks, of course, did not mean lack of participation in camp activities. While many Nisei received leadership training from organizing different social groups and classes, children and Issei women benefited enormously from these activities. For many Issei women, camp life meant emancipation from cultural and practical expectations and allowed them the opportunity to develop new skills and adopt a new mindset.

High education level also emerged as a central characteristic of those with power. In the political network, previous prestige seems to have aided the older Issei men regardless of education, but the younger the individual, the more evident this became. And for women, being well educated was even more important. Indefinite leave resettlers were particularly well educated, while those that responded "no-no" to the loyalty questionnaire had, on average, a much lower education level. This speaks to the inequality of resettling, or at least a perception thereof. Those with a lot of education, a solid employment history, and extensive relations with people beyond the Japanese American community were better equipped to leave the camps.

The research literature generally accepts that, initially, about 50 percent of all inmates in all ten incarceration camps resettled away from the West Coast, as was the case for Heart Mountain.[4] The movement *within* the coastal states, by contrast, has not been explored much, although about half of those returning to the coast found new hometowns. The number of places of residence also increased in California, Oregon, and Washington, though all settled to smaller Japanese American communities than before the war. In this sense, the WRA policy worked: there were fewer Japanese Americans on the West Coast and, in addition to former communities becoming smaller, the population became more spread apart.[5]

Compared to members of other networks, politicians left the camp late, about the same time as the average unconnected resident. However, they resettled significantly more often. This means that a sense of purpose kept them in camp rather than the inability or unwillingness to move. Their persistent demands that the WRA keep the camps open or provide more assistance did not stem from their own needs but from what they saw as their peers' needs.

In 1944, prominent councilmember Kumezo Hatchimonji proposed that the WRA hire staff to advance business opportunities, especially for resettling Issei.[6] This call was met with the hiring of Thomas Sashihara as a "relocatee business advisor" for the Great Lakes Area, based in Cleveland, Ohio. Sashihara seems to have started in this capacity at Heart Mountain before moving to Cleveland. An exception to the trend of young and single resettlers, Sashihara had camp connections especially in the political realm. Born in Japan in 1900, he had come to Heart Mountain via the Tujunga (California) Internment Camp. He returned to his family by September 1942.

Sashihara's story also takes us back to the value of studying networks. Depending on the network under scrutiny, he appears in multiple lights. Being an interned Japanese citizen would suggest that he was not on the best terms with the WRA. Yet he was active in camp politics (three consecutive council terms in addition to committee memberships), he was employed in the community enterprises, he served as an official of the Heart Mountain Golf Club, and then he was employed by the WRA outside the camp. He had also attended college in the United States and was a Christian, so by those standards he was an excellent partner for the WRA to advance the resettlement of the Issei. At the same time, he was a controversial person even within the community council. Upon his departure, project attorney Byron Ver Ploeg wrote that Sashihara had many "enemies, especially among the Hayashida group."[7] Ver Ploeg seems to refer to disputes over the organization of the community enterprises. Sashihara was the chairman of the Community Enterprises Board of Trustees that favored the trust model, while the Hayashida group famously supported the cooperative. Although the cooperative was originally the WRA's preferred form of conducting the services, it seems that at least the project attorney valued Sashihara's leadership qualities over his compliance to WRA propositions.

What network analysis gives us in regard to Heart Mountain, and regarding any historical community, is the clear understanding that historical events are not just a series of actions taken by individual "great men." At Heart Mountain, multiple, previously lesser-known people and groups wove an interconnected web where each actor had a role in relation to other individuals and the whole community.

METHODOLOGICAL APPENDIX

At minimum, an individual conducting network analysis needs a spreadsheet program (such as Microsoft Excel) and a network analysis software program (such as Gephi). Others exist, but Gephi is among the most advanced and versatile. It is also free and open source, meaning that users can create plug-ins and other improvements to the program. This methodological appendix is as general as possible but it contains some points about Gephi.

Basic Components of a Network

The basic components of a network are *nodes* and *edges*.[1] Nodes represent objects or entities and edges represent relationships between the entities. For example, a node might represent a person, a place, an event, an organization, a document, an idea, a religious affiliation, or any other concept, either abstract or concrete. The edges between nodes can be *directed* or *undirected*. Directed edges point in one direction only: for example, person A making a phone call to person B. Undirected edges, on the other hand, display reciprocal relationships, such as the marriage of persons A and B.

In addition to the basic concepts of nodes and edges, a few other properties, at minimum, must be understood to be able to analyze a network. *Degree* represents the number of links a node has to other nodes. *Average degree* describes the average number of those links in the network. In directed networks, *out(going) degree* represents the number of links pointing from a node toward other nodes, while *in(coming) degree* represents the number of edges pointing toward a node. In my study, individual activity or influence is often measured by *outdegree* (the number of connections a person has to institutions) and the prominence of an institution is determined by *indegree* (the number of individuals connecting to the institution).

Nodes and edges can also be assigned *weights* according to their importance. For example, in some cases it might be beneficial to know how long a couple has been married instead of just the fact that they are married. *Path length* is an important concept indicating the distance between any two nodes. Depending on the question, it might, for example, be important to discover the *shortest path* between two individuals of interest (how easily two individuals can reach each other).

Finally, a significant concept in many historical studies is *centrality*. Network analysis has several centrality calculations, which assess the importance of a node in relation to other nodes. Indegree and outdegree are sometimes used to evaluate a node's position, but in essence, they only suggest the number of connections a node—for example, an individual—has. They do not measure whether the individual is connected to important individuals or organizations, or whether the individual is perhaps a bridge between otherwise isolated parts of a network.

Closeness centrality measures the position of a node in relation to other nodes with high degree: an individual with few direct connections (outdegree) might have a high closeness centrality value, because she is connected mostly to individuals that, by contrast, have many connections. *Eigenvector centrality* takes this measure a step further, with a high score indicating that a node is connected to other nodes that are important (i.e., to nodes that score highly on a combination of these measures). Finally, *betweenness centrality* is a measure I discuss a lot in my networks, as it measures the bridging capabilities of a node. A high betweenness centrality score means that the node connects parts of the network that otherwise have few (or no) other links.

Creating and Cleaning the Data

It is possible to turn almost anything into network data. My starting point was a large database the US authorities collected during World War II. It might also be desirable to track, for example, the recipients of someone's correspondence, or the co-occurrence of mentions of people in the history of a journal. The format of the data (is it already in table format, digitized text, or entirely hand-written?) determines the number of steps needed before the network analysis stage. Let us, nevertheless, jump to the phase where all the data has been collected in a spreadsheet.

In collecting and cleaning data, it is advisable to include all found errors alongside the corrected information, even in cases where it seems redundant. As an example, in my third dataset, I matched names mentioned in the *Heart Mountain Sentinel* with WRA IDs, retaining the *Sentinel* spellings of the names if they differed from the entry data or final rosters. Further development of a dataset becomes easier if all deviant spellings are in one dataset. Adding data from new sources is faster when all variations of previous data are in one table.

Knowledge of one's data reveals the types of connections and networks that pertain to a specific community. Similarly, exploring the data shows the types of fields that are needed in the final dataset(s). In some cases, for example, it may be beneficial to add "yes/no" types of fields, such as the "Member of FPC" field in my combined dataset. This enables filtering and partitioning on that criterion. In this study, the datasets created by the authorities (the entry and final roster datasets) had fifty-two fields, of which forty-six were unique. I added another fifty-six fields based on the data, including the above-mentioned yes/no field of "Member of FPC" and others that contained more variable information, such as "Destination state" and "Times elected to community council."

This kind of metadata (data that is not directly linked to the *network* but rather to its members) is usually much more limited in studies of traditional social networks, depending somewhat on the researcher's choices. Downloading a dataset of Twitter social networks, for example, will give the researcher a wide variety of information on the Twitter behavior of a given user, but not, for example, the user's age, gender, or nationality. As another example, a researcher gathering data on a given company's information flows can often determine beforehand what types of background questions are asked, but not everything is necessarily available due to company policy or participant reluctance to provide data. Thus, the researcher can only study the networks in a limited context, allowing for fewer *ad hoc* lines of study to emerge.

The general rule of thumb for editing any, and especially historical, data, is to be as precise as possible. It is always better to collect data that will be discarded from the final model than to regret missing information. Similarly, it is helpful to break each data point into particles that are as small as possible (or reasonable). For example, if a person is listed as living in Los Angeles on January 1, 1942, at least the following should be collected: city of residence (Los Angeles), state of residence (California), and date of residence (01-01-1942)—three columns in all. Additionally, one might want to break the date into month, day, and year. This would make it easier to filter out people that lived in the city during a specific month of a certain year. Adding exact addresses or counties might be worthwhile depending on the type of queries one is planning. The more detailed the data, the more precise the questions one can ask.

Formatting the Data for Network Analysis Software

My focus here is on creating appropriate data for use in Gephi, but most network analysis software requires a similar structure.

Gephi looks at network data through two kinds of tables: the node table and the edge table. For the node table, only one column is compulsory, the ID. Each item must have a unique ID that can be a combination of numbers and letters. For my data, I used the WRA-generated individual IDs for people and self-generated IDs for organizations (such as CC194303 for Community Council, March 1943). Other columns depend on the structure, detail, and researcher's selection of data (see table 2). Here, I have given each node a label and a description, determined its size and type, and determined end dates. The dates are here expressed as decimals, but more traditional formats can also be used as described in the data-cleaning section above.

For the edge table, the obligatory fields are "source" and "target," denoting the link between nodes. For example, an individual's involvement in the above-mentioned community council would be expressed as Source [23646A] Target [CC194303] (see table 3).

The structure of the data also dictates the researcher's data-modeling choices. Depending on the types of questions being asked, graphs should be built either as directed, undirected, or mixed. In the present study, I selected the directed graph with a predetermined edge direction as the basic modeling paradigm. At its core are the relationships of individuals to institutions and places. The graph could also flow the other way around, with an institution "owning" its members. This would emphasize the notion that it is not only the individuals that form an organization but also the organization membership that shapes individuals. I have taken these influences into account in my consideration of different types of networks without changing the data structure. Undirected graphs proved useful for creating multimode projections of individual-to-individual and organization-to-organization relationships. Overall, the direction of edges makes a bigger difference when using many of the mathematical functions of network analysis. In a directed graph, the most central nodes (apart from individuals with high outdegree) are always institutions, which tells the researcher what some of the key groups and organizations were but does not reveal powerful individuals. Individual prominence is better discovered in an undirected, and preferably projected, graph. I used mixed graphs to uncover power families. Making the other network connections directed but family group membership undirected enabled large family groups to stand out. The largest institutional nodes would swallow the family groups, if they were created with directed edges.

Additionally, it is possible to create an edge ID, as I have done in the example, or to let the software generate the ID. If there are many types of edges (such as an individual's connections to different types of organizations, family

TABLE 2. A Sample of a Node Table

Id	Label	NodeDescription	NodeSize	NodeType	NodeStartDate	NodeEndDate
CC194210	Council 1942 Oct	1st temp. council	30	Council	1942.72	1943.15
CC194303	Council 1943 March	2nd temp. council	30	Council	1943.16	1943.55
CC194308	Council 1943 August	1st council	30	Council	1943.56	1944.07

TABLE 3. A Sample of an Edge Table

Id	Source	Target	Type	Weight
CC23646ACC194303	23646A	CC194303	Directed	1
CC15022ACC194210	15022A	CC194210	Directed	1

groups, places), it might make it easier to create the edge IDs following a logic that distinguishes between the different types. The fields "type" (undirected or directed) and "weight" (1 unless you want to make a distinction) are useful to key in, although Gephi will draw a graph without them. Finally, it is possible to determine an edge "kind." This can be used to distinguish, for example, membership in a family group. My dataset identifies the following kinds: "primary" (i.e., birth family), "adopted," and "marriage."

Regardless of where data is being edited (e.g., Microsoft Excel, Microsoft Access, or other programs), it needs to be saved in comma separated value format (CSV).

Understanding the Graph

Once the data tables are ready and imported into the network analysis software, it is possible to begin exploring the graph. In visualizing the network, there are no right or wrong choices—researchers must explore their particular data to see what works for their purposes. It is typically necessary to employ some kind of layout to make sense of the graph, which usually resembles a hairball in the beginning. In Gephi, one of the most useful layouts is Force Atlas 2. Often, it is desirable to increase the figure in "scaling" and tick the box for "prevent overlap." It is also helpful, especially in the beginning, to size and color the nodes. For example, there might be a column with gender information—maybe exploring the placement of sexes in the graph will be relevant. There are multiple tutorials online for these basic functions.

Gephi and other network analysis software come with a default set of tools and several optional plug-ins. It is possible to do all the basic analysis without installing any plug-ins, but some of them can be very helpful in making more sophisticated graphs. For this book, the main plug-ins installed were the Geo Layout (enabling the creation of a network graph with latitude and longitude data, further enabling the creation of maps with network elements) and the MultiMode Projection tool.

Analyzing the Network

The MultiMode Projection tool allows users to convert a multimode network into a single-mode one. In other words, if a user has started by creating edges between different types of nodes (for example, an individual's connection to an organization), they can reverse the process to create links based on shared membership. They can either create interpersonal links (where A and B get a mutual connection if they are both members of organization C), or they can link organizations to each other based on shared members (organizations D and E get a link if individual A is member of both). The main difference is whether they project individual onto institution or institution onto individual in the first step.

For this, a user must do two things:

1. Convert node types to represent two types only. For example, in my original data table, the types of nodes were named "individual, administrative, council, social group, organization, department, section, and division" but after adding a new NodeType2 column, I only had "individual" and "institution."
2. Convert all edges into undirected. In other words, save CSV file with a new name and change all cells in the type column into undirected.

The main benefit of this tool is that it allows users to see how different individuals interact in a network without having to collect such data separately. While in a multimode network organizations have the highest centralities (because an organization typically has more members than a single individual has memberships), in a projected network, users can find the people that have the highest betweenness score, for example.

Another way to uncover some of the underlying influences in my network was to search for families with several members in the networks. I did this by calculating the "Page rank" and filtering for families.[2] Page rank is not useful in this type of a network for measuring overall importance of nodes because, again, large organizations and even powerful individuals ranked higher than any of the family groups. After filtering out undesirable node types (organizations and political groups, leaving just individuals and family groups) to identify extended power hubs, Page rank works as it should. This requires the creation of a mixed graph in which edges between individuals and institutions are directed but edges between family members are undirected.

The results of a Page rank calculation in this specific case reflect the connections counted only once. If several members of the family participate in the same organization, it could also be argued that the strength of those connections becomes stronger with several family members knowing the same set of people personally. Here, I was more interested in the overall extent of family connections than the possible strength of those ties. I have given examples of the accumulative effect of memberships in chapters 6 and 7—though I also point out families where collective influence remains quite meager because they only have shared contacts and few unique relations.

NOTES

Preface

1. War Relocation Authority Photographs of Japanese-American Evacuation and Resettlement, Online Archive of California, https://oac.cdlib.org/ark:/13030/ft800007n3/?order=2&brand=oac4.

Chapter 1

1. The peak population of Heart Mountain was 10,767, making it the fourth-largest of the ten camps. It was also the third-largest community in Wyoming in its time. The loyalty questionnaire refers to a government-imposed questionnaire to determine the loyalty of all incarcerated individuals. Those claiming disloyalty were segregated at the Tule Lake Center in California. Initially, 48 percent of Heart Mountaineers resettled outside the West Coast.

2. Daniels, "Introduction: Heart Mountain—After Sixty Years," 22.

3. "Mainstream American" is a term frequently used in primary materials to compare Japanese Americans to White Americans, to suggest that the majority leads a homogeneous "American" life desirable to all.

4. See, for example, Hoxie, *A Final Promise*, 38; Wu, *The Color of Success*, 12–13.

5. Barabási, *Network Science*, Section 1.3.

6. Barabási, *Network Science*; Scott, *What Is Social Network Analysis?*, 21; Giuffre, *Communities and Networks*, 33; Freeman, "The Development of Social Network Analysis," 53–55. Critics of social network analysis like Mustafa Emirbayer and Jeff Goodwin (themselves, in fact, network analysts) have claimed that SNA emphasizes community at the expense of individual agency. Community network analysts, such as Barry Wellman, Charles Wetherell, and Robert Michael Morrissey, respond that, while they focus their research on the community level, one of their main arguments is that individuals within a community act consciously and purposefully. What is more, they point out, network analysis gives new viewpoints for identifying significant individuals. Wetherell, "Historical Social Network Analysis," 126; Emirbayer and Goodwin, "Network Analysis, Culture, and the Problem of Agency," 1413; Wellman and Wetherell, "Social Network

Analysis of Historical Communities," 98; Morrissey, "Archives of Connection," 69. On these tensions, see also Knox, Savage, and Harvey, "Social Networks and the Study of Relations."

7. Padgett and Ansell, "Robust Action," 1265–68; Morrissey, "Archives of Connection," 69; Kamp-Whittaker, "Diaspora and Social Networks."

8. Carley, "Dynamic Network Analysis," 136.

9. See, for example, Kivelä et al., "Multilayer Networks," 204.

10. See Bastian, Heymann, and Jacomy, "Gephi." There are several computer software tools for analyzing social networks, most notably UCINET, Pajek, and Gephi. Gephi is a free, open-source program. I used it for its ability to create dynamic networks and for its diverse file input and output forms, which enabled me to use various programs to create the tables analyzed in Gephi. "Pajek," http://mrvar.fdv.uni-lj.si/pajek; "UCINET," https://sites.google.com/site/ucinetsoftware/home; "Gephi," www.gephi.org.

11. Guiliano and Ridge, "The Future of Digital Methods": 21–22; Mäkelä, "Humanities/Social Sciences: Computing Interaction."

12. *Issei* (first-generation immigrants), *Nisei* (second-generation individuals who are US citizens), *Sansei* (third-generation), and *Kibei* (Nisei educated in Japan) are established terms both within the Japanese American community and among researchers. Collectively, Japanese living abroad are called *Nikkei*.

13. The numbers for incarcerated individuals as well as the population of each camp vary depending on the source. These numbers depend on the inclusion or exclusion of children born in incarceration and individuals in camps operated by the Department of Justice. A slightly different copy of this dataset is also available at Densho: The Japanese American Legacy Project.

14. The camp itself closed in November 1945.

15. The *Sentinel* published two editorials opposing the Fair Play Committee but did not write news articles on the organization apart from the trials of the draft resisters. See "Editorial," *Heart Mountain Sentinel* 3, no. 11, March 11, 1944, 1 and 4; "Editorial," *Heart Mountain Sentinel* 3, no. 12, March 18, 1944, 4. For the paper's rebuttal of accusations of being the administration's mouthpiece, see "Editorial," *Heart Mountain Sentinel* 3, no. 13, March 25, 1944, 4. Frank S. Emi's letter is in the same issue, p. 5.

16. Boys' and girls' clubs were part of the larger YMCA and YWCA umbrella organizations. They divided into several smaller units or divisions based on the members' age, with the youngest members being six years old and the oldest members reaching adulthood. See O'Mara, Community Activities Final Report, for a thorough breakdown of these clubs.

17. For use of the word "assimilation," see, for instance, "Memorandum, Nisei Assimilation," July 21, 1943, which states that "assimilation may most easily be defined as the acquisition of the cultural traits of a particular society." War Relocation Authority, Community Analysis Report No. 6, July 21, 1943, Papers of Philleo Nash, HSTPL, https://www.trumanlibrary.gov/library/research-files/

memorandum-nisei-assimilation-july-21-1943-papers-philleo-nash. For the authorities' assessment of the characteristics of assimilated and unassimilated persons, see, for example, Asael T. Hansen, Community Analyst Trend Report for October 5 to 25, 1945, JAERR, reel 136/2, 294; Anderson, Heart Mountain Relocation Center Community Government Final Report.

18. For contemporary views of the War Relocation Authority, see War Relocation Authority, *Wartime Exile*.

19. Ngai, *Impossible Subjects*, 179. President McKinley was the first to use the term in his proclamation outlining United States colonization policies in the Philippines.

20. Dillon S. Myer, who was the Director of the War Relocation Authority in charge of the incarceration, later led the Bureau of Indian Affairs (BIA). During his years in charge, the BIA adopted the "Indian Termination and Relocation Program," which shared the ideology and many practices of Japanese American resettlement. See, for example, Kekki, "Entangled Histories of Assimilation;" Kurashige, "Unexpected Views of the Internment,"110–111. For assimilation as a linear process, see Gordon, *Assimilation in American Life*. On the network theoretical integration of ethnic minorities, see, for example, Granovetter, "The Strength of Weak Ties," 201–233; Greve and Salaff, "Social Network Approach," 7–16.

21. Gordon, *Assimilation in American Life*, 103–04, 29; Kurashige, "Unexpected Views of the Internment," 110–111.

22. Yang, "We Asian Americans Are not the Virus."

23. For the authorities' assessment of the characteristics of assimilated and unassimilated persons, see, for example, Asael T. Hansen, Community Analyst Trend Report for October 5 to 25, 1945, JAERR, reel 136/2, 294; Anderson, Community Government Final Report.

24. Hayashi, *Democratizing the Enemy*, xiv; Ishizuka, *Lost & Found*, 109–10; Robinson, *By Order of the President*, 260–61; Robinson, *A Tragedy of Democracy*, 21–22.

25. Article 78, Geneva Convention relative to the Protection of Civilian Persons in Time of War, 12 August 1949, https://www.un.org/en/genocideprevention/documents/atrocity-crimes/Doc.33_GC-IV-EN.pdf. The article does not provide for the wholesale internment of people; each case must be individually deliberated.

26. For most recent discussion, see "What's in a Word?"; National JACL, Power of Words Committee, *Power of Words Handbook*, 149.

27. Ishizuka, *Lost & Found*, 13, 72; Hayashi, *Democratizing the Enemy*, xiv-xv; Robinson, *A Tragedy of Democracy*, 11; Densho, "Terminology."

28. See, for example, Kashima, "Japanese American Internees Return"; Dempster, *Making Home from War*, xxiii. Dempster, however, suggests that his own thinking has shifted toward considering resettlement as an ongoing process extending to the present day.

29. "The '72-Year Rule' (92 Stat. 915; Public Law 95–416; October 5, 1978) restricts access to decennial census records to all but the individual named on the record or their legal heir." US Department of Commerce, Census Bureau, "The '72-Year Rule.'"

Chapter 2

1. Spickard, *Formation and Transformations*, 8–18; Robinson, *A Tragedy of Democracy*, 9.

2. Robinson, *A Tragedy of Democracy*, 9–11. See also Wang, "The Double Burdens of Immigrant Nationalism."

3. US Department of the Interior, Census Office, "Statistics of the Population of the United States at the Tenth Census, June 1, 1880," xxxviii.

4. Spickard, *Almost All Aliens*, 171–226.

5. Robinson, *A Tragedy of Democracy*, 10–11; Spickard, *Formation and Transformations*, 22, 33–34, 60; Robinson, *After Camp*, 5; Williams, *American Sutra*. In Japan, as well as among the Japanese in the United States, religion was a more private matter. People were more tolerant of all religions and faiths and the practice of religion was less institutionalized than in the US. As a result, people may have claimed one religion in the census but regularly attended another group's services. Kitano, *Japanese Americans*, 58. This tendency is evident in the entry database, where a remarkable number of parents listed different religions from their (young) adult children, suggesting that the children may have listed whichever congregations they had most recently attended.

6. Prefectures were distinguishable in speech and customs, and people were expected to marry within the prefecture. Thomas and Nishimoto, *The Spoilage*, 4; Kitano, *Japanese Americans*, 34–38; LaViolette, *Americans of Japanese Ancestry*, 42.

7. LaViolette, *Americans of Japanese Ancestry*, 19–21; Kitano, *Japanese Americans*, 34–38. LaViolette was a WRA community analyst (anthropologist conducting studies and maintaining statistics of camp life) among other camps at Heart Mountain. The study in question is based on prewar research.

8. Yoo, *Growing up Nisei*, 3; Spickard, *Formation and Transformations*, 35.

9. Yoo, *Growing up Nisei*, 3; Lyon, *Prisons and Patriots*, 19–20. It should be noted that a new but much smaller wave of immigration from Japan occurred after 1965. These first-generation immigrants would also be referred to as Issei, but the children of the newer immigrants are often called *Shin-Nisei* (literally "new Nisei"). The anthropologist Takeyuki Tsuda, himself a Shin-Nisei, suggests that "proper" Japanese Americanness arises from the incarceration experience, making it more difficult for the newer generations to identify as Japanese Americans. Tsuda, *Japanese American Ethnicity*, 2–3.

10. Takaki, *Strangers from a Different Shore*, 214–23; Spickard, "The Nisei Assume Power"; Yogi, "Japanese American Literature"; Yoo, *Growing up Nisei*, 3; Robinson, *A Tragedy of Democracy*, 109–10; Robinson, *After Camp*, 5. For the more deviant views, see especially Spickard and Najima, "Not Just the Quiet People."

11. See, for example, *Personal Justice Denied*, 21–22, 41–43.

12. Muller, *American Inquisition*, 13–14; Spickard, *Formation and Transformations*, 96–98.

13. Community Analysis Report No. 8, January 28, 1944, "Japanese Americans Educated in Japan," box 7, folder 10, FSEP, HMWF; Muller, *American Inquisition*, 13–14; Spickard, *Formation and Transformations*, 96–98.

14. Okihiro, *Whispered Silences*, 125–26, 42–45.

15. LaViolette, *Americans of Japanese Ancestry*, 177.

16. ten Broek, Barnhart, and Matson, *Prejudice, War, and the Constitution*, 99; Congressional Record, 78th Cong., 1st Sess., vol. 89, pt. 6, October 18, 1943, 8469; Congressional Record, 79th Cong., 1st Sess., vol. 91, pt. 6, July 17, 1945, 7642. Emphasis added.

17. US Department of Commerce, Census Bureau, "Thirteenth Census of the United States Taken in the Year 1910," 155–56, 66; Journal of the Senate of the State of California (1905), 1164–1165, quoted in Daniels, *The Politics of Prejudice*, 27.

18. Mae N. Ngai discusses the topic at length in *Impossible Subjects*.

19. Robinson, *A Tragedy of Democracy*, 11–13.

20. LaViolette, "The American-Born Japanese and the World Crisis," 18–19; Sowell, *Ethnic America*, 162–63; Fuchs, *The American Kaleidoscope*, 116; Lyon, *Prisons and Patriots*, 21–26. Australia had restricted Chinese immigration already in the 1850s and banned Japanese immigration in 1896. This served as a precedent for the United States and Canada. Robinson, *A Tragedy of Democracy*, 11.

21. "Washington's Farewell Address in 1796," http://avalon.law.yale.edu/18th_century/washing.asp.

22. Fuchs, *The American Kaleidoscope*, 5–6; Gordon, "Assimilation in America," 60.

23. Salins, *Assimilation, American Style*, 7; Yoo, *Growing up Nisei*, 22.

24. Kitano, *Japanese Americans*, 25.

25. Kitano, 3, 121.

26. Robinson, *A Tragedy of Democracy*, 20.

27. Robinson, 26.

28. Weglyn, *Years of Infamy*, 34. Weglyn discusses the report in detail in her first chapter, 33–54. The entire Munson Report can be found in Munson, *Report on Japanese on the West Coast*.

29. Robinson, *By Order of the President*, 75. The first days after the Pearl Harbor attack are discussed in more detail in Robinson, 73–76. Personal narratives by Japanese Americans can be found, for instance, in Houston and Houston, *Farewell to Manzanar*, 3–9; Uchida, *Desert Exile*, 46–51; Sone, *Nisei Daughter*, 145–64; Gruenewald, *Looking Like the Enemy*, 2–7; Oppenheim, ed., *Stanley Hayami, Nisei Son*, 23.

30. Robinson, *A Tragedy of Democracy*, 60–61.

31. Robinson, 86.

32. Executive Order 9066, February 19, 1942, General Records of the Unites States Government; Record Group 11, NARA; ten Broek, Barnhart, and Matson, *Prejudice, War, and the Constitution*, 100.

33. Weglyn, *Years of Infamy*, 39. For oral histories describing voluntary relocation, see, for example,. Lily Hioki, "Lily C. Hioki Interview, December 1, 2010," interview by Tom Ikeda and Stephen S. Fugita, Japanese American Museum of San Jose Collection, Densho Digital Repository https://ddr.densho.org/media/ddr-jamsj-2/ddr-jamsj-2-10-transcript-9d062c6dcc.htm; Mary T. Karatsu, "Mary T. Karatsu Interview, August 24, 2011," interview by Sharon Yamato, Densho Visual History Collection, Densho Digital Repository, https://ddr.densho.org/media/ddr-densho-1000/ddr-densho-1000-362-transcript-2c94fd5381.htm; Harry K. Yoshikawa, "Harry K. Yoshikawa Interview, April 14, 2010," interview by Martha Nakagawa, Densho Visual History Collection, Densho Digital Repository, https://ddr.densho.org/media/ddr-densho-1000/ddr-densho-1000-278-transcript-782440fede.htm.

34. Muller, *American Inquisition*, 2.

35. US Department of Commerce, Census Bureau, "Sixteenth Census of the United States: 1940, Population, Volume II: Characteristics of the Population, Part 1," 698.

36. W. R. Silver to Nels H. Smith, December 15, 1941.

37. Ehrlich, *Heart Mountain*.

38. Weglyn, *Years of Infamy*, 77.

39. Takaki, *A Different Mirror*, 379; Weglyn, *Years of Infamy*, 86–89; Ishizuka, *Lost & Found*, 75.

40. Canada first evicted adult Japanese males from the West Coast in February (with a mid-January announcement), which could be considered a precedent for the United States to incarcerate its Japanese population. The two countries had expressed a desire to coordinate policy, but there is no evidence that Canada did so prior to making the decision. Canada's announcement received little attention in the United States. Later, President Roosevelt signed Executive Order 9066, evicting all people of Japanese descent. That order was followed by the Canadian decision to do the same. Weglyn, *Years of Infamy*, 56–57; Sunahara, *The Politics of Racism*; Robinson, *A Tragedy of Democracy*, 77–79.

41. Ishizuka, *Lost & Found*, 73–76; Weglyn, *Years of Infamy*, 57–66. For Peruvian internees, see, for example, Gardiner, *Pawns in a Triangle of Hate*.

42. Muller, "Of Coercion and Accommodation," 3–6; War Relocation Authority, *Administrative Highlights of the WRA Program*, 105, 85–87; Kekki, "Entangled Histories of Assimilation."

43. Drinnon, *Keeper of Concentration Camps*, 19; Robinson, *By Order of the President*, 130–31.

44. Drinnon, *Keeper of Concentration Camps*, 6–7; Robinson, *By Order of the President*, 132.

45. Starn, "Engineering Internment," 702.

46. Kekki, "Japanese American Internment," 29–46.

47. For the anthropologists' reports, see JAERR.

48. Robinson, *By Order of the President*, 245.

49. Weglyn, *Years of Infamy*, 79; Ishizuka, *Lost & Found*, 86. Internment here refers to the internment of the aliens, although Crystal City internment camp in Texas was later designated as a "family internment camp" and housed US citizens as well.

50. The purpose of the land reclamation projects, which began in the early twentieth century and continued into the 1960s, was to create land suitable for farming in the western states and thus to promote the economic development in those states. One of the most famous projects is the Hoover Dam on the Colorado River, see "About Us," US Department of the Interior.

51. Drinnon, *Keeper of Concentration Camps*, 8. More about the disputes between Indian tribes and authorities over the construction of the camp in Poston in, for example, Hayashi, *Democratizing the Enemy*, 88–89.

52. Weglyn, *Years of Infamy*, 48. For more about conditions and daily life in camp, see, for example, Weglyn, *Years of Infamy*, 76–92; Ishizuka, *Lost & Found*, 57–113. The autobiographies of Sone, Wakatsuki, Uchida, Gruenewald, and Hayami provide personal accounts.

53. Drinnon, *Keeper of Concentration Camps*, 8. The term "Caucasian" is an interesting detail in the euphemistic terminology related to incarceration, as among the three thousand employees were also African Americans.

54. Nisei girls' rate of educational attainment was nevertheless higher than that of the general population: in 1940, 54 percent of Nisei girls were in high school, compared to 38 percent of girls in the general population. Nakano, *Japanese American Women*, 110–12.

55. ten Broek, Barnhart, and Matson, *Prejudice, War, and the Constitution*, 143–44.

56. The final roster only accounts for indefinite leave and "terminal departure." People going on short-term and seasonal leave were expected (if not required) to return and were thus not recorded. ten Broek, Barnhart, and Matson, *Prejudice, War, and the Constitution*, 147–48; Drinnon, *Keeper of Concentration Camps*, 51–53.

57. ten Broek, Barnhart, and Matson, *Prejudice, War, and the Constitution*, 149–50; Muller, *American Inquisition*, 34–38.

58. Robinson, *By Order of the President*, 165–70.

59. ten Broek, Barnhart, and Matson, *Prejudice, War, and the Constitution*, 168; Okihiro, *Whispered Silences*, 215. More about Nisei soldiers in, for example, Crost, *Honor by Fire*; Tamura, *Nisei Soldiers Break Their Silence*.

60. The term "no-no" refers to all individuals who responded in the negative to both of the crucial questions in the loyalty questionnaire. Discussion usually centers around "no-no boys," who are erroneously confused with draft resisters.

61. ten Broek, Barnhart, and Matson, *Prejudice, War, and the Constitution*, 164. For more extensive discussions of the situation at Tule Lake, see Thomas and Nishimoto, *The Spoilage*; Weglyn, *Years of Infamy*, 156–73; Drinnon, *Keeper of Concentration Camps*, 62–82.

62. Drinnon, *Keeper of Concentration Camps*, 43. More about the strike and the riots in Hayashi, *Democratizing the Enemy*, 130–36; Robinson, *By Order of the President*, 200–01; Weglyn, *Years of Infamy*, 121–25; Muller, "Of Coercion and Accommodation."

Chapter 3

1. Mackey, *Remembering Heart Mountain*, 51–52.
2. War Relocation Authority, *Community Government*, 2.
3. These job titles are based on descriptions at the *Heart Mountain Sentinel*.
4. War Relocation Authority, *Administrative Highlights of the WRA Program*, 4.
5. Scott Taggart, "Brief History of the Development of Heart Mountain Business Enterprises, August 12, 1942 to June 30, 1944," 1944, JAERR, reel 135/3, 100–15; Thomas and Nishimoto, *The Spoilage*, 36; Inouye, "Immediate Origins of the Heart Mountain Draft Resistance Movement, 123; Mackey, *Heart Mountain*, 30, 39.
6. War Relocation Authority, *Community Government*, 4–5.
7. War Relocation Authority, 15, 27.
8. Confusingly, the WRA booklet states that councils were Nisei only and block managers could be Issei. War Relocation Authority, *Community Government*, 49–51. However, especially in the early months of the camp's operation, the material from the *Heart Mountain Sentinel* lists exactly opposite compositions.
9. "Need of Resident Governing Group Found in Election of Councilmen," *Heart Mountain Sentinel* 3, no. 33A, August 12, 1944, 8.
10. Nelson, *Heart Mountain*, 33–34; Hayashi, *Democratizing the Enemy*, 107–47; Mackey, *Heart Mountain*, 43.
11. These "divisions" do not seem to reflect any actual geographical or cultural classification. Areas that the Japanese traditionally considered very different from each other were lumped together, while, for example, Okinawa is not listed as its own area at all.
12. Although Mexico interned some of its Japanese residents and some were reportedly held at least at the Kooskia internment camp in Idaho, the individual who was born in Mexico had lived in the United States prior to these events.
13. US Department of Commerce, Census Bureau, "Sixteenth Census of the United States: 1940, Population, Volume II: Characteristics of the Population, Part 1," 568.
14. Jack Kunitomi, "Jack Kunitomi Interview, October 26, 2011," interview by Martha Nakagawa, Segment 4, Densho Visual History Collection, Densho Digital Repository, https://ddr.densho.org/interviews/ddr-densho-1000-355-1/.
15. Social Service Department, Memo to Reports Division, June 1, 1944, 3, JAERR, reel 135/1, 87.
16. Marjorie Matsushita Sperling interview by Tom Ikeda, February 24, 2010, Densho Visual History Collection, segment 17, https://ddr.densho.org/media/ddr-densho-1000/ddr-densho-1000-273-transcript-6f6a81a167.htm; Lillian Nakano interview by Megan Asaka, July 8, 2009, Densho Visual History Collection, segment 5, https://ddr.densho.org/media/ddr-densho-1000/ddr-densho-1000-254-transcript-0d151f25db.htm; Mits Koshiyama interview by Alice Ito, July 14, 2001, Densho Visual History Collection, segment 8, https://ddr.densho.org/media/ddr-densho-1000/ddr-densho-1000-130-transcript-2c86c3cd9d.htm; Frank Sumida interview by Tom Ikeda and Barbara

Takei, Densho Visual History Collection, September 23, 2009, segment 26, https://ddr.densho.org/media/ddr-densho-1000/ddr-densho-1000-261-transcript-94f6aab359.htm.

17. Community Analyst Trend Report from May 4 to 9, 1945, 1–3, JAERR, reel 136/2, 217–19.

18. George Yoshinaga interview by Alisa Lynch, August 10, 2010," Manzanar National Historic Site Collection, segment 22, https://ddr.densho.org/media/ddr-manz-1/ddr-manz-1-107-transcript-38525c22b7.htm.

19. See, for example, Heart Mountain Community Council meeting minutes, September 16, 1943, September 30, 1943, JAERR, reel 133/1, 194, 198; Community Analysis Section, Quarterly Report, October 1 to December 31, 1942, 4, JAERR, reel 136/1, 380. At least for parts of the year 1944, councilmembers were, after election, appointed as block coordinators and received a salary. Asael T. Hansen, Weekly Report for September 29–October 5, 1944, October 6, 1944, 1, JAERR, reel 136/2, 86.

20. See, for example, "Former Center Girl Employed as Media Maker," *Heart Mountain Sentinel* 2, no. 39, September 25, 1943, 5; "Successful Resettlement in Kansas City Told," *Heart Mountain Sentinel* 3, no. 24, June 10, 1944, 5.

21. See, for example, Heart Mountain Reports Office, Monthly Report for Month Ending March 31, 1945, 2, JAERR, reel 134/2, 129.

22. See, for example, evacuee case file for Akira Matsumoto, Records about Japanese Americans Relocated during World War II, record group 210, Records of the War Relocation Authority.

23. Katie T. (Koga) Hironaka interview by Barbara K. Uchiyama, December 5, 1997," *REgenerations Oral History Project,* 100, https://oac.cdlib.org/view?docId=ft600006b-b&brand=oac4&doc.view=entire_text, OAC.

Chapter 4

1. Asael T. Hansen, Combined Weekly Reports for September 1–21, 1944, September 22, 1944, 2, JAERR, reel 136/2, 75.

2. On the use of the word "politics" by inmates, see, for example, Rikio Tomo to Block Managers, April 7, 1943, folder 08.10.1, RHP, HMWF.

3. "Relocation" in the names of these committees refers to resettling, moving away from the camps, and especially moving to parts of the country other than the West Coast.

4. These nodes are grouped close to each other at the center of the network graph.

5. "Job List to Be Compiled by Relocation Group," *Heart Mountain Sentinel* 2, no. 15, April 10, 1943, 8.

6. Community Government Quarterly Report, August 1943, 2–3, JAERR, reel 136/1, 212–213.

7. The categories reflect the United States Bureau of Labor occupation lists, which differentiate between, for example, various types of managers like hotel and restaurant

managers, retail managers, and wholesale managers. Most politicians self-reported as "retail managers," which means they were likely to have operated small produce stores.

8. Thomas, Kikuchi, and Sakoda, *The Salvage*, 43–43.

9. Welfare Director Virgil Payne's memorandum to the Reports Division, April 1, 1944, JAERR, reel 135/1, 72.

10. Thomas and Nishimoto, *The Spoilage*, 109–12.

11. See, for example, Hansen, Community Analyst Trend Report from February 9 to 22, 1945, February 23, 1945, 4, JAERR, reel 136/2, 153; Hansen, Community Analyst Trend Report for March 16 to 22, 1945, March 23, 1945, 3, JAERR, reel 136/2, 175.

12. "Informal discussion on relocation between Isseis and the relocation team," February 2, 1944, 10–12, JAERR, reel 136/3, 37–39.

13. Relocation Division Monthly Report for the Month Ending October 31, 1944,"2, JAERR, reel 134/2, 287; Melford O. Anderson, Community Management Division Narrative Report, July 31, 1945, 3, JAERR, reel 134/2, 234; Clarence I. Nishizu, "War Relocation Authority and Relocation," March 1944, 14, JAERR, reel 136/3, 81; Hansen, Community Analyst Trend Report from December 22 to 28, 1944, December 29, 1944, 2, JAERR, reel 136/2, 110.

14. Eiichi Sakauye interview by Joe Yasutake, July 25 and October 4, 1997, *REgenerations Oral History Project*, 362-63, 379, https://oac.cdlib.org/view?docId=ft600006bb&query=&brand=oac4.

15. See, for example, Hayashi, *Democratizing the Enemy*, 110. Hayashi's analysis focuses on the Manzanar (California) and Poston (Arizona) camps, where political dynamics were very different from those at Heart Mountain. Because Manzanar, especially, was such a politically active camp, its practices (e.g., the fact that block managers had more power than councilmembers) have come to represent all camps, although dynamics clearly varied in different camps.

16. Memorandum Ruth Hashimoto to Hospital, Survey of infants without small pox or diphtheria shots, June 16, 1943, folder 08:10.4, RHP, HMWF; Block 6 Volunteer Firemen, n.d., folder 08:10.4, RHP, HMWF; Santa Claus's Route, 1943, folder 08:10.2, RHP, HMWF.

17. Quarterly Report, Heart Mountain Community Government, October 1–December 31, 1942, 2–3, JAERR, reel 134/2, 146-47; Frank S. Emi interview by Alan Koch, March 11, 1993 and February 20, 1994, *Japanese American World War II Evacuation Oral History Project*, 370, http://www.oac.cdlib.org/view?docId=ft1f59n61r&brand=oac4&doc.view=entire_text; Judy Murakami interview by Carolyn Nayamatsu, October 13, 2009," Twin Cities JACL Collection, segment 5, https://ddr.densho.org/media/ddr-densho-1014/ddr-densho-1014-17-transcript-5c9a0c6eb9.htm. Brian Hayashi discusses the relations between the community councils and block managers, Issei and Nisei, although his camps of focus (Manzanar, Poston, and Topaz) had a different government structure. Hayashi, *Democratizing the Enemy*, 108–14.

18. John Y. Hayakawa interview by Tom Ikeda, March 21, 2012, Densho Visual History Collection, segment 20, https://ddr.densho.org/media/ddr-densho-1000/ddr-densho-1000-401-transcript-9ce8e851f8.htm, Densho Digital Archive.

19. See, for example, Hansen, Weekly report for April 7–13, 1944, April 14, 1944, 2, JAERR, reel 136/2, 2; Block managers to Assistant Project Director Douglas M. Todd, February 1, 1943, folder 08:10.1, RHP, HMWF.

20. "Delegates Hit New WRA Co-Op Regulations: Air Doubts in Stormy Session," *Heart Mountain Sentinel* 2, no. 2, January 9, 1943.

21. Sentinel Supplement Series, no. 236, September 26, 1944, 1; Byron Ver Ploeg to Philip M. Glick, October 5, 1944, 2, JAERR, reel 134/1, 66.

22. Scott Taggart, "Brief History of the Development of Heart Mountain Business Enterprises, August 12, 1942 to June 30, 1944," JAERR, reel 135/3.

23. The project attorney and community analyst explained the dispute at length in their reports. For examples of their analyses, see Hansen, Weekly Report for October 6–12, 1944, October 13, 1944, JAERR, reel 136/2, 93; Hansen, Community Analyst Trend Report for May 18 to 25, 1945, 2, JAERR, reel 136/2, 229; Byron Ver Ploeg to Philip M. Glick, September 21, 1944, JAERR, reel 134/1, 54.

24. Block managers' memorandum to Shig Masunaga, Tom Oki, George Nakaki, and Min Yonemura, August 16, 1943, folder 08:10.1, RHP, HMWF.

25. Nakaki, Community Government—Evacuee Viewpoint.

26. Sentinel Supplement Series, no. 179, March 14, 1944; Byron Ver Ploeg to Edwin M. Ferguson, November 2, 1944, JAERR, reel 134/1, 86.

27. "Nine Will Face Gambling Count," *Heart Mountain Sentinel* 4, no. 11, March 10, 1945, 1; "Gamblers Fined by Judge Metz," *Heart Mountain Sentinel* 4, no. 14, March 31, 1945, 8. For more on gambling in Japanese American culture, see Lau, "Japanese Immigrant Gambling."

28. Hansen, Community Analyst Trend Report from June 1 to June 7, 1945, June 8, 1945, JAERR, reel 136/2, 237.

29. Hansen, Community Analyst Trend Report from February 9 to 22, 1945, February 23, 1945, 14, JAERR, reel 136/2, 163.

Chapter 5

1. Suski, *My Fifty Years in America*, 42.

2. See Hinnershitz, *The Camps and Coerced Labor* for the first book-length exploration of the labor conditions in Japanese American incarceration camps.

3. The available information is inconsistent in detail: some individual records include the name of the position, division, and department of employment, as well as the start and end dates of employment, while others lack any time reference and might indicate only a division or line of work, not the exact office or workplace. Nevertheless, I am confident that the employment network presented here is representative of the whole. I have been able to find employees for each section and division of the WRA administration. During data collection, I looked at the statistics of the network at various stages with different numbers of employees, and the core numbers (share of citizens/non-citizens, women/men, etc.) remained the same. Furthermore, although some units are sparsely

populated, we can detect the relative significance of the workplaces based on number of listed employees; the more important an office was considered, the more often it would have been mentioned.

4. "44% of Population Working on Project," *Heart Mountain Sentinel* 1, no. 2, October 31, 1942, 2; Weglyn, *Years of Infamy*, 82; Robinson, *A Tragedy of Democracy*, 161–62.; Community Analyst Trend Report from June 22 to June 28, 1944, 2, JAERR, 2, reel 136/2, 245; Nelson, *Heart Mountain*, 81; Mackey, *Heart Mountain*, 45; Robertson, Project Director Final Report. I also get the impression from Mackey and the *Sentinel* that some of the inmates working in nearby fields operated by Wyoming farmers were counted in the camp workforce, although this is not explicitly stated. Mackey, *Heart Mountain*, 34. Full records of employment were either not kept or were not archived with the rest of the camp records.

5. Hayashi, *Democratizing the Enemy*, 8; "Life in Camp."

6. See Robinson, *The Unsung Great*, 267,272.

7. Sakauye interview, 369.

8. "Washington, U.S., Arriving and Departing Passenger and Crew Lists," Ancestry.com, M1383 arriving Seattle 1890–1957, frames 160, 023, 035, 061; "U.S., World War I Draft Registration Cards," National Archives/Ancestry.com, frame 02, draft card O. The registration card does not give Iwajiro Otsuki's draft classification, but there is no evidence that he would have volunteered.

9. "U.S., School Yearbooks," Ancestry.com; 1940 Federal Census, Ancestry.com. Otsuki's mother passed away in early 1941. "Oregon, U.S., Death Index," Ancestry.com; *The Michigan Alumnus*, 341; *University of Michigan Official Publication*, 203.

10. "33 Residents Leave to Sail on Gripsholm," *Heart Mountain Sentinel* 2, no. 35, August 28, 1943, 8.

11. "Crops Harvested Total 2,069,735 Pounds," *Heart Mountain Sentinel* 2, no. 48, November 27, 1943, 8.

12. Deckrow, "A Community Erased," 178–79.

13. General Information Bulletin, Series 24, October 10, 1942, 5; Sentinel Supplement Series, no. 274, February 1, 1945.

14. "The Heart Mountain Night School for Adult Education," 1, box 1, folder 1, FSEP, HMWF.

15. "Sewing Class Graduation Set," *Heart Mountain Sentinel* 4, no. 13, 3; "Sign-Up for Adult Education Classes Set," *Heart Mountain Sentinel* 4, no. 13, 8.

16. Takashi Hoshizaki interview by Tom Ikeda and Jim Gatewood, July 28, 2010, segment 16, Densho Visual History Collection, https://ddr.densho.org/media/ddr-densho-1000/ddr-densho-1000-290-transcript-1585f1946d.htm.

17. Spickard, *Formation and Transformations*, 90.

18. Art Okuno interview by Kirk Peterson, September 1, 2009, segment 17, Manzanar National Historic Site Collection, https://ddr.densho.org/media/ddr-manz-1/ddr-manz-1-80-transcript-a8087657a1.htm.

19. O'Mara, Community Activities Final Report.

20. Fugita and Fernandez, "Religion and Japanese Americans' Views of their World War II Incarceration," 116–17. See also Williams, *American Sutra*, 117–118.

21. In the entry dataset, "Christian/Protestant" was the largest selected Christian denomination, but there were also eleven other categories that fall under Christian churches. Some of them, like the Christian Union or the Disciples of Christ, only had a handful of members in the camp.

22. The Community Activities Section reported weekly participation as six thousand individuals. O'Mara, Community Activities Final Report. See also Matsumoto, "Japanese American Women during World War II," 9; Mackey, *Heart Mountain*, 75.

23. See, for example, "150 Attend Judo Class," *Heart Mountain Sentinel* 1, no. 1, October 24, 1942, 6.

24. Memorandum Virgil Payne to Reports Division, April 1, 1944, JAERR, reel 135/1, 66.

25. Sakauye interview, 336.

26. Spickard, *Formation and Transformations*, 75–76.

27. Russell, "Arthur and Estelle Ishigo," 7–9. See also Ishigo, *Lone Heart Mountain*.

28. Although some of these unidentified spouses could have been found in the full WRA entry database, I decided to limit searches to individuals at Heart Mountain.

29. "Okuda-Mamiya," *Heart Mountain Sentinel* 2, no. 2, January 9, 1943, 3.

30. Spickard, *Formation and Transformations*, 92; Matsumoto, "Japanese American Women during World War II," 74.

31. Ted Hamachi interview by Kirk Peterson, March 4, 2010, Manzanar National Historic Site Collection, segment 12, https://ddr.densho.org/media/ddr-manz-1/ddr-manz-1-91-transcript-3e7540511f.htm.

32. Toshi Nagamori Ito, interview by Martha Nakagawa, November 9, 2010, Densho Visual History Collection, segment 19, https://ddr.densho.org/media/ddr-densho-1000/ddr-densho-1000-309-transcript-6e22c08ddc.htm.

33. See, for example, "Girl to Attend New York School," *Heart Mountain Sentinel* 2, no. 34, August 21, 1943, 2; Sone, *Nisei Daughter*, 226–232; Adeline S. Kell, Memo to Reports Division, December 30, 1944, 3, JAERR, reel 135/1, 158. See also Community Analysis Section report, November 1–4, 1942, 4, JAERR, reel 136/1, 365.

34. Matsushita Sperling interview; Kaneshiro interview, segment 13.

35. (Okida) Zaima interview, 644.

36. There is a discrepancy between the reported Japanese language school attendance of Heart Mountain residents and the general research literature that emphasizes that every Nisei growing up before the war studied Japanese. This might partly derive from the organization of the camp entry questionnaire form that left language school information to be recorded in the Voluntary "other information" field.

37. Japanese language training for the US Navy started at Harvard and the University of California, Berkeley in 1941 but moved to the University of Colorado when the Japanese were removed from the West Coast. The school had as many as 150 Japanese American instructors. Camp Savage Language School in Minnesota, meanwhile, was

a Military Intelligence Service Language School (MISLS) and originated in San Francisco. At its highest in 1946, the MISLS had 160 teachers. Nakamura, "Military Intelligence Service Language School,"; Niiya, "Navy Japanese Language School."

38. Precise job titles were available for five hundred resettlers.

39. The Japanese American Student Relocation Council was sponsored by the American Friends Service Committee and is credited for helping four thousand students to resettle. See, for example, Austin, *From Concentration Camp to Campus*. See also Ito, "Japanese American Women and the Student Relocation Movement." One underexplored aspect of religion and resettlement is that student resettlement aid often came from Christian churches, resulting in an overrepresentation of Christians in the student resettlers. See Fugita and Fernandez, "Religion and Japanese Americans' Views of Their World War II Incarceration," 118.

40. (Hirooka) Kunitsugu interview, 250.

41. For example, "Classifieds," *Heart Mountain Sentinel* 3, no. 25, June 17, 1944, 2; "Classifieds," *Heart Mountain Sentinel* 3, no. 32, August 5, 1944, 2.

42. Asael T. Hansen, Community Analyst Weekly Report for April 7–13, 1944, April 14, 1944, 2, JAERR, reel 136/2, 2; "Informal Discussion on Relocation between Isseis and the Relocation Team," February 2–3, 1944, 11, JAERR, reel 136/3, 38; "Reasons Given for Not Relocating," n.d. (but probably winter/spring 1944), JAERR, reel 135/1, 321.

43. Sentinel Supplement Series, no. 228, August 31, 1944, 1.

44. Miyo Minnie (Nakae) Uratsu interview by Martha Nakagawa, May 25, 2011, Densho Visual History Collection, segment 15, https://ddr.densho.org/media/ddr-densho-1000/ddr-densho-1000-335-transcript-ca47e2aaa5.htm.

Chapter 6

1. Researchers continue to rely on the 1959 division of power into coercive, reward, legitimate, referent, expert, and informational power. See French and Raven, "The Bases of Social Power."

2. He was a candidate in the second election of 1943 but lost the election. "4 Nisei, 15 Issei Selected to Council Posts/Hayashida Defeated in Block 8," *Heart Mountain Sentinel* 2, no. 33, August 14, 1943, 8.

3. "Heart Mountain Community," n.d., 10, JAERR, reel 136/3, 123.

4. "Heart Mountain Community," n.d., 4, 10, JAERR, reel 136/3, 117, 123; Letter from Community Council (signed Minejiro Hayashida, Chairman) to Dillon S. Myer, March 22, 1943, JAERR, reel 136/2, 197; Nelson, *Heart Mountain*, 67. The House Committee on Un-American Activities, generally known as the Dies Committee, investigated allegations that the incarceration camps housed Japanese soldiers and that inmates were receiving more and higher quality food than American soldiers. See, for example, Myer, *Uprooted Americans*, 96–97.

5. Asael T. Hansen, "Ryoichi Fujii's Program to Reorient Issei Thinking, with Added Comments on the War as the Issei Now View It," November 14, 1944, 3, JAERR, reel 136/2, 316. On Fujii, see also "Finding Aid for the Ryoichi Fujii Papers, 1919–1999," Online Archive of California, https://oac.cdlib.org/findaid/ark:/13030/kt6v19q42b/.

6. Hansen, "Ryoichi Fujii's Program to Reorient Issei Thinking," November 14, 1944, 3, JAERR, reel 136/2, 316.

7. Ralph J. Moore, "Handling of Attempted Rape of Child at Heart Mountain," extract of a letter by Heart Mountain project attorney Jerry W. Housel to WRA acting solicitor Lewis Singler, April 29, 1943, May 12, 1943, JAERR, reel 133/1, 111. The case referred to in the title of Moore's report was of a mentally disabled young man attempting an attack on a child, which the Judicial Committee was handling. Tomo was accused of trying to meddle in the committee's procedure.

8. "Heart Mountain Community," n.d., 11, JAERR, reel 136/3, 124.

9. Rikio Tomo to Douglas M. Todd, April 6, 1943, folder 08:10.1, RHP, HMWF.

10. See chapter 8.

11. For more on the Judicial Committee, see Muller, "Of Coercion and Accommodation."

12. "Fujioka Polls 885 Votes to Win Prep Election," *Heart Mountain Sentinel* 2, no. 6, February 6, 1943, 8.

13. Yoshinaga interview, segment 14.

14. War Relocation Authority, *Wartime Exile*, 41.

15. Rhodes, *The Ethnic Press*, 19.

16. See Sakanosuke Imura biography at "50 Objects/Stories."

Chapter 7

1. Robinson, *The Unsung Great*, 62–72; See also Matsumoto, "Desperately Seeking 'Deirdre.'"

2. This is her name in camp records. She later remarried and became Hironaka, the name she used in the interview referenced in this chapter.

3. (Koga) Hironaka interview, 94.

4. See, for example, McKay, *The Courage Our Stories Tell*, 2; Fujita-Rony, "Remaking the 'Home Front;'" Yamaguchi, *Experiences of Japanese American Women*. In fact, more works document women's service in the army than their experiences in incarceration, for example, Moore, *Serving Our Country*; Robinson, *Nisei Cadet Nurse*.

5. "70 Hospital Aides Receive Caps at Ceremony," *Heart Mountain Sentinel* 2, no. 32, August 7, 1943, 8.

6. See, for example, "YWCA Plans Education to Speed up Relocation," *Heart Mountain Sentinel*, 2, no. 7, February 13, 1943, 3.

7. Wakida, "Through the Fire."

8. Asael T. Hansen, Weekly Report for September 29–October 5, 1944, October 6, 1944, 4, JAERR, reel 136/2, 90.

9. In comparison, in the 1940 census, about 25 percent of the adult population in the United States had completed at least high school, and about 5 percent had completed a bachelor's degree. An equivalent statistic with attendance figures was not found. Ryan and Siebens, *Educational Attainment in the United States*, 3–4.

10. "Mrs. Hashimoto Only Woman Administrator," *Heart Mountain Sentinel* 2, no. 2, January 9, 1943, 8. The entry database simply gives her occupation as "secretary," demonstrating that occupational categories may not always have revealed the full extent of a person's work situation even at a given moment.

11. "Report on Dietetic Survey: An Analysis of the Project Menu with Emphasis on the Necessity of Diet Kitchens," Heart Mountain block managers, March 20, 1943 and "Survey of Residents Requiring Special Food Preparation Dietetic Cases," n.d., folder 2008.010, RHP, HMWF.

12. Block manager meeting minutes, April 16, 1943, folder 2008.010, RHP, HMWF; "Block Mothers Complete 10-Day Training Course," *Heart Mountain Sentinel* 2, no. 29, July 17, 1943, 8; "70 Hospital Aides Receive Caps at Ceremony," *Heart Mountain Sentinel* 2, no. 32, August 7, 1943, 8.

13. (Nagamori) Ito interview, segment 1.

14. (Nakae) Uratsu interview, segment 4.

15. Oral Interview of the Ichishita Sisters, Betty, Mary, and Alice, their sister-in-law, Haru (Helen) Ichishita, and her daughter, Elaine Raine, by Paul Tsuneishi, September 26, 1997, 53, Home Games, HMWF.

16. "Twenty-Four Prep Girls Help Meet Nurses' Aide Shortage," *Heart Mountain Sentinel*, 2, no. 26, June 26, 1943, 8; Kessel, *Behind Barbed Wire*, 34.

17. Matsumoto, "Japanese American Women during World War II," 6.

18. Mrs. Seiichi Nako to David Yamakawa, July 28, 1943 and David Yamakawa to Mrs. Seiichi Nako, July 30, 1943, envelope 10, DYC, HMWF.

19. (Koga) Hironaka interview, 97.

20. McKay, *The Courage Our Stories Tell*, 90–91, 93; "Infant Feeding Unit," *Heart Mountain Sentinel* 2 no. 28, July 10, 1943, 4.

21. (Koga) Hironaka interview, 94.

22. Community activities monthly report, November 31, 1944, 1, and Community activities monthly report, March 31, 1945, 1, JAERR, reel 135/3, 9, 35.

23. Matsumoto, *City Girls*, 8.

24. Shig Yabu interview by Tom Ikeda, February 23, 2010, Segment 15, Densho Visual History Collection, https://ddr.densho.org/media/ddr-densho-1011/ddr-densho-1011-10-transcript-6d611743c5.htm.

25. (Yabe) Yasui interview, segment 8. See also "Victory Gardens to Be Grown Here," *Heart Mountain Sentinel* 2, no. 17, April 24, 1943, 8. Victory gardens were planted across the country to support food production and boost morale.

26. (Okida) Zaima interview, 640.

27. Kunio Otani interview by Alice Ito and Rebecca Walls, May 31, 1998, segment 17, Densho Visual History Collection, https://ddr.densho.org/media/ddr-densho-1000/ddr-densho-1000-75-transcript-b2cf8084b6.htm.

28. Kaneshiro interview, segment 14.

29. Community Analyst Trend Report for July 27 to September 27, 1945, September 28, 1945, 2, JAERR, reel 136/2, 275.

30. University of Michigan, General Register, 2, no. 96, 62.

31. Forrest E. LaViolette, Report of Meeting, Y.W.C.A General Panel Discussion, May 22, 1943, 1–3, JAERR, reel 136/3, 102–04.

32. LaViolette, Report of Meeting, May 22, 1943, 1–3, JAERR, reel 136/3, 102–04.

33. Sentinel Supplement Series, no. 248, November 7, 1944, 1. Emphasis original.

34. "Two Ex-Heart Mountain Girls Making Good in Philadelphia," *Heart Mountain Sentinel* 3, no. 12, March 18, 1944, 8; "Schmoe Arrives Here April 16," *Heart Mountain Sentinel* 3, no. 15, April 8, 1944, 1.

35. (Hirooka) Kunitsugu interview, 16–17, 24.

36. (Koga) Hironaka interview, 97–98.

37. Robinson, *The Unsung Great*, 62–72.

Chapter 8

1. Japanese American Internee Data File for Tamio Miyahara in Records about Japanese Americans Relocated during World War II, record group 210, NARA; WRA Evacuee Case File for Tamio Miyahara, record group 210, NARA.

2. "Citizen's short term leave statements," WRA Evacuee Case File for Tamio Miyahara, record group 210, NARA.

3. McKay, *The Courage Our Stories Tell*, 88–89. This appears to be some kind of cultural inferiority issue. The nurse had worked in Japan, seeing that people bow to each other, perhaps assuming she was being belittled when her coworkers did not bow to her. Working culture in America—despite the workers having Japanese roots—was different, however, and especially the Nisei working with White people were not accustomed to such displays of esteem. For the mothers' petitions, see Shimabukuro, *Relocating Authority*.

4. Community Analyst Trend Report for July 27 to September 27, 1945, 3, JAERR, reel 136/2, 276.

5. For the renewed heroism of resisters in opposition to no-noes, see also Lyon, *Prisons and Patriots*.

6. Summary and Report, Office of Provost Marshal General, Japanese American Section, record group 210, NARA, Washington, DC.

7. Myer, *Uprooted Americans*, 72.

8. The numbers of resisters were as follows: Tule Lake, twenty-seven; Granada (Amache), thirty-one; Minidoka, thirty-two; Poston, 106. In addition, Topaz (Arizona) had five resisters and Jerome and Rohwer (Arkansas) each had four. Poston's overall

number of resisters was larger than that of Heart Mountain, but the population was much higher, so in proportion, Heart Mountain had the highest rate. At Poston, the instigation to resist came from a single individual instead of an organization. Muller, *Free to Die for Their Country*, 4, 76; Muller, "Draft Resistance."

9. Daniels, *Concentration Camps USA*, 118; Mackey, ed., *A Matter of Conscience*, 3, 42, 130; Castelnuovo, *Soldiers of Conscience*; Okada, *No-No Boy*.

10. Mackey, *Heart Mountain*, 103, 11. Frank T. Inouye himself later argued that the purpose of the congress had been to clarify the civil rights of the Nisei, but that the FPC later took things too far. See Inouye, "Immediate Origins of the Heart Mountain Experience."

11. Emi, "Protest and Resistance," 52.

12. Statement of United States Citizen of Japanese Ancestry, February 26, 1943, Evacuee Case File for Tamio Miyahara, record group 210, NARA; Tom Oki Oral History, June 29, 1996, interview by Frank Chin and Paul Tsuneishi, 47-48, Home Games, HMWF.

13. WRA Evacuee Case File for Kiyoshi Okamoto, record group 210, NARA; Muller, "Heart Mountain Fair Play Committee.""

14. Emi interview, 306.

15. Harry W. McMillen, "FBI report on the Fair Play Committee," 2, box 7, folder 5, FSEP, HMWF.

16. Emi interview, 366–367.

17. United States v. Fujii et al. 55 F. Supp. 928 (D. Wyo. 1944). All eighty-five should have been granted parole after one year, but Heart Mountain project director Guy Robertson and WRA director Dillon S. Myer organized a denial of parole because they did not want the so-called troublemakers back at Heart Mountain. For their "good behavior," all were freed after two years, in the summer of 1946. Muller, *Free to Die for Their Country*, 172–73; Mackey, *Heart Mountain*, 117.

18. The restriction of the number of correspondents permitted to each inmate in the federal penitentiaries is alluded to in many case files, but I have not found an explicit rule setting the number.

19. Teruo Matsumoto Oral History, September 13, 1996, interview by Frank Chin and Paul Tsuneishi, 26–27, Home Games, HMWF.

20. Guntaro Kubota, interview with the FBI, no date, box 14, folder 8, FSEP, HMWF.

21. Sylvia Toshiuki biography, box 44, folder 7, FSEP, HMWF. See also Emi interview, 367.

22. Gloria Kubota interview by Frank Abe and Frank Chin, August 28, 1993, segment 5, Frank Abe Collection, https://ddr.densho.org/media/ddr-densho-122/ddr-densho-122-13-transcript-0b091a4016.htm.

23. Hayashi, *Democratizing the Enemy*, xii.

24. Kats Kunitsugu and Paul Tsuneishi interview by Frank Abe and Frank Chin, August 22, 1995, segment 8, Frank Abe Collection, https://ddr.densho.org/media/ddr-densho-122/ddr-densho-122-17-transcript-c3528ffd28.htm.

25. McMillen, "FBI report on the Fair Play Committee," 78, box 7, folder 5, FSEP, HMWF. The camp newspaper was famously opposed to the Fair Play Committee. The

paper did not write any news items on the organization—apart from the trials—but did publish two consecutive editorials denouncing the resisters. See "Editorial," *Heart Mountain Sentinel* 3, no. 11, March 11, 1944, 1 and 4; "Editorial," *Heart Mountain Sentinel* 3, no. 12, March 18, 1944, 4. For the paper's rebuttal of accusations of being the administration's mouthpiece, see "Editorial," *Heart Mountain Sentinel* 3, no. 13, March 25, 1944, 4. To the paper's credit, it published Frank Emi's letter to the editor, which defended the FPC. *Heart Mountain Sentinel* 3, no. 13, March 25, 1944, 5.

26. WRA Evacuee Case File for Kenroku Sumida, record group 210, NARA.

27. Japanese American Internee Data File, record group 210, NARA.

28. See, for example, Emi interview, 352.

29. Asato, *Teaching Mikadoism*, 109.

30. Sakauye, *Heart Mountain*, 130.

31. Emi interview, 370.

32. Report by the 13th Naval District Office, quoted in George Nozawa and Harry Ueno interview by Frank Chin and Paul Tsuneishi, July 29, 1997, 14–15, Home Games, HMWF.

33. Emi interview; McMillen, "FBI Report on the Fair Play Committee," 3, box 7, folder 5, FSEP, HMWF.

34. Memorandum from Guy Robertson to Dillon S. Myer, December 10, 1943, WRA Evacuee Case File for Kiyoshi Okamoto, record group 210, NARA.

35. Community Analyst Report for April 1944, box 7, folder 11, FSEP, HMWF.

36. WRA Evacuee Case File for Kiyoshi Okamoto, record group 210, NARA.

37. See Muller, *Free to Die for Their Country*, 82, 90. For the trials, see also, for example, Daniels, *Asian America*, 270–73.

38. Letter from Phillip M. Glick to E. G. Arnold, June 17, 1944, WRA Evacuee Case File for Frank Seishi Emi, record group 210, NARA.

39. Summary of Leave Clearance Hearing Docket, March 30, 1944, WRA Evacuee Case File for Paul Takeo Nakadate, record group 210, NARA.

40. Hearing Board for Leave Clearance, March 30, 1944, WRA Evacuee Case File for Paul Takeo Nakadate, record group 210, NARA.

41. WRA Evacuee Case File for Paul Takeo Nakadate, record group 210, NARA.

42. Kiyono (Wakaye) Tominaga interview, October 1, 1998, by Paul Tsuneishi, Frank Chin, and Mits Koshiyama, 32–34, Home Games, HMWF. See also Chin, *Born in the USA*, 405.

43. "Hearing Board for Leave Clearance" for Ben Wakaye, April 3, 1944, in McMillen, "FBI Report on the Fair Play Committee," 45, 57–58, box 7, folder 5, FSEP, HMWF.

44. Tsukuda, "The Battle Between the Nisei Veterans and the Resisters of Conscience," 169.

45. Emi interview, 370.

46. Ray Motonaga Oral History, January 12, 1999, interview by Frank Chin and Paul Tsuneishi, 53, Home Games, HMWF.

47. Satoru Tsuneishi, "Testimony for the Commission on Wartime Relocation and Internment of Civilians," Los Angeles, California, July 28, 1981, box 44, folder 7, FSEP, HMWF.

48. Tayeko Matsuura and Jane Iwanaga Oral History, October 18, 1996, interview by Frank Chin and Paul Tsuneishi, 65, Home Games, HMWF.

49. The sociologist Dorothy S. Thomas named the three inmate groups as "salvage" (early resettlers), "spoilage" (segregates, or segregees in WRA terminology), and "residue" (those staying in camps as long as possible). Thomas, Kikuchi, and Sakoda, *The Salvage*, 5.

50. Naito interview, segment 20.

51. Myer used the image of "accident of ancestry" at least twice: Myer, "Relocation Problems and Policies," March 14, 1944; "Racism and Reason," October 2, 1944; "A Message from the Director of the War Relocation Authority [to evacuees resident in relocation centers]," January 1945, DSMP, HSTPL. I have chosen to refer to the inmates segregated in Tule Lake as segregates or double segregates, although the word's usage as a noun typically relates to the field of genetics. By giving the segregates a designation of their own, I want to recognize them as a distinct group within the incarcerated Japanese American community.

52. Jimi Yamaichi interview by Tom Ikeda and Stephen S. Fugita, January 26, 2011, segment 8, Densho Visual History Collection, https://ddr.densho.org/media/ddr-densho-1000/ddr-densho-1000-312-transcript-30d1b3a9e5.htm. For a firsthand account of the tensions between Californians and Pacific Northwesterners, see Gruenewald, *Looking Like the Enemy*, especially 90–92, 105–33. See also Weglyn, *Years of Infamy*, 163–74.

53. Interestingly, the number of those who professed no religion was equal to the number of Christians. Dorothy Thomas made the same observation, attributing "agnosticism" to "Occidental pattern," i.e., assimilation. Thomas and Nishimoto, *The Spoilage*, 106.

54. Thomas, Kikuchi, and Sakoda, *The Salvage*, 135–136.

55. The sociologist Mark Granovetter suggests that especially the number of "weak" ties—contacts to employers, coworkers, or other acquaintances—are vital for the integration of ethnic minorities into a dominant society. Granovetter, "The Strength of Weak Ties." See also Giuffre, *Communities and Networks*, 88–89, 91.

56. Gruenewald, *Looking Like the Enemy*.

57. In secondary literature, the number usually ranges between 990 and 998, so the differences in numbers are inconsequential.

58. Kessel, *Behind Barbed Wire*, 34.

59. Camp Attorney Byron Ver Ploeg to WRA Solicitor Edwin E. Ferguson, October 18, 1945, 2, JAERR, reel 134/2, 23.

60. One of the two councilmen was Kiyoshi Eugene Okamoto, sent to Tule Lake during the Fair Play Committee crisis. He was not connected to the rest of the network and was the only member of his family group in the graph.

61. The FBI was said to have spelled his last name Mori, which is a more common spelling. Williams, *American Sutra*, 295.

62. Naito interview, segment 15.

63. Yamaichi interview.

64. Naito interview, segment 16.

65. Marian Asao Kurosu interview by Alice Ito and Tomoyo Yamada, July 23-24, 2000, segment 63, Densho Visual History Collection, https://ddr.densho.org/media/ddr-densho-1000/ddr-densho-1000-118-transcript-f9c855a292.htm.
66. Hoshizaki interview, segment 29; Tono interview, 6.
67. Weglyn, *Years of Infamy*, 260–62.
68. Culley, "The Santa Fe Internment Camp," 63–64.
69. Naito interview, segment 19.
70. Naito interview, segment 29.
71. Weglyn, *Years of Infamy*, 268–69.
72. Emi interview, 349.
73. See Nakagawa, "Historic Apology Marks First Step in Reconciliation between JACL and Resisters of Conscience," and Hirai, "JACL Votes to Apologize to 'Tule Lake Resisters.'"

Chapter 9

1. Suski, *My Fifty Years in America*, 42–43.
2. See, for example, A. T. Hansen to M. O. Anderson, September 22, 1944, 2, JAERR, reel 136/2, 74.
3. Thomas, Kikuchi, and Sakoda, *The Salvage*, 135–36; Spickard, *Formation and Transformations*, 129.
4. The division of self-declared religions was as follows: 55 percent Christian, 36 percent Buddhist, 2.5 percent not willing to answer, and 6.5 percent unknown.
5. Some people were allowed to return to the West Coast upon application to and individual consideration by the Western Defense Command. Therefore, the dataset contains a handful of California returnees for 1944.
6. See, for example, Dorothy (Okura) Yonemitsu interview by Joyce Nabeta Teague, September 24, 1997, REgenerations Oral History Project, 275–302, https://oac.cdlib.org/view?docId=ft0n39n5t5&brand=oac4.
7. Mackey, *Heart Mountain*, 94.
8. Reports Office, monthly report for May 1944 and monthly report for August, 1944, JAERR, reel 134/2, 103, 115. On the accusations of treating the inmates better than American soldiers, see for example, Myer, *Uprooted Americans*, 96–97.
9. War Relocation Authority, "When You Leave the Relocation Center," n.d. (probably 1943), Densho Digital Repository. There are several editions of this pamphlet, but the introduction to my copy refers to the "relocation program" as relatively recent, hence the presumed publication date.
10. Letter to David Yamakawa, December 6, 1942; Letter to David Yamakawa, January 15, 1944, folder 6, DYC, HMWF.
11. (Okida) Zaima interview, 644–647; Kunitsugu interview, 252.

12. Further investigation reveals that the Hachiyas appreciated education. A February 23, 2018 obituary for the oldest son reports that he went on to become a psychiatrist, and his younger brother is also titled "Dr.," as are four of his five children, all of whom were born after incarceration. "Obituaries, February 23, 2018."

13. For Satsuki Hachiya, see, for example, "Mouri, Hachiya to Head Prep Groups," *Heart Mountain Sentinel* 2, no. 16, April 17, 1943, 8.

14. Field Bulletin no. 7, March 1945, for the Middle Atlantic Area, Envelope 2, DYC, HMWF.

15. "Student Relocation Handbook," September 1943, Voices in Confinement: A Digital Archive of Japanese-American Internees, https://oac.cdlib.org/ark:/28722/bk0016z3r98/?brand=oac4.

16. "A Tenth of a Million People," speech by Dillon S. Myer to the Des Moines Adult Education Forum, Des Moines, Iowa, October 26, 1944, Papers of Dillon S. Myer, HSTPL, https://www.trumanlibrary.gov/library/research-files/speech-tenth-million-people-dillon-s-myer-des-moines-adult-education-forum; Thomas, Kikuchi, and Sakoda, *The Salvage*, 5.

17. See, for example, Asael T. Hansen, Weekly Report for August 25–31, 1944, September 1, 1944, 8, JAERR, reel 136/2, 71; Project attorney Byron Ver Ploeg, letter to WRA solicitor Edwin E. Ferguson, October 18, 1945, 2, JAERR, reel 134/2, 23.

18. Keen Yanagi to David Yamakawa, November 9, 1945, folder 13, DYC, HMWF.

19. ten Broek, Barnhart, and Matson, *Prejudice, War, and the Constitution*, 154, 74; Drinnon, *Keeper of Concentration Camps*, 60; Robinson, *By Order of the President*, 250. For a short but useful survey of the first years after resettlement, see Smith, "Resettlement of Japanese Americans."

20. This is closer to the gender division of the entire camp, where 53 percent were men and 47 percent women. The proportion of men to women is surprisingly close, considering that such a large number of Japanese immigrants originally were men.

21. Hansen, Community Analyst Trend Report from April 27 May 3, 1945, May 4, 1945, 1, JAERR, reel 136/2, 212.

22. David Yamakawa to Nobu Tabata, January 19, 1944, folder 6, DYC, HMWF; David Yamakawa to Ricardo Ritchie, December 14, 1945, folder 13, DYC, HMWF.

23. David Yamakawa to Merlin T. Kurtz, March 5, 1947, folder 2, DYC, HMWF.

24. Ricardo Ritchie to David Yamakawa, December 20, 1945, 2, folder 13, DYC, HMWF.

25. Bill to David Yamakawa, December 16, 1945, 2, folder 2, DYC, HMWF.

26. Boy Scout Troop 333 interviews by Frances Clymer, August 26, 2002, McCracken Research Library, Buffalo Bill Center of the West.

27. This break-up of the Japanese American community should be studied further; this can be done only in limited detail in the scope of this study. While different camps had different compositions of people and, as a result, different prewar and postwar places of residence, I believe that trends can be detected through the investigation of just one camp.

28. US Department of Commerce, Census Bureau, "Sixteenth Census of the United States: 1940, Population, Volume II: Characteristics of the Population, Part 1," 346; US Department of Commerce, Census Bureau, "A Report of the Seventeenth Decennial Census of the United States: Census of Population: 1950 Volume II: Characteristics of the Population," 100.

29. Matsushita Sperling interview.

30. Sumi Okamoto interview by Megan Asaka, April 26, 2006, segment 13, Densho Visual History Collection, https://ddr.densho.org/media/ddr-densho-1000/ddr-densho-1000-192-transcript-63995a2c05.htm; Kazue (Nabata) Yamamoto interview by Megan Asaka, June 8, 2006, segments 14 and 20, Densho Visual History Collection, https://ddr.densho.org/media/ddr-densho-1000/ddr-densho-1000-197-transcript-59d71cb81e.htm.

31. Robinson, *A Tragedy of Democracy*, 257; Weglyn, *Years of Infamy*, 276.

32. Drinnon, *Keeper of Concentration Camps*, 60; Robinson, *By Order of the President*, 250.

33. Spickard, *Formation and Transformations*, 155; Wu, *The Color of Success*, 147; Drinnon, *Keeper of Concentration Camps*.

34. Kashima, "Japanese American Internees Return," 113.

35. Weglyn, *Years of Infamy*, 267; Okihiro, *Whispered Silences*, 91; Ishizuka, *Lost & Found*, 6–8; Robinson, *A Tragedy of Democracy*, 289–90.

36. Okihiro, *Whispered Silences*, 221.

37. Okihiro, *Whispered Silences*, 94–97; Robinson, *A Tragedy of Democracy*, 291.

38. *Personal Justice Denied*, 18; Ishizuka, *Lost & Found*, xiii, 2.

Epilogue

1. On WRA self-reflection, see Anderson, Community Government Final Report, 12. On inmate viewpoint, see Community Council meeting minutes, September 14, 1943, 2, JAERR, reel 133/1, 192.

2. Sakauye interview, 363.

3. "Report of visit to Heart Mountain," November 1–4, 1942, 1, JAERR, reel 136/1, 360.

4. United States War Liquidation Agency, *People in Motion*, 11.

5. General statistics, however, also show that at least 50 percent of the initial resettlers returned to the West Coast within a few years after the war's end. To study the return migration in more detail—including an exploration of the age, educational, and occupational backgrounds of the resettlers-turned-returnees—we will have to wait for the release of the 1950 census data in 2022.

6. "Informal Discussion on Relocation between Isseis and the Relocation Team," February 2–3, 1944, 12, JAERR, reel 136/3, 39.

7. Byron Ver Ploeg to Philip M. Glick, August 24, 1944, 5, JAERR, reel 134/1, 34.

Methodological Appendix

1. There is a subtle distinction between *network* and *graph*, although they are often used interchangeably. The students of a class, for example, form a network, whereas the representation of the relationships of the students within the class is called a graph. Mathematicians also tend to distinguish between the names of the components slightly differently: in networks, they refer to nodes and links, and in graphs to vertices and edges. Outside of purely mathematical considerations, however, nodes and edges are the standard terms. Barabási, *Network Science*, section 1.3.

2. Page rank, named after Google founder Larry Page, is an algorithm most typically used to measure the importance of websites through the number of links pointing toward a particular page.

BIBLIOGRAPHY

Primary Sources

1940 United States Federal Census [database online]. Ancestry.com. Accessed April 11, 2022. https://www.ancestry.com/search/collections/2442/.

Anderson, Melford O. Heart Mountain Relocation Center Community Government Final Report. Japanese American Relocation Digital Archive. Accessed April 21, 2022. https://oac.cdlib.org/view?docId=ft0d5n98jg&brand=calisphere.

"Boy Scout Troop 333 Interviews, August 26, 2002." By Frances Clymer. 2002. McCracken Research Library, Buffalo Bill Center of the West, Cody, WY.

David Yamakawa Collection. Heart Mountain Wyoming Foundation, Powell, WY.

Densho Visual History Collection. Densho Digital Repository. Accessed April 21, 2022. https://ddr.densho.org/ddr-densho-1000/.

Executive Order 9066, February 19, 1942. General Records of the Unites States Government; RG 11. NARA. Accessed April 22, 2022. https://www.archives.gov/milestone-documents/executive-order-9066.

Emi, Frank S. "Frank S. Emi Interview, March 11, 1993 and February 20, 1994." By Alan Koch. *Japanese American World War II Evacuation Oral History Project*. Munich: K. G. Saur, 1995. http://www.oac.cdlib.org/view?docId=ft1f59n-61r&brand=oac4&doc.view=entire_text.

Final Accountability Rosters of Evacuees, 1942–1946. Heart Mountain & Tule Lake. PDF document of Microfilm Publication M1865. NARA, College Park, MD.

"Finding Aid for the Ryoichi Fujii Papers, 1919-1999." Online Archive of California. Accessed April 12, 2022. https://oac.cdlib.org/findaid/ark:/13030/kt6v19q42b/.

Frank Abe Collection. Densho Digital Repository. Accessed April 21, 2022. https://ddr.densho.org/ddr-densho-122/.

Frank S. Emi Papers. Heart Mountain Wyoming Foundation, Powell, WY. Heart Mountain Relocation Center Collection, MS 396. McCracken Research Library, Buffalo Bill Center of the West, Cody, WY.

Heart Mountain Relocation Center Records. American Heritage Center, University of Wyoming, Laramie, WY. Accessed April 21, 2022. https://digitalcollections.uwyo.edu/luna/servlet.

Heart Mountain Sentinel Collection. Densho Digital Repository. Accessed April 21, 2022. https://ddr.densho.org/ddr-densho-97/.

Home Games: An Oral and Documentary History of the Japanese American Resistance at Heart Mountain. Recorded by Paul Tsuneishi and Frank Chin. Heart Mountain Wyoming Foundation, Powell, WY.

Japanese American Evacuation and Resettlement Records, 1930–1974, BANC MSS 67/14c, reels 133–136. Bancroft Library, Berkeley, CA. Also available at Online Archive of California. Accessed April 21, 2022. https://oac.cdlib.org/findaid/ark:/13030/tf5j49n8kh/.

Japanese American Internee Data File, 1942–1946, Records about Japanese Americans Relocated during World War II, created 1988–1989, documenting the period 1942–1946. Record group 210. Records of the War Relocation Authority. NARA, College Park, MD.

Japanese American Museum of San Jose Collection. Densho Digital Repository. Accessed April 21, 2022. https://ddr.densho.org/ddr-jamsj-2/.

Manzanar National Historic Site Collection. Densho Digital Repository. Accessed April 21, 2022. https://ddr.densho.org/ddr-manz-1/.

Nakaki, George Hidenobu. Community Government—Evacuee Viewpoint: Final Report. 1945. Japanese American Relocation Digital Archive. Accessed April 21, 2022. https://oac.cdlib.org/ark:/28722/bk000404k0f/?brand=oac4.

O'Mara, T. J. Heart Mountain Relocation Center Community Activities Section Final Report. 1945. Japanese American Relocation Digital Archive. Accessed April 21, 2022. http://www.oac.cdlib.org/view?docId=bk-000404j5p&brand=oac4&chunk.id=meta&NAAN=28722.

Oral History Collection 1998–2012, MS 201. McCracken Research Library, Buffalo Bill Center of the West, Cody, WY.

"Oregon, U.S., Death Index, 1898–2008." Ancestry.com. Accessed April 21, 2022. https://www.ancestry.com/search/collections/5254/. Original data: State of Oregon. Oregon Death Index, 1903–1998. Oregon State Archives and Records Center. Oregon Death Indexes, 1903–1970 and 1971–2008. Oregon State Library, Salem, OR.

REgenerations Oral History Project: Rebuilding Japanese American Families, Communities, and Civil Rights in the Resettlement Era. Vol. 2: Los Angeles Region. Japanese American National Museum/Online Archive of California. Accessed April 21, 2022. https://calisphere.org/item/ark:/13030/ft358003z1/

REgenerations Oral History Project: Rebuilding Japanese American Families, Communities, and Civil Rights in the Resettlement Era. Volume 3: San Diego Region. Japanese American National Museum/Online Archive of California. Accessed April 21, 2022. https://calisphere.org/item/ark:/13030/ft0n39n5t5/.

Robertson, Guy. Heart Mountain Relocation Center Project Management Division, Project Director Final Report. 1945. Japanese American Relocation Digital Archive. Accessed April 21, 2022. https://oac.cdlib.org/ark:/13030/ft5n39n93s/?brand=oac4.

Ruth Hashimoto Papers. Heart Mountain Wyoming Foundation, Powell, WY.

Sakauye, Eiichi. *Heart Mountain: A Photo Essay.* San Mateo, CA: AACP, 2000.

Silver, W. R. Letter to Nels H. Smith, December 15, 1941. Box 3, folder 4. Nels H. Smith Papers. University of Wyoming, American Heritage Center. Accessed April 21, 2022. https://digitalcollections.uwyo.edu/luna/servlet/uwydbuwy~52~52.

"Student Relocation Handbook," September 1943. Voices in Confinement: A Digital Archive of Japanese-American Internees. Accessed April 20, 2022, https://oac.cdlib.org/ark:/28722/bk0016z3r98/?brand=oac4.

Suski, P. M. *My Fifty Years in America*. Hollywood: Hawley Publications, 1990 (orig. pub. 1960).

The Michigan Alumnus. Vol. 45, *October 8, 1938 to September 16, 1939 Including Quarterly Review Numbers*. Ann Arbor, MI: The Alumni Association of the University of Michigan, 1938–1939. https://books.google.fi/books/about/The_Michigan_Alumnus.html?id=ACNYAAAAMAAJ&redir_esc=y.

"The War Relocation Authority and the Incarceration of Japanese Americans During World War II Research File." Papers of Philleo Nash and Papers of Dillon S. Myer. HSTPL, Independence, MO. https://www.trumanlibrary.gov/library/online-collections/war-relocation-authority-and-incarceration-of-japanese-americans.

Tono, Jack Kyoto. "Oral History Interview of Jack Tono, September 15, 2000." By unknown interviewer. Heart Mountain Wyoming Foundation, Powell, WY.

University of Michigan Official Publication. Vol. 43, no. 20, *School of Nursing*. Ann Arbor, MI: University of Michigan, 1941. https://books.google.fi/books?id=oZefAAAAMAAJ&dq=university+of+michigan+official+publication+vol.+43&source=gbs_navlinks_s.

University of Michigan Official Publication 47, no. 96, General Register Issue. Ann Arbor, MI: University of Michigan. https://books.google.fi/books?id=5pafAAAAMAAJ&dq=asa+munekiyo&source=gbs_navlinks_s.

"U.S., School Yearbooks, 1900–1999." Ancestry.com. https://www.ancestry.com/search/collections/1265/. Accessed April 11, 2022. Original data: various school yearbooks from across the United States.

"U.S., World War I Draft Registration Cards, 1917–1918." Ancestry.com. Accessed April 21, 2022. https://www.ancestry.com/search/collections/6482/. Original data: United States, Selective Service System. World War I Selective Service System Draft Registration Cards, 1917–1918. M1509, 4,582 rolls. NARA, Washington, DC.

War Relocation Authority Evacuee Case Files. Record Group 210. Records of the War Relocation Authority. NARA, College Park, MD.

War Relocation Authority Photographs of Japanese-American Evacuation and Resettlement. Online Archive of California. Accessed April 22, 2022. http://www.oac.cdlib.org/findaid/ark:/13030/tf596nb4h0/?&brand=oac4.

"Washington, U.S., Arriving and Departing Passenger and Crew Lists, 1882–1965." Ancestry.com. Accessed April 21, 2022. https://www.ancestry.com/search/collections/8945/. Original data: Selected Passenger and Crew Lists and Manifests. NARA, Washington, DC.

"When You Leave the Relocation Center." CSU Sacramento Japanese American Archival Collection, Densho Digital Repository. Accessed April 20, 2022, https://ddr.densho.org/ddr-csujad-55-792/.

Japanese American Museum of Oregon Visual History Collection. Densho Digital Repository. Accessed April 21, 2022. https://ddr.densho.org/ddr-one-7/.

Twin Cities JACL Collection. Densho Digital Repository. Accessed April 21, 2022. https://ddr.densho.org/ddr-densho-1014/

REgenerations Oral History Project: Rebuilding Japanese American Families, Communities, and Civil Rights in the Resettlement Era. Vol. 4: San Jose Region. Accessed April 21, 2022. https://calisphere.org/item/ark:/13030/ft600006bb/.

Secondary Sources

Asato, Noriko. *Teaching Mikadoism: The Attack on Japanese Language Schools in Hawaii, California, and Washington, 1919–1927*. Honolulu: University of Hawaii Press, 2006.

Austin, Allan W. *From Concentration Camp to Campus: Japanese American Students and World War II*. Urbana: University of Illinois Press, 2004.

Barabási, Albert-László. *Network Science*. 2012. http://networksciencebook.com.

Bastian, Mathieu, Sebastien Heymann, and Mathieu Jacomy. "Gephi: An Open Source Software for Exploring and Manipulating Networks." Paper presented at International AAAI Conference on Weblogs and Social Media, San Jose, California, May 17, 2009.

Carley, Kathleen M. "Dynamic Network Analysis." In *Dynamic Social Network Modeling and Analysis: Workshop Summary and Papers*, edited by Kathleen Carley and Philippa Pattison, 133–45. Washington, DC: The National Academies Press, 2003.

Castelnuovo, Shirley. *Soldiers of Conscience: Japanese American Military Resisters in World War II*. Lincoln, NE: Bison Books, 2010.

Chin, Frank. *Born in the USA: A Story of Japanese America, 1889–1947*. Lanham, MD: Rowman & Littlefield, 2002.

Crost, Lyn. *Honor by Fire: Japanese Americans at War in Europe and the Pacific*. Novato, CA: Presidio Press, 1994.

Culley, John J. "The Santa Fe Internment Camp and the Justice Department Program for Enemy Aliens." In *Japanese Americans: From Relocation to Redress*, edited by Roger Daniels, Sandra C. Taylor and Harry H. L. Kitano, 55–71. Seattle: University of Washington Press, 1991.

Daniels, Roger. *Asian America: Chinese and Japanese in the United States since 1850*. Seattle: University of Washington Press, 1988.

———. *Concentration Camps USA: Japanese Americans and World War II*. New York: Holt, Rinehart and Winston, Inc., 1971.

———. "Introduction: Heart Mountain—after Sixty Years." In *A Matter of Conscience: Essays on the World War II Heart Mountain Draft Resistance Movement*, edited by Mike Mackey, 1–7. Powell, WY: Western History Publications, 2001.

———. *The Politics of Prejudice: The Anti-Japanese Movement in California and the Struggle for Japanese Exclusion*. Berkeley: University of California Press, 1962.

Deckrow, Andre Kobayashi. "A Community Erased: Japanese Americans in El Monte and the Greater San Gabriel Valley." In *East of East: The Making of Greater El Monte*, edited by Romeo Guzmán, Caribbean Fragoza, Alex Sayf Cummings, and Ryan Reft, 174–84. New Brunswick, NJ: Rutgers University Press, 2020.

Dempster, Brian Komei. *Making Home from War: Stories of Japanese American Exile and Resettlement*. Berkeley: Heyday, 2011.

Densho: The Japanese American Legacy Project. Accessed April 21, 2022. http://www.densho.org.

Densho. "Terminology." Accessed May 4, 2018. https://densho.org/terminology/.

Drinnon, Richard. *Keeper of Concentration Camps: Dillon S. Myer and American Racism*. Berkeley: University of California Press, 1987.

Ehrlich, Gretel. *Heart Mountain*. New York: Viking Penguin Inc., 1988.

Emi, Frank S. "Protest and Resistance: An American Tradition." In *A Matter of Conscience: Essays on the World War II Heart Mountain Draft Resistance Movement*, edited by Mike Mackey, 51–61. Powell, WY: Western History Publications, 2002.

Emirbayer, Mustafa, and Jeff Goodwin. "Network Analysis, Culture, and the Problem of Agency." *American Journal of Sociology* 99, no. 6 (1994): 1411–54. https://doi.org/10.1086/230450.

Freeman, Linton C. "The Development of Social Network Analysis—with an Emphasis on Recent Events." In *The Sage Handbook of Social Network Analysis*. Thousand Oaks: SAGE Publications, 2011.

French, John R. P., and Bertram Raven. "The Bases of Social Power." In *Studies in Social Power*, edited by D. Cartwright, 150–167. Ann Arbor, MI: Institute for Social Research, 1959.

Fuchs, Lawrence H. *The American Kaleidoscope: Race, Ethnicity, and the Civic Culture*. Hanover, NH: Wesleyan University Press, 1990.

Fugita, Stephen S., and Marilyn Fernandez. "Religion and Japanese Americans' Views of Their World War II Incarceration." *Journal of Asian American Studies* 5, no. 2 (2002): 113–37.

Fujita-Rony, Thomas Y. "Remaking the 'Home Front' in World War II: Japanese American Women's Work and the Colorado River Relocation Center." *Southern California Quarterly* 88, no. 2 (2006): 161–204.

Gardiner, Clinton Harvey. *Pawns in a Triangle of Hate: The Peruvian Japanese and the United States*. Seattle: University of Washington Press, 1981.

Geneva Convention relative to the Protection of Civilian Persons in Time of War, 12 August 1949, Accessed April 5, 2022. https://www.un.org/en/genocideprevention/documents/atrocity-crimes/Doc.33_GC-IV-EN.pdf.

Giuffre, Katherine. *Communities and Networks: Using Social Network Analysis to Rethink Urban and Community Studies.* Cambridge: Polity, 2013.

Gordon, Milton M. "Assimilation in America." In *Forging the American Character. Reading in the United States History since 1877*, edited by John R. M. Wilson. Englewood Cliffs, NJ: Prentice Hall, Inc., 1991.

Gordon, Milton M. *Assimilation in American Life: The Role of Race, Religion, and National Origins.* New York: Oxford University Press, 1964.

Granovetter, Mark. "The Strength of Weak Ties: A Network Theory Revisited." *Sociological Theory*, no. 1 (1983): 201–33.

Greve, Arent, and Janet W. Salaff. "Social Network Approach to Understand the Ethnic Economy: A Theoretical Discourse." GeoJournal, no. 64 (2005): 7–16.

Gruenewald, Mary Matsuda. *Looking Like the Enemy: My Story of Imprisonment in Japanese American Internment Camps.* Troutdale: NewSage Press, 2005.

Guiliano, Jennifer, and Mia Ridge. "The Future of Digital Methods for Complex Datasets: An Introduction." *International Journal of Humanities and Arts Computing* 10, no. 1 (2016): 1–7.

Hayashi, Brian Masaru. *Democratizing the Enemy: The Japanese American Internment.* Princeton: Princeton University Press, 2004.

Hinnershitz, Stephanie. *Japanese American Incarceration: The Camps and Coerced Labor During World War II.* Philadelphia: University of Pennsylvania Press, 2021.

Hirai, Tomo. "JACL Votes to Apologize to 'Tule Lake Resisters.'" *Nichi Bei*, August 29, 2019. https://www.nichibei.org/2019/08/jacl-votes-to-apologize-to-tule-lake-resisters/.

Houston, Jeanne Wakatsuki, and James D. Houston. *Farewell to Manzanar.* New York: Dell Laurel-Leaf, 1973.

Hoxie, Frederick E. *A Final Promise: The Campaign to Assimilate the Indians, 1880–1920.* Lincoln: University of Nebraska Press, 1992.

Inouye, Frank T. "Immediate Origins of the Heart Mountain Draft Resistance Movement." In *Remembering Heart Mountain: Essays on Japanese American Internment in Wyoming*, edited by Mike Mackey, 121–31. Powell, WY: Western History Publications, 1998.

Inouye, Frank T. "Immediate Origins of the Heart Mountain Experience." *Peace & Change* 23, no. 2 (1998): 148–66. https://doi.org/https://doi.org/10.1111/0149-0508.00078.

Ishigo, Estelle. *Lone Heart Mountain.* Los Angeles, 1972.

Ishizuka, Karen L. *Lost & Found: Reclaiming the Japanese American Incarceration.* Chicago: University of Illinois Press, 2006.

———. "What's in a Word? History, Violence, and Erasure When the Words are 'Japanese Internment' and 'Muslim Registry.'" *Rewire*, November 22, 2016. https://rewire.news/article/2016/11/22/word-history-japanese-internment/.

Ito, Leslie A. "Japanese American Women and the Student Relocation Movement, 1942–1950. *Frontiers: A Journal of Women's Studies* 21, no. 3 (2000): 1–24.
Kamp-Whittaker, April. "Diaspora and Social Networks in a World War II Japanese American Incarceration Center." *International Journal of Historical Archaeology* 25 (2020): 828–50.
Kashima, Tetsuden. "Japanese American Internees Return, 1945 to 1955: Readjustment and Social Amnesia." *PHYLON: The Atlanta University Review of Race and Culture* 41, no. 2 (1980): 107–15.
Kekki, Saara. "Entangled Histories of Assimilation: Dillon S. Myer and the Relocation of Japanese Americans and Native Americans, 1942–1953." *American Studies in Scandinavia* 51, no. 2 (2019): 25–48.
———. "Japanese American Internment: Spectacularization, Americanization, and the Model Minority Myth." Master's thesis, University of Helsinki, 2009.
———. "Life at Heart Mountain: A Dynamic Network Model of a Japanese American Incarceration Camp." PhD diss., University of Helsinki, 2019.
Kessel, Velma Berryman. *Behind Barbed Wire: Heart Mountain Relocation Camp*. Casper: Mountain States Lithographing, 1992.
Kitano, Harry H. L. *Japanese Americans: The Evolution of a Subculture*. Prentice Hall Ethnic Groups in American Life. 2nd ed. Englewood Cliffs, NJ: Prentice Hall, Inc., 1976.
Kivelä, Mikko, Alex Arenas, Marc Barthelemy, James P. Gleeson, Yamir Moreno, and Mason A. Porter. "Multilayer Networks." *Journal of Complex Networks* 2, no. 3 (2014): 203–71. https://doi.org/10.1093/comnet/cnu016.
Knox, Hannah, Mike Savage, and Penny Harvey. "Social Networks and the Study of Relations: Networks as Method, Metaphor and Form." *Economy and Society* 35, no. 1 (2006): 113–40. https://doi.org/10.1080/03085140500465899.
Kurashige, Lon. "Unexpected Views of the Internment." In *Colors of Confinement: Rare Kodachrome Photographs of Japanese American Incarceration in World War II*. Edited by Eric L. Muller, with photographs by Bill Manbo. Chapel Hill: University of North Carolina Press, 2012.
Lau, Chrissy Yee. "Japanese Immigrant Gambling in Early 20th-Century California." *Oxford Research Encyclopedia of American History* (2019). Accessed April 22, 2022. https://oxfordre.com/americanhistory/.
LaViolette, Forrest E. "The American-Born Japanese and the World Crisis." *The Canadian Journal of Economics and Political Science* 7, no. 4 (1941): 517–27.
———. *Americans of Japanese Ancestry*. The Asian Experience in North America: Chinese and Japanese. New York: Arno Press, 1978.
"Life in the Camp." Heart Mountain Interpretive Center. Accessed April 22, 2022. https://www.heartmountain.org/history/life-in-the-camp/.
Lyon, Cherstin M. *Prisons and Patriots: Japanese American Wartime Citizenship, Civil Disobedience, and Historical Memory*. Philadelphia: Temple University Press, 2011.
Mackey, Mike. *Heart Mountain: Life in Wyoming's Concentration Camp*. 2nd ed. Powell, WY: Western History Publications, 2008.

———. *A Matter of Conscience: Essays on the World War II Heart Mountain Draft Resistance Movement*. Powell, WY: Western History Publications, 2002.

Mäkelä, Eetu. "Humanities/Social Sciences: Computing Interaction." Paper presented at the Heldig Humanities Forum, University of Helsinki, Finland, March 16, 2018.

Matsumoto, Valerie J. *City Girls: The Nisei Social World in Los Angeles, 1920–1950*. New York: Oxford University Press, 2014.

———. "Desperately Seeking 'Deirdre': Gender Roles, Multicultural Relations, and Nisei Women Writers of the 1930s." *Frontiers: A Journal of Women Studies* 12, no. 1 (1991): 19–32. https://doi.org/10.2307/3346573.

———. "Japanese American Women During World War II." *Frontiers: A Journal of Women Studies* 8, no. 1 (1984): 6–14. https://doi.org/10.2307/3346082.

McKay, Susan. *The Courage Our Stories Tell: The Daily Lives and Maternal Child Health Care of Japanese American Women at Heart Mountain*. Powell, WY: Western History Publications, 2002.

Moore, Brenda L. *Serving Our Country: Japanese American Women in the Military during World War II*. New Brunswick, NJ: Rutgers University Press, 2003.

Morrissey, Robert Michael. "Archives of Connection." *Historical Methods: A Journal of Quantitative and Interdisciplinary History* 48, no. 2 (2015): 67–79.

Muller, Eric L. *American Inquisition: The Hunt for Japanese American Disloyalty in World War II*. Chapel Hill: University of North Carolina Press, 2007.

———. "Draft Resistance." Densho Encyclopedia. Updated August 24, 2020. http://encyclopedia.densho.org/Draft%20resistance/.

———. *Free to Die for Their Country: The Story of the Japanese American Draft Resisters in World War II*. Chicago: University of Chicago Press, 2003.

———. "Heart Mountain Fair Play Committee." Densho Encyclopedia. Updated July 2, 2020. http://encyclopedia.densho.org/Heart_Mountain_Fair_Play_Committee/.

———. "Of Coercion and Accommodation: Looking at Japanese American Imprisonment through a Law Office Window." *Law and History Review* 35, no. 2 (2017): 277–319.

Munson, Curtis B. *Report on Japanese on the West Coast of the United States*. Washington, DC: Government Printing Office, 1946.

Myer, Dillon S. *Uprooted Americans. The Japanese Americans and the War Relocation Authority During World War II*. Tucson: University of Arizona Press, 1972.

Nakagawa, Martha. "Historic Apology Marks First Step in Reconciliation between JACL and Resisters of Conscience." Resisters.com: Japanese American Resistance to Wartime Incarceration. Updated May 17–June 6, 2002. https://resisters.com/conscience-and-the-constitution/jacl/the-jacl-apology-to-the-heart-mountain-resisters/historic-apology-marks-first-step-in-reconciliation-between-jacl-and-resisters-of-conscience/.

Nakamura, Kelli Y. "Military Intelligence Service Language School." Densho Encyclopedia. Updated October 16, 2020. http://encyclopedia.densho.org/Military_Intelligence_Service_Language_School/.

Nakano, Mei T. *Japanese American Women: Three Generations, 1890–1990*. San Francisco: National Japanese American Historical Society and Mina Press, 1990.
National JACL Power of Words Committee. *Power of Words Handbook: A Guide to Language About Japanese Americans in World War II. Understanding Euphemism and Preferred Terminology*. San Francisco: Japanese American Citizens League, 2013.
Nelson, Douglas W. *Heart Mountain: The History of an American Concentration Camp*. Madison: State Historical Society of Wisconsin for the Dept. of History, University of Wisconsin, 1976.
Ngai, Mae M. *Impossible Subjects: Illegal Aliens and the Making of Modern America*. Princeton and Oxford: Princeton University Press, 2004.
Niiya, Brian. "Navy Japanese Language School." Densho Encyclopedia Updated July 20, 2016. http://encyclopedia.densho.org/Navy%20Japanese%20Language%20School/.
Okada, John. *No-No Boy*. Seattle: University of Washington Press, 2014.
Okihiro, Gary Y. *Whispered Silences: Japanese Americans and World War II*. Seattle: University of Washington Press, 1996.
Oppenheim, Joanne, ed. *Stanley Hayami, Nisei Son: His Diary, Letters, & Story from an American Concentration Camp to Battlefield, 1942–1945*. New York: Brick Tower Press, 2008.
Padgett, John F., and Christopher K. Ansell. "Robust Action and the Rise of the Medici, 1400–1434." *American Journal of Sociology* 98, no. 6 (1993): 1259–319.
Personal Justice Denied: Report of the Commission on Wartime Relocation and Internment of Civilians. Seattle: University of Washington Press, 1997.
Rhodes, Leara. *The Ethnic Press: Shaping the American Dream*. New York: Peter Lang, 2010.
Robinson, Greg. *After Camp: Portraits in Midcentury Japanese American Life and Politics*. Berkeley: University of California Press, 2012.
———. *By Order of the President: FDR and the Internment of Japanese Americans*. Cambridge: Harvard University Press, 2001.
———. *A Tragedy of Democracy: Japanese Confinement in North America*. New York: Columbia University Press, 2009.
———. *The Unsung Great: Stories of Extraordinary Japanese Americans*. Seattle: University of Washington Press, 2020.
Robinson, Thelma M. *Nisei Cadet Nurse of World War II: Patriotism in Spite of Prejudice*. Boulder: Black Swan Mill Press, 2005.
Roper & Sons. "Obituaries, February 23, 2018." Updated February 23, 2018. http://www.roperandsons.com.
Russell, Dakota. "Arthur and Estelle Ishigo: A Heart Mountain Love Story." *Kokoro Kara*, Autumn (2017): 7–9.
Ryan, Camille L., and Julie Siebens. *Educational Attainment in the United States: 2009: Population Characteristics*. United States Census Bureau (2012). Updated

October 8, 2021. https://www.census.gov/library/publications/2012/demo/p20-566.html.

Salins, Peter D. *Assimilation, American Style*. New York: BasicBooks, 1997.

Scott, John. *What Is Social Network Analysis?* London: Bloomsbury Academic, 2012.

Shimabukuro, Mira. *Relocating Authority: Japanese Americans Writing to Redress Mass Incarceration*. Boulder: University Press of Colorado, 2016.

Smith, Elmer R. "Resettlement of Japanese Americans." *Far Eastern Survey* 18, no. 10 (1949): 117–118.

Sone, Monica. *Nisei Daughter*. Seattle: University of Washington Press, 2002, orig. pub. 1953.

Sowell, Thomas. *Ethnic America: A History*. New York: Basic Books, 1981.

Spickard, Paul. *Almost All Aliens: Immigration, Race, and Colonialism in American History and Identity*. New York: Routledge, 2007.

———. *Japanese Americans: The Formation and Transformations of an Ethnic Group*. Revised ed. New Brunswick, NJ: Rutgers University Press, 2008.

———. "The Nisei Assume Power: The Japanese American Citizens League, 1941–1942." *Pacific Historical Review* 52, no. 2 (1983): 147–74.

Spickard, Paul, and Blackie Najima. "Not Just the Quiet People: The Nisei Underclass." *Pacific Historical Review* 68, no. 1 (1999): 78–94.

Starn, Orin. "Engineering Internment: Anthropologists and the War Relocation Authority." *American Ethnologist* 13, no. 4 (1986): 700–20.

Sunahara, Ann Gomer. *The Politics of Racism: The Uprooting of Japanese Canadians During the Second World War*. Toronto: James Lorimer Limited, Publishers, 1981.

Takaki, Ronald. *A Different Mirror: A History of Multicultural America*. Boston: Little, Brown, and Company, 1993.

Takaki, Ronald. *Strangers from a Different Shore: A History of Asian Americans*. New York: The Penguin Group, 1990.

Tamura, Linda. *Nisei Soldiers Break Their Silence: Coming Home to Hood River*. Seattle: University of Washington Press, 2012.

ten Broek, Jacobus, Edward N. Barnhart, and Floyd W. Matson. *Prejudice, War, and the Constitution*. Berkeley: University of California Press, 1958.

Thomas, Dorothy Swaine, Charles Kikuchi, and James Minoru Sakoda. *The Salvage*. Berkeley: University of California Press, 1952.

Thomas, Dorothy Swaine, and Richard S. Nishimoto. *The Spoilage*. Berkeley: University of California Press, 1946.

Tsuda, Takeyuki. *Japanese American Ethnicity: In Search of Heritage and Homeland across Generations*. New York: NYU Press, 2016.

Tsukuda, George. "The Battle between the Nisei Veterans and the Resisters of Conscience." In *A Matter of Conscience: Essays on the World War II Heart Mountain Draft Resistance Movement*, edited by Mike Mackey, 153–74. Powell, WY: Western History Publications, 2002.

US Department of Commerce, Census Bureau. "The '72-Year Rule.'" Updated January 26, 2022. https://www.census.gov/history/www/genealogy/decennial_census_records/the_72_year_rule_1.html#:~:text=April%202%2C%202012.,collected%20for%20the%20decennial%20census.

US Department of Commerce, Census Bureau. "A Report of the Seventeenth Decennial Census of the United States: Census of Population: 1950 Volume II: Characteristics of the Population." Washington, DC: Government Printing Office, 1952.

US Department of Commerce, Census Bureau. "Sixteenth Census of the United States: 1940, Population, Volume II: Characteristics of the Population, Part 1." Washington, DC: Government Printing Office, 1942.

US Department of Commerce, Census Bureau. "Thirteenth Census of the United States Taken in the Year 1910, Vol. II, Population 1910." Washington, DC: Government Printing Office, 1913.

US Department of the Interior. Bureau of Reclamation "About Us." . Updated January 7, 2020. http://www.usbr.gov/main/about.

US Department of the Interior, Census Office. "Statistics of the Population of the United States at the Tenth Census, June 1, 1880." Washington, DC: Government Printing Office, 1882.

Uchida, Yoshiko. *Desert Exile: The Uprooting of a Japanese-American Family*. Seattle: University of Washington Press, 1982.

Ukai, Nancy. "Nameplates." 50 Objects/Stories. Accessed November 25, 2021. https://50objects.org/object/nameplates/?fbclid=IwAR39nOyJKHnPRgk8M4QexB7XYEzvz_ylQWR_kjGjx3d6mAmg1Chjod87YQ.

United States v. Fujii, 55 F. Supp. 928 (D. Wyo. 1944). Accessed April 19, 2022. https://law.justia.com/cases/federal/district-courts/FSupp/55/928/2312600/

United States War Liquidation Agency. *People in Motion: The Postwar Adjustment of the Evacuated Japanese Americans*. Washington, DC: Government Printing Office, 1947.

Wakida, Patricia. "Through the Fire: Louise Suski." Discover Nikkei. April 23, 2013. http://www.discovernikkei.org/en/journal/2013/4/23/louise-suski/.

Wang, Joan S. "The Double Burdens of Immigrant Nationalism: The Relationship between Chinese and Japanese in the American West, 1880s-1920s." *Journal of American Ethnic History* 27, no. 2 (2008): 28–58.

War Relocation Authority. *Administrative Highlights of the War Program*. Washington, DC: Government Printing Office, 1946.

War Relocation Authority. *Community Government in War Relocation Centers*. Washington, DC: Government Printing Office, 1946.

War Relocation Authority. *Wartime Exile: The Exclusion of the Japanese Americans from the West Coast*. Washington, DC: Government Printing Office, 1946.

"Washington's Farewell Address in 1796." Goldman Law Library. Yale Law School. Accessed May 8, 2018. http://avalon.law.yale.edu/18th_century/washing.asp.

Weglyn, Michi Nishiura. *Years of Infamy: The Untold Story of America's Concentration Camps*. New York: Morrow, 1976.

Wellman, Barry, and Charles Wetherell. "Social Network Analysis of Historical Communities: Some Questions from the Present to the Past." *The History of the Family, An International Quarterly* 1, no. 1 (1996): 97–121.

Wetherell, Charles. "Historical Social Network Analysis." *International Review of Social History* 43, supplement S6 (1998): 125–44.

Williams, Duncan Ryuken. *American Sutra: A Story of Faith and Freedom in the Second World War*. Cambridge: Harvard University Press, 2019.

Wu, Ellen D. *The Color of Success: Asian Americans and the Origins of the Model Minority*. Princeton, NJ: Princeton University Press, 2015.

Yamaguchi, Precious. *Experiences of Japanese American Women during and after World War II: Living in Internment Camps and Rebuilding Lives Afterwards*. Lanham, MD: Lexington Books, 2014.

Yang, Andrew. "We Asian Americans Are Not the Virus, but We Can Be Part of the Cure." *The Washington Post*, April 1, 2020. https://www.washingtonpost.com/opinions/2020/04/01/andrew-yang-coronavirus-discrimination/.

Yogi, Stan. "Japanese American Literature." In *An Interethnic Companion to Asian American Literature*, edited by King-Kok Cheung, 125–155. New York: Cambridge University Press, 1997.

Yoo, David. *Growing up Nisei: Race, Generation, and Culture among Japanese Americans of California, 1924–49*. Urbana: University of Illinois Press, 2000.

INDEX

References to illustrations appear in italic type.

Abe, Yukio, 133; as a bridge, 93. *See also* Fair Play Committee (FPC)
activities in camp, 37, 40, 41, 48, 65–66, 71, 73–79, 113–14, 169, 191n22
Agricultural Committee, 48, 53, 142
Akizuki, Chitoshi, 79
Albert, Réka, 3
alien land laws, 20, 154. *See also* land ownership
aliens ineligible for citizenship, 20
American Association of University Women, 69, 106, 117
American Civil Liberties Union (ACLU). *See* Fair Play Committee (FPC)
Americanization. *See* assimilationism
Ansell, Christopher K., 4
anthropologists in incarceration camps. *See* community analysts
Aoyama, Betty, 34, 57. *See also* block managers
Asao, Marian. *See* Kurasu, Marian Asao
Asato, Noriko, 131
assault. *See* crimes among inmates
assembly centers, 26, *27*, 31, 33, 52
assimilationism, 9–10, 14, 17, 21, 29, 71
Attorney's Office, 68

baishakunin ("go-between," "matchmaker"), 15, 81–82. *See also* family
Barabási, Albert-László, 3

Bepp, Yoneo, 61. *See also* cooperative disputes
betweenness centrality. *See* centrality
Bismarck internment camp. *See* internment camps
block clerks, 41, 110, 117
block clubs, 40–41, 75, 78, 114, 131, 133–34
block managers, 34, 41, 46–47, 54, 56–63, 85, 88–89, 108–9, 132, 167, 186n8, 188n15, 188n17
bridge, 5, 34, 40–41, 69, 91–94, 133–35, 142, 168, 172
Buddhists. *See* religious denominations
Bureau of Indian Affairs, 25, 181n20

California, state of, 17, 19–20, 23, 26, 52, 80, 106; Japanese Californians, 15, 31, 34–36, 42–43, 131, 137, 140–41, 159, 198n52; return and resettlement to, 12, 148, *149*, 154, *160–62*, 169, 199n5
camp administration, 9, 12, 30, 32, 34, 57, 60, 88–89, 138, 154, 158, 170, 189n23, 196n17. *See also* War Relocation Authority (WRA)
camp closure, 53–54, 91, 157
Camp Savage, Minn., 84, 191n37. *See also* Japanese language schools: for soldiers
Carroll, W. J., 138
Castelnuovo, Shirley, 124
Catholics. *See* religious denominations
centrality: betweenness, 5, *38*, 91–92, 172, 177; closeness, 172; degree, 5, 9, 41–42,

215

centrality: betweenness (continued) 50–52, 86–87, 90, 94, 101, 104, 171–72, 174; eigenvector, 172
Chicago, Ill., 89, 121, 146, 152, 154, 159, 161, 163
children's networks, 8
Civil Liberties Act of 1987, 2. *See also* redress
Cleveland, Ohio, 119, 146, 154, 158, 161, 170
closeness. *See* centrality
Cody, Wyo., 31, 154, 158. *See also* relations to the outside
Commission on Wartime Relocation and Internment of Civilians (CWRIC), 165. *See also* redress
Community Activities Board, 47–48, 59, 86
Community Activities Section, 40, 48, 65–67, 71, 75, 79, 82–83, 92–93, 95, 99, 106–7, 111–14, 117, 143, 152, 155, 157–58, 168, 180n16, 191n22
community analysts, 25, 36, 54, 66, 87, 107, 117, 126, 135, 141, 182n7, 189n23
community council, 2, 33–34, 40, 41, 46–48, 49, 51–54, 56–59, 61, 63–64, 85–88, 93, 98, 107–8, 138, 142, 170, 173–74, 188n17
Community Enterprises Advisory Council, 49
Community Enterprises Board of Trustees, 48, 170
Community Enterprises Liquidation Committee, 47–48
Community Enterprises Section, 33, 40, 53, 55, 60–62, 62, 64, 71, 117, 134–35, 167, 170. *See also* cooperative disputes
Community Enterprises Trust Committee, 40, 47–48, 51–52, 60, 64
community government in WRA camps, 8, 9, 33–34, 46, 89, 110, 167. *See also* community council
Community Management Division, 32, 65, 110

concentration camps. *See* incarceration sites; euphemisms
constitutionality of incarceration. *See* Civil Liberties Act of 1987
cooperative disputes, 33, 60–61, 170, 189n23. *See also* Community Enterprises Section
Coordinating Council for Girls' Clubs and Scouts, 106, 108
Coordinating Council for the Prevention and Disposition of Juvenile Delinquency, 106, 108
crimes among inmates, 58, 63, 89, 93, 151, 193n7. *See also* gambling
Crystal City, Tex. *See* internment camps

Daniels, Roger, 2, 124
data: data cleaning, 172, 174; dataset, 5–7, 131, 154, 172–73, 176, 180n13, 191n21, 199n5; entry database, 6–7, 52, 99, 131, 143, 172, 182n5, 191n21, 191n28, 194n10; final roster, 6–7, 44, 69, 141, 147–48, 172–73, 185n56; metadata attributes, 4, 133, 173
defense work, 60, 85. *See also* Tooele Ordnance Depot, Utah
Denver, Colo., 7, 121, 128, 152, 154
Dies Committee, 88, 192n4
disputes: cooperative/community enterprises, 33, 60–61, 170, 189n23; draft, 2, 7, 18, 29, 93; loyalty of inmate politicians, 46, 87, 88
Doi, Kiyochi, 63
draft, 45, 71, 84–85
draft resistance: in other camps, 123–24, 195n8. *See* Fair Play Committee (FPC)
Durkheim, Émile, 3

edge. *See* networks
education: for adults in camp, 65, 67, 69–72, 72, 77, 92–94, 98, 100, 102, 111, 113, 115, 141, 152, 168; inmate levels of,

43, 51–52, 68, 70–71, 78, 84, 95, 101, 108, 117, 143–44, 154, 157, 169; leaving camp for, 28, 45, 84, 107, 155–56, 192n39; schools in camp, 36, 67, 70, 84, 96, 110, 129, 152, 155–56
Ehrlich, Gretel, 23
eigenvector centrality. *See* centrality
Eisenhower, Milton, 25, 43
Elliott, Alfred J., 19
Emi, Arthur, 135, 137. *See also* Fair Play Committee (FPC)
Emi, Frank S., 7, 125–26, 128, 131, 133–38, 150, 166, 197n25. *See also* Fair Play Committee (FPC)
Emi, Susie, 114
Endo, Ada Otera, 114
Endo-Otera-Sashihara family group. *See* power families
Endo, Mitsuye, 122
ethnic enclave. *See* Japantown
euphemisms, 11
evacuation, 11–12, 24–26, 35, 37, 42, 68, 144, 148
Evacuation Claims Act, 164. *See also* losses
Executive Order 9066, 11, 22–23, 25, 184n40
expatriation, 69, 146, 148

factions: city v. country, 36–37; co-op v. trust, 61; generational, 17; Los Angeles v. San Francisco, 42; perceived assimilationism, 61, 147
Fair Labor Practice Committee, 47–48
Fair Play Committee (FPC), 37, 40, 43, 58, 62–63, 77–79, 90, 92–93, 101, 123, 126–40, 141, 146, 150–51, 168, 196n10; and American Civil Liberties Union (ACLU), 136; and attorneys Samuel Menin and A. L. Wirin, 136; and family relations, 129–30, 132–34, 138–39, 146; pardon of resisters, 150; relations with JACL, 18, 150–51; and

Rocky Shimpo, 136; trial of resisters, 18, 126, 128, 180n15, 197n25; and women, 128
family: before the war, 16–17, 51, 80; in camp, 27, 32, 35, 55–56, 69, 71, 78, 94–100, 106, 108, 114, 116–18, 122; and loyalty questionnaire, 140–47, and resettlement, 84–85, 120–21, 148, 155–56, 163
family numbers (groups), 4, 29, 80, 98, 100, 108, 141, 146, 148, 168, 174, 176–77
Farm Advisory Board, 46, 48
farming: at Heart Mountain, 31, 70, 97, 110; upon leaving camp, 56, 85, 146, 163; on West Coast, 20, 28, 51, 55–56, 109, 113, 122, 127. *See also* victory garden
final roster. *See* data
Form 26. *See* data: entry database
Fort Snelling, Mich., military base, 45, *162*
Fujii, Ryoichi, 88, 89
Fujimoto, Shinji, 36, 54. *See also* factions
Fujioka family. *See* power families
Fujioka, Chiyo, 94–97, *97*, 107. *See also* power families: Fujioka
Fujioka, Dick, 91, *97*. *See also* power families: Fujioka
Fujioka, Ted (Teruo), 95–97, *97*, 166. *See also* power families: Fujioka
Fujiwara, Kiyoshi, 132; as a bridge, 93

gambling, 63
gender roles, 28, 80, 101, 107, 109, 111, 119–20
generations, generational conflict, 17, 19, 28–29, 34, 51, 61, 79–80, 115, 117, 134, 137, 150, 180n12, 182n9
Gentlemen's Agreement, 20, 58
Gephi, 171, 173–74, 176, 180n10
Gila River, Ariz., incarceration camp. *See* incarceration sites

Hachiya family, 155–56, 200n12
Hamachi, Ted, 82
Hanfrisaka, Ai, *112*
Hansen, Asael T., 36, 54, 64, 66, 87, 89, 107, 126, 135–36
Hashimoto, Harry, 99. *See also* power families: Sato
Hashimoto, Ruth, 34, 41, 57, 103–6, 108–9, 121
Hashimoto Sato, Kiyo. *See* power families: Sato
Hatchimonji, Kumezo, 54, 70, *88*, 166, 170
Hawaii, 22, 29, 35, 62–63, 89, 126; incarceration of Japanese Hawaiians, 24, 36; inmates return to, 146, 152, *162*; Japanese immigration to, 15
Hayami, Stanley, 166
Hayashi, Brian Masaru, 12, 34, 188n15, 188n17
Hayashida group, 61, 170
Hayashida, Minejiro, 54, 61, 82, 86–87, 93, 166, 168, 170; as bridge, 91–92, 167
Hayashima, Daitetsu, 100
Heart Mountain, characteristics, 7, 31–33
Heart Mountain canal, 31
Heart Mountain Scholarship Fund Committee, 40, 46, 86, 91, 95, 107
Heart Mountain Sentinel, 37, 71; as data source, 6–8, 13, 47, 66, 74, 76, 80, 172, 186n8, 190n4; reporting style and bias, 7, 43, 74, 76, 81, 104, 119, 138, 167, 180n15, 196n25; as workplace, 67, 82–83, 98–101, 104, 108, 111–12, 118
Heart Mountain Sixty-Three. *See* Fair Play Committee (FPC)
Hirabayashi, Gordon, 122
Hiraoka, Kei. *See* Nagamori, Kei Hiraoka
Hirashiki, Hisa, 77, 104, 106
Hirohata, Misao, 112
Hirooka, Katsumi. *See* Kunitsugu, Katsumi Hirooka

Hohri, William, 124
Hollywood, Calif., 42
Homma, Mary, 111
Honda, Teresa, 61
Honda, Toshiko, *112*
Honda family. *See* power families: Honda
Horikoshi, Aiko, 123
Horino, Minoru, 79, 86, 90, 131. *See also* Fair Play Committee (FPC)
Horino, Sam, 135. *See also* Fair Play Committee (FPC)
Hoshizaki, Takashi, 73, 145
Hosokawa, William (Bill), 7, 37, 81, 166
hospital, 41, 92, 104, 109, 114; as workplace, 43, 65, 67–69, 71, 82–83, 94–96, 98–101, 107, 110–13, 116–18, 123, 142, 152
House Committee on Un-American Activities. *See* Dies Committee
Housel, Jerry W., 89

Ichishita, Haru, 110
Idaho, state of, 26, 44, 124, 161, 186n12
ie (household). *See* family
immigration: early, 14–15; restriction of, 15, 183n20. *See also* Gentlemen's Agreement
Imura, Haruo, 81, 98. *See also* power families: Imura
Imura family. *See* power families: Imura
incarceration of Japanese: in Canada, 24, 184n40; in Peru, 24
incarceration sites: Gila River, Ariz., 27, 164; Granada, Colo., 26, *27*, 124, 195n8; Jerome, Ark., 26–27, *27*, 35, 195n8; Manzanar, Calif., 26–*27*, 30, 188n15, 188n17; Minidoka, Ida., 26–27, *27*, 58, 123–24, 195n8; Poston, Ariz., 27, 30, 83, 124, 164, 185n51, 188n15, 188n17, 195n8; Rohwer, Ark., 26–27, *27*, 195n8; Topaz, Utah, 26–27, *27*, 123, 188n17,

195n8; Tule Lake, Calif., 2, 13, 26–27, 27, 29–30, 36–37, 44, 52–53, 59, 124, 126–27, 129, 137, 139, 140–44, 146–51, 161, 179n1, 186n61, 195n8, 198n51, 198n60. See also segregation
indefinite leave, 7, 28, 43–45, 53, 59–60, 68, 84, 99, 118, 120–21, 127, 140, 146, 153–54, 159, 163, 169, 185n56. See also resettlement program
inmate administration. See block managers; community council
Inoshita, Yayoi, 107
Inouye, Frank, 125, 166, 196n10. See also Fair Play Committee (FPC)
Inouye, Kiyoye, 71
institutionalization, 120, 153. See also resettlement program: resistance to
internment, 11, 26–27, 52, 63, 93, 123, 143, 146–48, 181n25, 185n49, 186n12; of German Americans and Italian Americans, 22, 26, 139
internment camps: Bismarck, N.Dak., 147–49, 149; Crystal City, Tex., family internment camp, 27, 149, 185n49; Santa Fe, N.Mex., 27, 93, 137, 147–49
interracial relationships, 80, 87
inu ("dog," spy), 87–88. See also disputes
Ishigo, Estelle, 80
Ishizuka, Karen L., 11
Issei, 11, 15, 18, 23, 28, 51, 54, 77–78, 80–81, 115–16, 128, 137–39, 180n12, 182n9; camp employment of, 65–66, 69–71, 73, 84, 109, 112–13; citizenship, 29, 124, 164; discrimination of, 19–20, 60, 154; education of, 21, 72, 109, 112; power of, 22, 33–34, 41, 46, 49, 52, 56–57, 61–64, 87–90, 102, 107–8, 166–69, 186n8, 188n17; resettlement of, 43, 54–56, 60, 85, 153, 163–64, 170. See also generations, generational conflict; women: Issei women
Ito, James, 82

Ito, Toshio (Nagamori), 82, 109
Iwamoto, Aimee, 142
Iwamoto, Shyogo, 142
Iwamoto, Toragusu, 142

Japanese American Citizens League (JACL), 7, 17–18, 58, 123, 130, 137, 144; relation to no-noes and resisters, 150
Japanese American Student Relocation Council, 28, 84, 192n39
Japanese Canadian incarceration. See incarceration of Japanese
Japanese cultural values, 18–19, 21–22, 52, 78, 109, 117, 144, 155–56, 169. See also family
Japanese language schools: for children, 21, 84, 130–31, 191n36; for soldiers, 18, 45, 84, 117, 121, 191n37
Japanese Mexican incarceration. See incarceration of Japanese
Japanese names, 6–7
Japanese Peruvian incarceration. See incarceration of Japanese
Japantown, 2
Judicial Committee, 47–48, 59, 63, 87, 93–94, 98, 107, 132–33, 152, 193

Kaneshiro, Sachi (Tamaki), 83, 116
Kansas City, Mo., 82,
Kashima, Tetsuden, 164
Kawai, Nobu, 130
Keegan, J. Clyde, 80
ken (prefecture), 14, 16, 119, 182n6
Kessel, Velma, 142
Kibei, 17–18, 50–51, 93, 128–30, 144, 163, 180n12. See also generations, generational conflict
Kimoto, Toyosake, 59
Kitamura, Tadao, 133–35
Kodama, Robert Yoshio, 79; as a bridge, 92–93
Koshiyama, Mits, 36

Kubota, Gloria, 128
Kubota, Guntaro, 128, 135
kucho (district head), 46. *See also* block managers
Kunitsugu, Katsumi Hirooka, 120, 129, 144, 155
Kurasu, Marian Asao, 145
Kurtz, Merlin T., 158
Kuwahara, Julia (Suski), 106

land ownership, 20, 54, 154
language school. *See* Japanese language schools
LaViolette, Forrest, 16, 182n7
Leavenworth, Kans., federal penitentiary at, 126, 137. *See also* Fair Play Committee (FPC)
leaving camp. *See* resettlement program
Little Tokyo, Lil Tokyo. *See* Japantown
Long Beach, Calif., 121
Los Angeles, Calif., 35, 42, 131, 146, 148, 159, 161, 173
losses: caused by incarceration, 116, 150, 164; of property before incarceration, 22–24
loyalty, 2, 10, 16, 17–19, 26, 29, 37, 43, 53, 58, 61, 75, 78, 123–27, 129–30, 136–41, 143–44, 151, 157, 168–69, 179n1, 185n60; questionnaire, 2, 29, 53, 123–27, 137, 139–41, 143–44, 151, 157, 168–69, 179n1, 185n60. *See also* disputes
Lyon, Cherstin M., 17

Mackey, Mike, 34, 124, 190n4
Madison, Wisc., 155
Mamiya, Albert, 80
Manpower Commission, 49, 86
Manzanar, Calif. *See* incarceration sites
marriage, 4, 18, 65, 79–82, 87, 100, 109, 118, 171, 176. *See also* family
Masaoka, Joe Grant, 18
Masaoka, Mike, 18

Masuda family. *See* power families: Masuda
Masunaga, Shigeo, 58, 61–62. *See also* Japanese American Citizens' League
Matsui, Ryozo (Rosie), 82
Matsumoto, Valerie, 112, 114
Matsumoto, Teruo, 128
Matsushita Sperling, Marjorie, 36, 83
Matsuura, Frank, 139
Matsuura, Tayeko, 139
McKay, Susan, 123
McNeil Island, Wash., 127, 145. *See also* Fair Play Committee (FPC)
Mechau, Vaughn, 99
Menin, Samuel. *See* Fair Play Committee (FPC): and attorneys
Mess Hall Advisory Board, 48, 53, 63, 100, 134, 142
mess halls, 27–28, 33, 44, 67, 71, 73, 109–10, 114, 142
mess hall workers' club, 77, 92, 142
metadata. *See* data
Military Intelligence Service. *See* Japanese language schools: for soldiers
military police, 2, 27, 30
military service, 29, 37, 75, 122–23, 125–26
Mimeograph Department, 67, 98–99
Minneapolis, Minn., 154
miscegenation laws. *See* interracial relationships
Mittwer, Mary Oyama, 103, 121
Miyahara, Tamio, 79, 122, 125, 127, 131, 168; as bridge, 133–35
model minority myth, 164
modularity. *See* networks
Mohri, Reichi, 100, 143, 198n61
Montana, 44, 161
Morrissey, Robert Michael, 4, 179n6
Motonaga, Ray, 139
Mountain View, Calif., 36, 42, 121–22
Muller, Eric L., 124
multiculturalism, 10, 20

multilevel, multilayer, multimode network, 3–4, 90, 174, 176–77
multiracial inmates, 80
Munekiyo family. *See* power families: Munekiyo
Munson, Curtis B., 22
Murakami (Nomura), Judy, 58
Muranaka, May Shirao, 107
Myer, Dillon S., 25, 124, 136, 181n20, 196n17; and assimilationism, 10, 25–26, 140, 156, 198n51. *See also* Bureau of Indian Affairs

Nabata family, 163
Nagamori, Kei Hiraoka, 109
Nagamori, Toshi. *See* Ito, Toshio
Nagata, Samuel, 88–89
Nagata, Toshiye, 78–79, 103–4, 106–7, 121, 166, 168
Naito, Hitoshi, 140, 144–45, 147–48
Nakadate, Paul Takeo, 37, 92, 125–26, 135, 137, 166, 168
Nakae, Miyo. *See* Uratsu, Miyo (Nakae)
Nakaki, Hidenobu George, 41, *50*, 52, 59, 61–63, 86, 90, 94, 166
Nakamoto family. *See* power families: Nakamoto
Nakamura, Mary Lucy, 106–7
Nako, Tsuji, 112–13
Nelson, Douglas, 34
networks: dynamic, 3–5, 9, 180n10; edge (link), 3–5, *38*, 40–41, 58, 66–67, 73, 76, 79, 86, 90–94, 98, 102, 104, 106, 116–17, 131, 134, 171–72, 174, 176–77, 202n1; modularity (community), 5, 40, 76–77, 91–93, 104; network model, 1, 3, 5, 8, 37, 89, 97, 103, 135, 137, 141; node, 3–6, *38*, 40–42, *50*, 57, 78, 90–91, 97–98, 100, 104–5, 113, 170–72, 174, 176–77, 187n4, 202n1; page rank, 177, 202n2; structure of network, 1, 3, 9, 65, 71, 75, 104, 116, 168–69, 173–74. *See also* centrality

New York City, 154, 161
night school. *See* education: for adults in camp
Nisei, 7, 11, 16–18, 22, 41–42, 45, 54, 74, 76–77, 81, 89, 102, 110, 119, 126–31, 141, 144, 146, 148, 150, 164, 180n12, 182n9; Americanism of, 17–19, 21, 115, 123–25; education of, 28–29, 51, 59, 131, 156, 185n54, 191n36; employment of, 65, 68, 70, 73, 84, 112–13, 195n3; power of, 33–34, 46, 51–52, 57, 61–64, 105, 107, 109, 114–15, 143, 166–67, 169, 186n8, 188n17; resettlement of, 43, 85, 119–20, 152, 154–56; socioeconomic status of, 51. *See also* generations, generational conflict; military service
Nisei clubs. *See* block clubs
Nishi Hongwanji. *See* religious denominations
Nishizu, Clarence, 55
node. *See* networks
Nomura, Howard, 58. *See also* Japanese American Citizens League (JACL)
"no-no"/"no-no boys," 29, 123–26, 139–42, 144–45, 150, 168–69, 185n60, 195n5. *See also* loyalty: questionnaire
Nose, Amy, 104–7, 163
Nose, James, 163

Oka, Charles Tozaburo, 63
Okada, Hana, 115
Okada, John, 125
Okamoto, Kiyoshi Eugene, 61–62, 125–26, 128, 134–36, 166, 198n60
Oki, Tom, 61, 125
Okihiro, Gary, 18–19
Okinawa, 15, 186n11
Okuda, Haru, 80
Okuda, Tom, 98
Omura, James, 128, 136. *See also* Fair Play Committee (FPC)
optical character recognition (OCR), 6

Oregon, state of, 17, 23, 35; Japanese Oregonians, 31, 42–43, 154; return to and resettlement in, 12, 148, 159, 161, 169
Otamura, Howard, 85
Otani, Kunio, 116
Otera, Ada. *See* Endo, Ada Otera
Otera, Allen, 100
Otera, Jacob, 100
Otsuki, Chieko, 69; as bridge, 94
Otsuki, Hichi, 69
Otsuki, Iwajiro, 69, 190n8
Oyama, Mary. *See* Mittwer, Mary
Ozawa v. United States. See aliens ineligible for citizenship

Pacific Northwest Japanese Americans, 35, 43, 131, 140–41, 153–54, 198n52. *See also* factions
Padgett, John F., 4
page rank. *See* networks
Palo Alto, Calif., 35
Pearl Harbor, Hawaii, 11, 17–19, 22–23, 29, 35, 45, 52, 95, 108, 143, 183n29
Philadelphia, Pa., 119
Physical Education Board, 48
picture brides, 15, 109
Pomona, Calif., assembly center, 31, 35, 52, 73
Poston, Ariz. *See* incarceration sites
Powell, Wyo., 31, 158. *See also* relations to the outside
power families: concept of, 55, 94, 101, 108, 116; Endo-Otera-Sashihara, 100–101; Fujioka, 94–97, 117, 168; Honda, 116–17; Imura, 98; Masuda, 99, 118; Munekiyo, 117; Nakamoto, 116–17, 168; Sakauye, 96–98, 168; Sato, 99–102; Tanouye, 96
prefecture. See *ken*
project attorneys, 89, 170, 189n23
property loss. *See* losses

racism: before incarceration, 10, 14, 19, 21, 154; late twentieth century, 165; twenty-first century, 10
Red Cross, 74, 76–78, 102, 107, 113, 115, 152
redress, 164–66
relations to the outside, 31, 154–55, 158
religion, 15–16, 21, 76, 140, 182n5, 192n39, 198n53, 199n4
religious denominations: Buddhists, 16, 73, 76, 77, 81, 100, 115, 130, 138, 140, 141, 142, 143, 144, 154, 163, 199n4; Catholics, 76; Christians, 11, 15, 76–77, 81, 102, 104, 109, 123, 130, 140, 153–54, 158, 191n21, 192n39, 198n53, 199n4; Nishi Hongwanji, 143; Seventh Day Adventists, 76
relocation from camps. *See* resettlement program
relocation camp. *See* incarceration sites
Relocation Committee, 47, 49, 88, 91, 94, 106–7
Relocation Coordination Committee, 86–88
Relocation Planning Commission, 47–49, 52–53, 59, 86, 91, 95, 132
repatriation, 29, 129, 144, 146–48, 150. *See also* segregation
Reports Division, 67, 98, 118
resettlement program, 2, 163; resistance to, 2, 28, 45, 56, 64, 84–85, 98, 152. *See also* disputes
Reynolds, Rose, 119
rho clubs. *See* women's clubs
Ritchie, Ricardo, 159
Robertson, Guy, 32, 136, 138, 158, 196n17
Robinson, Greg, 11–12, 25, 29
Rafu Shimpo, 106
Rocky Shimpo, 136.
Roosevelt, Eleanor, 22
Roosevelt, Franklin Delano, 9, 22, 25–26, 29, 184n40

Sakauye family. *See* power families: Sakauye
Sakauye, Eiichi Edward, 41, *50*, 55–56, 59, 69, 78, 85, 93, 96–97, 132, 166–67
Salt Lake City, Utah, 161
San Francisco, Calif., 31, 36, 42, 158
San Jose, Calif., 35–36, 42, 58, 146, 148, 159, 161
Santa Anita, Calif., assembly center, 31, 52, 96, 122
Sashihara, Chiyoko Nina, 6–7, 108, 112
Sashihara, Thomas, 108, 170
Sato family. *See* power families: Sato
seasonal leave, 36, 43, 114, 123, 127, 154, 185n56
Seattle, Wash., 16, 131, 137, 163
segregation, 30, 122, 137, 140–45, 148. *See also* loyalty: questionnaire; "no-no"/"no-no boys"; Tule Lake, Calif.
senior boys' clubs, 40, 43, 74, 76, 78–79, 93, 96, 133–34, 142–43
Sentinel. See *Heart Mountain Sentinel*
Seventh Day Adventists. *See* religious denominations
schools. *See* education
scouting, 8, 36, 40, 65, 73, 75, 83, 92, 102, 106, 108, 112–14, 123, 131, 143, 155
Sheppard, Harry R., 19–20
Shimakoji, Nobu, 159
Silver, W. R., 23
Simmel, Georg, 3
Smith, Nels H., 23
Space and Coordinating Committee of the Community Activities Board, 86–87
Spokane, Wash., 154, *160*, 163
sports, 4, 7, 8, 36–37, 40–41, 48, 73–74, 76–79, 92, 101, 113–14, 127, 131, 142–43
Starn, Orin, 25
Stimson, Henry, 98
Strogatz, Steven H., 3

Study Committee for Opening the West Coast, 48, 86–87
Sumida, Frank, 36
Sumida, Kenroku, 130
Suski, Joe, 106
Suski, Julia. *See* Kuwahara, Julia (Suski)
Suski, Louise, 104, 106
Suski, Peter-Maria (P. M.), 65, 152–53

Takaki, Ronald, 24
Tamaki, Sachi. *See* Kaneshiro, Sachi (Tamaki)
Tamesa, Minoru, 135, 137, 139
Tamesa, Uhachi, 137, 139
Tanouye family. *See* power families: Tanouye
tau clubs. *See* women's clubs
terminal departure. *See* resettlement program
Thomas, Dorothy, 51, 140–41, 156, 198n49, 198n53
Todd, Douglas M., 60, 88–89, 154
Tomo, Rikio, 63, 89, 193n7
Tono, Jack, 146
Tooele Ordnance Depot, Utah, 85, *160*, *162*. *See also* defense work
Toppenish, Wash., 35, 134
Toriumi, Donald, 91, 158
Toriumi, Sophie, 77
Toshiyuki, Silvia, 128
Truman, Harry S., 150
Tsukuda, George, 138
Tsuneishi, Satoru, 139
Tsunokai, Minokichi, *50*, 86–87, 90
Tule Lake, Calif. *See* incarceration sites

Uchiyama, Katie Koga, 44, 103, 114, 120–21
United Service Organizations (USO), *38*, 74, 76, 78–79, 91, 98, 104, 106, 118, 133
University of Nebraska at Lincoln, 155
University of Wisconsin, 84, 120

University of Wyoming–Laramie, 84
USO parents, 74, 96
Uratsu, Miyo (Nakae), 85, 109
Utah, 26, 85, 121, 161

Ver Ploeg, Byron, 60, 63, 170
victory garden, 115, 194n25. *See also* farming
Vocation, Wyo., 1, 152
vocational training. *See* education: for adults in camp
voluntary evacuation, 23, 184n33
voluntary incarceration, 80, 87, 128
voluntary internment, 44, 185n49
voluntary military service, 7, 29, 62, 71, 96, 125, 139, 144, 190n8

Wakaye, Ben, 134–35, 137
Wapato, Wash., 35, 42
War Relocation Authority (WRA), 6, 9, 13, 17, 18, 28–29, 32–34, 43, 45, 47–48, 57–58, 64, 87; administration, 25–26, 28, 69; perception of the Japanese, 2, 9, 26, 52, 61, 63, 71, 77, 123–24, 137, 140, 156; relations with Heart Mountain inmates, 40, 54, 60, 75, 81, 85, 88–91, 101, 142–44, 152–58, 167–69
War Savings Committee, 86, 106–7
Wartime Civilian Control Agency (WCCA), 26–27
Washington, state of, 23, 95; Japanese Washingtonians, 31, 35, 42–43, 86, 106, 131, 134, 154; return and resettlement to, 12, 159, 161–63, 169
Watanabe, Hama, 119
Watanabe, Texie, 79
Watanabe, Yoneko, 119–20
Watts, Duncan, 3
Western Defense Command, 23, 28, 199n5
White, Harrison C., 3
Wirin, A. L. *See* Fair Play Committee (FPC): and attorneys

women, 41, 74, 76–77, 80, 103–5, 158, 163, 168–69; camp duties, 28, 66, 78, 115–16; in camp politics, 49, 57, 106–9; clubs for, 43, 74, 76, 78, 96, 98, 104, 107, 113, 117–18; education of, 109, 117; Issei women, 28, 169; job prospects, 69–71, 83, 85, 98, 101, 109–13, 118–21; resistance of, 122–23; *See also* gender roles; picture brides; Young Women's Christian Association
Wounded Soldier Fund, 48
WRA. *See* War Relocation Authority

Yabe, Miyuki. *See* Yasui, Miyuki (Yabe)
Yakima, Wash., 31, 35–36, 163
Yamaichi, Jimi, 140, 145
Yamakawa, David, 83, 112–13, 155, 157–59
Yamamoto Sato, Fred. *See* power families: Sato
Yamamoto Sato, Tom. *See* power families: Sato
Yanagi, Irene, 152
Yanagi, Keen, 152–53, 157
Yang, Andrew, 10
Yasui, Minoru, 18. *See also* Japanese American Citizens League (JACL)
Yasui, Miyuki (Yabe), 115
yellow peril, 10, 15
Yokoi, Jutaro, 85
Yonemura, Min, 61–62
Yoo, David, 17
Yoshinaga, George, 36, 96
Young Buddhists' Association (YBA), 73, 78–79, 96, 118, 131
Young Men's Christian Association (YMCA), 40, 73, 91, 180n16
young people's clubs. *See* block clubs
Young Women's Christian Association (YWCA), 73–74, 78, 106–9, 113–14, 118, 180n16

Zaima, Tetsuko Okida, 83, 115–16, 155